BILL BEAUMONT'S RUGBY MASTERPIECES

BILL BEAUMONT'S RUGBY MASTERPIECES

Bill Beaumont

with Neil Hanson

SIDGWICK & JACKSON

LONDON

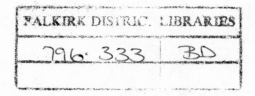
First published 1992 by Sidgwick & Jackson Ltd,

A division of Pan Macmillan Publishers Limited
Cavaye Place London SW10 9PG
and Basingstoke

Associated companies throughout the world

ISBN 0 283 06131 6

1 3 5 7 9 8 6 4 2

A CIP catalogue record for this book is available from the
British Library

Phototypeset by Intype, London

Printed in England by Clays Ltd, St Ives plc

All the pictures used in this book are reproduced by
courtesy of Coloursport, except for the photograph of
Prince Obolensky which is reprinted by permission of
Hulton-Deutsch.

Contents

Introduction

'Where is our Cardus?' The rhetorical question is almost as old as rugby itself. The contention is that while cricket has thoroughbred writers like Cardus and C.L.R. James to celebrate its virtues, rugby union has had to content itself with a bunch of selling-platers. This not only does disservice to the many fine writers who cover the game of rugby, it also ignores the excellent writing on rugby by 'outsiders' to the game. We may have no Cardus, but Dylan Thomas, Myles na Gopaleen and Louis MacNeice are by no means inadequate substitutes.

Perhaps I am being unfair in singling out isolated works by writers far more celebrated in other fields, but the fact remains that there are several rugby writers who stand comparison with the best on any other sport. Is there a better history of a sport than the magnificent investigation of the social and historical roots of Welsh Rugby *Fields of Praise* by Gareth Williams and David Smith? Has anything captured the flavour of a sporting tour as vividly as Denis Lalanne's *The Great Fight of the French XV*? Is there a better sporting biography than Alex Veysey's *Colin Meads – All Black*, or a more thoughtful analysis of a game than John Morgan and Geoffrey Nicholson's *Report on Rugby*?

Rugby is certainly now at least back-page news, which it was not when I started playing, when soccer dominated the headlines. As a result of the game's higher profile, the sports editors are sending more top-line journalists to cover the big rugby matches, but the game is also blessed with excellent writing from those who cover the sport regularly, watching wintry club matches on freezing cold afternoons, as well as the great occasions at the great showpieces of the game.

Columnists and reporters of the calibre of Stephen Jones, John Reason and Steve Bale in England, Alan Watkins from Wales, Irishmen Edmund van Esbeck and Sean Diffley, and Scot Norman Mair, rank with the best in any sport. If cricket appears better served, it is in the nature of the game, rather than the talents of the writers, that the reason should be sought.

Rugby is an all-action sport. There is little time for the contemplative writing which the gentler pace of cricket allows. The deadlines under which a lot of rugby reporters operate also mean that they almost miss the last twenty minutes of the game! In cricket a writer is able to sit down and paint a picture, describing not only the game, but the characters and mannerisms of the players, observed over six hours in the field. By contrast rugby is fast-moving and explosive, a high-action eighty minutes. Like all codes of football, as Geoffrey Moorhouse has pointed out, it is

quite simply over and done with too quickly to exhibit much more than the athletic skills of those involved, and the courage accompanying them . . . there have always been journalists as capable as any novelist of writing creatively and imaginatively; that is with an intuitive ability to see possibilities, to perceive connections, to make allusions, to *enlarge* upon the bare bones of the matter to hand . . . The restriction of column inches, however, and the very nature of reporting (which means presenting information as a chief priority) ensure that in practice very few sports writers get the chance to exercise whatever imagination they may possess.

Great Game, Great People

If that is the reason why 'There is no Cardus' of rugby, there are fine writers and fine writings in abundance. I have chosen work from and about every major rugby nation, and about great players and teams from my own and every other generation. I hope I will be forgiven for including among the Great Occasions three which were of great personal significance for me: the Lions' victory against the All Blacks in the second Test at Lancaster Park in 1977, the Northern Division's famous defeat of the All Blacks at Otley two years later and, sweetest of all for me, England's first Grand Slam in twenty-three years in 1980, the finest moment of my rugby career.

I have also chosen my favourite grounds in every major rugby-playing country, but the one closest to my own heart is inevitably Twickenham. I still get a buzz when I go to Twickenham. It's still my ground in a way. This is where I played all my rugby, where I had some of my greatest moments and some of my lowest ones. I still look out on that field and think that it would be great to get out there again.

Amongst my heroes, I have paid tribute to two great forwards, Colin Meads and Willie John McBride, who were my role models when I was serving my apprenticeship in the second row. I have also looked back to a great forward from an earlier, and very different era, Wavell Wakefield. The standards that he set were extremely high. In my own career as an England player and certainly as an England captain, I tried to emulate great players and great captains and Wavell Wakefield was one of the greatest. Even when he was in his eighties, he would walk into a room and someone would say 'That's Wavell Wakefield' and everyone would know who Wavell Wakefield was. For me, he epitomizes everything that is good in the game.

Great Changes

My own playing era was a little more recent but even in the decade since I retired, the game has changed a great deal. The whole focus of rugby is now on the World Cup, whereas for players of my era, the Five Nations Championship and the British Lions were the pinnacles. If you were selected for the Lions, you were on a different level from the other Five Nations players and that was something you always aimed for.

Now there are not as many Lions tours and the World Cup is very big business indeed, but all the money made from the World Cup is ploughed back into the game, and that is great. There are posters of Will Carling and Rory Underwood hanging next to those of Gary Lineker, while ten years ago, with the best will in the world, there was no poster of Bill Beaumont, Fran Cotton or Steve Smith!

I believe that the great change to the game brought about by the World Cup will result in players' careers becoming shorter. Prop forward Jason Leonard, for example, has played eighteen times for England in the space of eighteen months, whereas in the past, players would have had to wait four or five years before playing eighteen games for England. I played successive games from 1975 to 1982 and ended up with thirty-four caps, but players can now earn six or seven caps in one World Cup campaign. I think that is great for players, but I do believe that their careers will become shorter. They will build up for a World Cup and then retire after it.

Without a doubt the World Cup has also devalued the Lions. In the past, the home nations officials were very keen to get their players on a Lions tour, whereas now they are more likely to be saying 'Let's keep them together as a side'. In future England, Ireland, Wales and Scotland will go away on tour as individual nations far more often than the Lions. The home countries will focus so much on the next World Cup that they will be reluctant to let their players face extra pressure like a Lions tour.

That is a shame, because a Lions tour is a lot of fun. It is hard rugby, but you do have a lot of fun and it is probably the only time that players get together with nothing to do but play rugby. You also mix with guys from the four home countries whom you would otherwise not come across a great deal. That was very valuable in building bridges between players. If there had been a bit of trouble in a Five Nations game, with vendettas building up, it was all forgotten about on a Lions tour, all four nations pooled their resources. I can see a time when Lions tours will be scrapped altogether, which will be sad, but with the World Cup becoming bigger and bigger, Lions tours will inevitably go by the board.

A lot of people in rugby were reluctant to accept the idea of the World Cup, because they saw commercial pressures arising from it, which they feared would irrevocably change the game, but I do not share their reservations. I would love to have played in a World Cup. It must be a magnificent feeling for those English and Australian players to have played in a World Cup final at Twickenham – what greater moment can you have in your own sport?

A lot of administrators would have been quite happy to preserve the status quo, but the game has to move into the twenty-first century and I think the impact of league rugby on the domestic game and the World Cup on the game worldwide has been tremendous. One or two of the old brigade were probably reluctant to accept it because the game is now involved in the world of television, when you have to kick off at a certain time to suit the television company or a sponsor who wants this or that around the ground.

Professionalism

The World Cup has also had an impact on the players' off-field earning potential. England have got the 'Run with the Ball' campaign, there are players' pools and that sort of thing. If a company wants five of the England players to endorse their products, then I cannot see anything wrong with that whatsoever, but I would not actually like to see anyone getting paid to play the game.

What they do off the field is up to them, as long as they do not bring the game into disrepute. If they are prepared to put in all the hard work and the graft and someone wants to reward them because of their success on the rugby field, then that is fair enough. Anything else would simply lead to a gang of mercenary players going round from club to club just for what they could get out of it.

It is inevitable that some players will do better than others, of course, but I don't see any potential for friction in the difference between the earning potential of stars like Will Carling and Jeremy Guscott and the less high-profile players like Jason Leonard or Martin Bayfield. We all realize that there are mere mortals like us, and the superstars. It is just the same in soccer, where you get stars like Gary Lineker alongside the old goalkeeper that no one wants to interview. As long as there is a players' pool and they all pool their resources from a team point of view, to look after the guys who are never going to be interviewed, there should not be a problem.

The captain is always going to be in demand, but I don't think anyone will ever take up this game for what they can get out of it. Even if the game did ever become professional at the top level, which I would profoundly regret, it would not affect rugby at the grassroots, because most clubs are practically bankrupt; they have no money and are running five or six teams, providing rugby for fifty or sixty guys every Saturday. That is what those guys look forward to in their mundane work hours, that is what they want to do and the game will always continue in that vein.

Playing by the Rules

There are other pressures which come from the increasing coverage of the sport, particularly pressures to change the rules to speed up the game or make it more attractive for television viewers. There are one or two law changes being mooted at the moment but I would not want to see too many cosmetic changes to give the game a bigger global appeal on a television screen.

There are some changes I would favour, however. I would like to see the scrummage law changed to stop sides just wheeling the scrum defensively, because I think it takes away the art of scrummaging. There is an art to scrummaging in rugby union and it is a part of the game, whereas in rugby league the scrums are just a joke. I would like to see the laws tightened up on that, not altered along the lines of one proposal, now, which would stop pushing in scrums. That would just make the rugby union scrums like rugby league, with the side getting the put-in winning the ball. The art of scrummaging would go and I think that would be a shame. I would like to see the line-out laws changed, though, to legalize lifting, because everyone lifts anyway and if you legalize it, four players out of the seven involved in the line-out will at least be doing something constructive instead of destructive.

That would be enough tinkering with the laws to satisfy me, and as I have said, I would not want further changes made just to pander to television audiences. The game is about playing; as the French say, the game is about piano players and piano pushers and there has to be a role for everybody in that. Not everybody is athletic and can sprint around the field, there are little fat fellows who can play, as well as tall and lean guys, and I think that is what the game should be about. The game has always had that feature, that whatever shape or size you were, there was a position where you could play.

The best thing about rugby for me is playing the game, the players, the crack that you have in any team game and the characters that you meet within the game – the rugby way of life that attracted me initially to the sport. Despite the changes in the game, you still get that from rugby. I still feel that rugby should remain an amateur game, something that you do and look forward to on a Saturday afternoon and I would hate to think that it ever became anything other than that. I realize that there are sacrifices that players have to make but when it comes to the crunch, if they do not want to do it, they can simply jack the game in.

Grand Slam

As an Englishman I have been immensely proud of the achievements of the England side in the last couple of years, but my own proudest moment has to be my own Grand Slam in 1980. Having played for five years with hardly any success, then to go from wooden-spoonists to champions was a great English achievement, and the guys who were in that team are still my friends. We have a lot in common, for we have been through a lot together.

It is great to see England succeeding again and England always should be at the top, with the resources that we have and the number of people playing the game. In the past our size has been our weakness, but now it is our strength and I am sure that England will continue to go from strength to strength.

To the people who criticize the style in which England have played, I would say 'Look at the results'. They are the only things for which players are remembered. The 65,000 people at Twickenham singing 'Swing Low' could not care how England get the result, as long as they get it. As a player you like to win in style, but then everybody likes to drive a Rolls-Royce, but most of us have to drive a Sierra and you still get there in the end. It is nice to do things in style, but if you do not and you still succeed, that is what you are remembered for just the same. As I said to my great friend Tony Neary, the day after England had been criticized for the way in which they beat Wales 24–0 to secure the 1992 Grand Slam, 'We would have given our right arms to have beaten Wales 4–0, never mind 24–0.'

Rugby Fellowship

The fellowship of rugby extends far beyond the field of play and far beyond one's own playing days. I owe a debt of gratitude to many people who have helped in the compilation of this book, far more than I can adequately pay tribute to here. I am grateful to all the many fine writers who have given permission for their work to be reproduced here, but I must also single out Rex King, Librarian at Twickenham, who gave unstintingly of his time and his knowledge, and William Armstrong, Managing Director of Sidgwick & Jackson, for the chance to embark on this labour of love. To them and to all the many others who contributed to *Masterpieces of Rugby*, my sincere thanks. I hope it gives the reader as much pleasure as Neil Hanson and I have had in compiling it.

Bill Beaumont
Preston, April 1992

Editor's Note

I had not met William Blackledge Beaumont until we began working on this book together, but I already had a picture in my mind, one shared by sports fans throughout the world. Like Henry Cooper, Billy Beaumont has transcended his own sport and indeed all sports, a man whose warmth, honesty, self-deprecating humour and humanity have endeared him to people whose only contact with sport is a flutter on the Grand National and who think Rugby is a town in the Midlands.

Bill Beaumont is the same off-camera as on, in public or private, a warm and likeable man, modest about his own achievements, quick in praise of those of others and a man enthused with a love of the game of rugby. That shines through in the work included in this anthology, work that covers the great moments of Billy Beaumont's own career but also spans the history of the sport, its great personalities, great matches and great teams, as well as the wit and the spirit that make the game unique.

It is characteristic of W.B. Beaumont that he should not want me to include any tribute to himself in this anthology; it is characteristic of me that having agreed to that, I should sneak two in anyway . . .

Neil Hanson

Straight Down the Middle

John Robbie

Billy Beaumont was the captain and I have no praise high enough for him as a leader, a person and a player. Of course he knew that a lot of Welshmen wanted a Welsh captain; the Welsh nation felt they had been cheated that year when Paul Ringer was sent off against England. This must have put Billy under a lot of pressure, especially at the beginning of the tour. But he just played it straight down the middle. He was always available for a chat, was good fun and obviously decided never to ask any of his players to do anything he wasn't prepared to do himself. I was amazed, at training sessions, at the way he ran. I had grown up at Irish squad sessions where the backs ran on and the donkeys trundled far, far behind. I expected that all sides allowed their forwards to jog along *à la* Moss Keane, Phil Orr and Willie Duggan. Not so. Billy set a standard and big guys like Maurice Colclough, Alan Tomes and Graham Price were more than happy to match his efforts.

Billy was an excellent player as well. I sometimes think that he gets a lot of praise for his captaincy, but that history has neglected to give him credit for his playing ability. He isn't tall for a modern lock, but with timing and clever variation managed to win a lot of line-out ball. He was also very mobile and drove very hard; he had great guts and despite an injured knee on tour gave everything with no complaint.

From *The Game of My Life*
(Pelham Books, London, 1989)

William Blackledge Beaumont

Clem Thomas

When Bill's rugby career was cut short by injury, that fine writer Clem Thomas penned a moving tribute to 'a big man in every sense', who, as Thomas predicted 'may have finished as a player, but not as a rugby man and we will, I know, hear and see a lot more of him yet.' Indeed we have and what a pleasure it has been.

N.H.

William Blackledge Beaumont is a splendid name, but then he is a splendid man. The premature passing of his career will be mourned as much by the Welsh, Irish and Scots as by his own Englishmen, for whom he is the archetypal example of the very best characteristics of his breed.

The injury which finally snuffed out Bill's delightful career was a culmination of three hard blows on the head in a year. The worst of these by far was sustained at Béziers at the start of the current season and the final one came while playing for his beloved Lancashire two weeks ago.

A computerized brain scan revealed that there were grave risks of permanent injury if he continued to play. Wisely he read the medical evidence correctly and ended one of the most distinguished careers in the history of the Rugby Football Union.

I am not surprised that he acquired so many head injuries, for he was never an instinctive footballer. His greatest attributes were honesty, integrity and courage. He will not be remembered for jumping like a stag in the line-out; instead he was a compressor at the front of the line where his concentration and determination invariably saw him snatch a fair share of the ball.

His principal strength was that, in the idiom of the game over the past decade, he was a marvellous ground player. He would drive fiercely into rucks and mauls, using his head like a battering ram, propelled by what Steve Smith called his outboard motor, which is perhaps the most famous and prominent posterior in the game. His courage in driving into a maelstrom of flying boots and bodies was his danger and eventually his downfall. He contested everything.

Bill will never be forgotten for the charm of his captaincy. He led England a record twenty-one times, winning eleven times and drawing twice. In 1980 he took England to the Grand Slam for the first time since 1957 when they were led by another Lancastrian, Eric Evans.

If it is a cliché to say that he led by personal example, it is nevertheless entirely true. He had an immense charisma, both on and off the field, and perhaps a reflection of his strength of character was that he was always at his best when things were going badly. In adversity in South Africa in 1980 he could shrug his shoulders and say 'Come on, lads', and then take ten minutes to get to the coach as he politely signed autographs.

The first major impression he made on me was in 1977 when he arrived in New Zealand as a replacement for Nigel Horton on that difficult, ill-fated tour. I will never forget the Lions meeting him at the airport. Willie Duggan stepped forward to shake his hand and said, 'If I were you, Bill, I would flick off home again on the next plane.' Bill smiled and said, 'Not Pygmalion likely.' Immediately he established himself alongside Gordon Brown as an automatic choice for the Tests.

I used to look at Bill Beaumont and wonder what he reminded me of; and finally decided that he was like a St Bernard, a lovable, bulky, gentle old thing possessing great strength under the gracefully floppy exterior, someone who would always come to your rescue.

Yes, Beaumont was everybody's favourite. You see, he always had an advantage over the kind of man who recently broke Geoff Wheel's nose in two places with two punches at the last line-out of the game. It would never have occurred to Bill to act like that. The very idea would be abhorrent because he loved the game, its ethics and its people; and the little man who feels that punching or kicking is part of the game would never morally or physically survive against Beaumont who was a big man in every sense. He may have finished as a player but not as a rugby man and we will, I know, hear and see a lot more of him yet.

From the *Guardian*, 1982

1
GREAT TRADITIONS

The Spirit of Rugger

William Wavell Wakefield

Willam Wavell Wakefield is one of my rugby heroes, a formidable player and captain of Sedbergh School, the RAF, Cambridge University, Harlequins and England, for whom he won thirty-one caps, an astonishing number in an era with few tours to boost the totals. Beyond this, however, 'Wakers' was the first man to apply organization to the chaos of forward play as it then existed. A back-rower himself, he specified roles for each of the forwards for the first time ever and devised the strategies that transformed back-row forwards from anonymous donkeys in a pack toiling from set-piece to set-piece, to hunter-destroyers, targeting the midfield backs.

Wakefield was a great player, a visionary thinker about the game and a tough administrator, but he never forgot the essential spirit of the game, a spirit he encapsulated in a piece written in 1927, which remains just as fresh and as relevant today.

W.B.B.

Without doubt it is a hard game, and that is one of its chief virtues. A man who plays it must be ready to give and take hard knocks, but he will take and give them with a grin. He will need courage and determination and a sense of humour, and he must learn the meaning of unselfishness. It may be that Rugger has an element of danger about it, and people often ask whether it is worth risking serious injury in what, after all, is only a game. It would, I think, be a poor sort of game that had no sort of risk to be faced, and it is one of the glories of Rugger that you can put your shoulder into a man with all your strength and bring him down with a crash, knowing that if you stave in a rib or two of his he will bear no grudge against you, while if he knocks your teeth out in handing you off it is merely your own fault for tackling him too high. Such accidents are relatively rare, but when they do happen they are just the fortune of war.

There really is the crux of the matter, for Rugger is war, though it is friendly and controlled war, if such a conception be possible. We all have our primitive instincts, and one of the strongest is the love of a good fight, which no amount of civilization has been able to eradicate. I see no reason, as a matter of fact, why it should be eradicated, for it is merely the natural desire of a healthy man to pit his strength against another's, and for this desire we have in Rugger the best possible outlet. Of all games it is the least hampered by restrictions, and though a player may not be a Hercules, he may have speed or subtlety to put to the test, and in modern conditions every quality and every physique has its chance. It is because of the freedom of Rugger and its consequent risks that it breeds hardiness, which in these days of cocktails and lounge-lizards is a quality to be encouraged.

But I do not want to give the impression that Rugger is no more than brute force directed by courage rather than intelligence. If it were only that it would not be so increasingly popular, nor would it be so widely played in the schools. It is above all the game for the tactician and for the man who is mentally alert, for so quickly does it move and so unexpected are its phases, that only a keenly intelligent player can seize openings which come and are gone in a flash, or can check his opponents when prompt decision and action are essential.

Plainly there is more in Rugger than mere strength, and I would go so far as to say that it calls for quicker and deeper thought than any other game. But though I have tried to show how it breeds courage and hardiness, unselfishness, self-control and strength of character and mind, I have said nothing of the spirit underlying it all.

The spirit of any game is an elusive quantity, for we play without analysing our motives. There is, however, something in the spirit of Rugger which is worth defining, difficult though it is to express. Mrs Battle demanded for her whist 'a clean hearth and the rigour of the game', and somehow that expresses my feelings about Rugger. A clean hearth – well, that is plain enough; our game is to be played swept clean of all those mean and petty infringements of the rules which could so easily creep in; infringements and obstructions which no man who understands the spirit of Rugger could ever practise. And the rigour of the game, that we must have, a wholehearted joy in the hardness of it, a desire to do our best, to play fair and ask no favour. And, above all, there is no fear of defeat, but simply an effort to win because that is the object of the game. If defeat comes our way, it is a lesson rather than a loss, while if we win we are satisfied that our best should have proved good enough.

From *Rugger* by W.W. Wakefield and H.P. Marshall
(Longmans, Green & Co., London, 1927)

The Spirit of the Game

John Morgan and Geoffrey Nicholson

John Morgan and Geoffrey Nicholson also mused on the spirit of the game in their thoughtful and influential *Report on Rugby*, published in 1959.

W.B.B.

At the present time there are people interested in Rugby who wonder if the *ethos* will survive the game's new expansion. Their argument runs along these lines: more and more people are playing and many of them will be people, perhaps, who will not *understand* the Spirit of the Game, who will try to seek mean advantage out of the referee's sight, who may, if they think it safe, trip, late-tackle or offend against more subtle manifestations of the *ethos*. Will new laws have to be formulated, they wonder, to guard against this; will the unwritten laws, in fact, have to be written? Ourselves, we think this fear exaggerated. All kinds of people have been playing Rugby for a long time without the moral tenor fluctuating wildly or the degree of roughness varying greatly – although some people will dispute this according to their particular *bête noire* – in different parts of the country. It is really a question of the clubs keeping their houses in order.

In some circumstances, of course, rough play is more likely than others. One circumstance is when it's thought by team and spectator that a vital importance attaches to the result of a match, when it is easy for a player's excitement to grow to a high pitch, for his temper to fray at the edges, and to increase the prospect of his falling victim to the temptations of malpractice which lie so thick around him. And here one meets another facet of *ethos*. The game is more important than the result. While playing to win you must accept defeat gracefully. It is obligatory to cheer your opponents from the field. Here again our hypothetical stranger will be puzzled. For seventy or eighty minutes these men have been tearing into each other, knocking, to all appearances, the living daylights out of each other, yet here they are shaking hands, applauding one another, calling for three cheers. Is this not hypocrisy? It is not, of course. They are genuinely feeling happy, tired perhaps, but well disposed towards their rivals. They will be having a meal together afterwards. (It wasn't always like this everywhere. Matches between local rivals used to be played in a bitter spirit in places where parochial loyalties were intense. But even in South Wales nowadays matches are almost invariably friendly and quarrels rarely break out among spectators, even though the desire to defeat a neighbouring town's side may still be keen.) It is this notion that the result is not important which sets the faces of so many Rugby people firmly against competition. Ireland and Scotland and New Zealand do have their competitions, of course. In England there is the powerful force of the County Championship. In Wales there is no formal competition, but, then, it is difficult to imagine any system of league or cup which might create a keener spirit of competition between Cardiff and Newport, or Swansea and Cardiff, or Llanelly and Neath, or Swansea and Llanelly. In this one can only suggest that the *ethos* is not intolerant. Somehow these matches must be played in the Spirit of the Game and usually they are, even International matches, which form part of a championship, whatever *ethos* might say, of acute importance to players and spectators. Yet even in International matches the Spirit burns and try-scorers do not exult in success or seek congratulation from colleagues who never offer it with any wildly emotional show. A man scoring his first try in an International may be forgiven a smile, even a small jig, but no more. Self-control is evident here, and the notion that the game is more important than the result, and the idea that it was the team that scored, not the individual.

But as remarkable as anything about the Spirit of the Game is that so many Rugby men feel it central not only to the existence of their form of sport but to their lives away from field and club-house. It is perfectly understandable why it should be the former: Rugby could not be played without it. It is a game which otherwise would lend itself too easily to dangerous play and would offer pleasure to no one but the bruiser instead of, as it does now, to all manner of men. But that the Spirit should be so much talked about away from the field is less immediately comprehensible. The claims made are that the game moulds character and creates gentlemen, and sometimes they are made so strongly that the implication clearly is that someone who doesn't play Rugby has an inadequate character and can't *really* be a gentleman. Only the wilder spirits would make this claim.

There is a suggestion that Rugby is the only game men – *real* men – play. This is not a view we share. Naturally, people devoted to any activity tend to see it as the only valuable activity and to say so at after-dinner speeches among people who share their views, more or less; or perhaps they are creating a thesis about a game's larger values out of respect for the fact that they have devoted their lives to it and must necessarily find their lives adequate. Most people who play or watch Rugby or like talking about it in club-house or bar and arguing about International sides or quarrelling with selectors or recalling old matches and praising famous men or planning a trip or roaring out anecdotes or remembering old rogues or weighing up the prospects, are not given to making speeches. They just like it. The Spirit is important to the game, but the game is more important than the Spirit, is more than a moral exemplar. Within its closed world is contained pleasure and sadness and excitement and comedy and moments of great emotional intensity.

From *Report on Rugby* by John Morgan and Geoffrey Nicholson
(William Heinemann, London, 1959)

The Loom of Youth

Alec Waugh

For most rugby players, the beginnings of their life-long love of the game were at school. 'Tom's First Match' from *Tom Brown's Schooldays* is traditionally chosen for rugby anthologies – I must have twelve versions of it on my shelves by now! Instead of that I have chosen Alec Waugh's account of 'a first House match'. Published towards the end of the First World War, it looks back to a public school age that was already passing into history, but Waugh's account of pre-match nerves still strikes a chord with anyone who has ever played the game.

W.B.B.

Nothing is more horrible than the morning before a first House match. Gordon woke happy and expectant, but by break he had begun to feel a little shivery, and at lunch-time he was done to the world. He ate nothing, answered questions in vague monosyllables, and smiled half nervously at everyone in general. He was suffering from the worst kind of stage fright. And after all, to play in an important match before the whole school is a fairly terrifying experience. As he sat trembling in the pavilion, waiting for the whistle to blow, Gordon would have welcomed any form of death, anything to save him from the ordeal before him. The whistle blew at last. As he walked out from the pavilion in his magenta-and-black jersey, an unspeakable terror gripped him; his knees became very weak; his tongue stuck to the roof of his mouth, and then something seemed to snap in his brain. He walked on quite cheerfully. He was as a spectator. It seemed that it was not really he, but his ghost that was walking on to the field. Subconsciously he lined up with the rest. The School side in their white jerseys, the Colts with their red dragons, seemed miles away. Collins kicked off. Gordon did not know he was playing. A roar of 'House' rose from the touch-line. Involuntarily he joined it, thinking himself a looker-on, then suddenly Livingstone, the Buller's inside three-quarter, caught the ball and ran towards him. At once Gordon was himself. He forgot the crowd on the touch-line, forgot his nervousness, forgot everything except that he was playing for the House, and somehow or other had to drive the ball over that line. He crashed into Livingstone, and the pair rolled into touch. A cheer rippled down the line. Gordon did not hear it.

The Fernhurstian described this match as 'perhaps the finest ever witnessed on the School ground,' and the reporter was not far wrong. Certainly that first mad rush of the

House forwards was the most glorious moment in Gordon's football career. It was all so unexpected, so essentially wonderful. On the touch-line Mansell shouted himself hoarse. The cries of 'House' completely drowned those of 'School'. For the first quarter of an hour the School pack never got the ball out of their half. It seemed that the House must score. Time after time, the School were forced to touch down. Stewart was brought down just the wrong side of the line. Lovelace performed prodigies of valour. A gloom descended over Buller's. On the Masters' side of the line 'the Bull' fumed and ground his teeth: 'Go low, Reice, you stinking little funk. Get round, forwards, and shove; you are slacking the lot of you. Buck up, Philson.' Up and down he stamped, cursing at his men. Lovelace could hardly refrain from laughing.

'Now, lads,' shouted Stewart, 'fair or foul; shove the ball over the line!' Like a sledge-hammer Gordon crashed into the scrum. Wilkinson was in his light, but Gordon was seeing red, his feet stamped on Wilkinson, and found the ball. His elbows swung viciously, as he cut his way through the scrum. Then someone caught him by the ankle. He went down hard. A boot caught him on the side of the head. He got up blind with wrath. 'Fight! Fight!' he yelled. The House grovel swarmed in; the outhouse pack shivered for a moment, then gave way. Collins and Gordon burst through, the ball at their toes; Wilkinson dashed across and dived for the ball; he clawed it for a second, Gordon's feet smashed it from his hands, and Collins steered it past the back, and kicked it just over the line and fell on top of it.

From the touch-line, there burst a roar that must have been heard five miles away. 'Well done, laddie!' bawled Mansell. Even Ferguson waved his stick in the air. It was a great moment.

As the School lined up behind their line, 'the Bull' strode behind them. 'What are you doing? Put some life into your game. Buck up, all of you; it is a filthy show. Guts!'

Lovelace took the kick. It was far out; the ball hardly rose from the ground. In a state of feverish panic Livingstone dropped out. For a second or two the School pressed. But it was impossible to withstand the wild attack of the House for long. Collins, elated by his success, brought off a magnificent dribble, and was forced into touch only a few yards from the line. Half-time was not far off. And the House struggled fiercely to get over the line once more. Up and down between the goal line and the twenty-five the two scrums fought. It seemed only a matter of time for another try to send the House across with a lead of six points; but there is as much luck in rugger as in any game. The House had heeled perfectly, Foster cut past one man, and passed out to Richards. A roar of 'House!' went up. A try was imminent, Richards passed to Lovelace. But Livingstone was one of those three-quarters who will miss an easy kick one minute and bring off a superb collar the next. As Richards passed, he dashed between him and Lovelace, intercepted the pass, and raced up the field. Collins caught him only a foot away from the line, and from the line out Grienburg, a heavy Buller forward, caught the ball and fell over the line by the flag, just as the whistle was about to blow for half-time. It was very far out, and the kick failed. The sides crossed over 3–3.

Simonds came on during the interval almost incoherent with excitement. 'Splendid, you fellows! Magnificent! Never saw anything like it. Stick to it and you're bound to win. Simply putrid luck that last try . . . keep it up!'

On the touch-line there was no doubt as to the final result. 'We shall walk away with the Cup,' said Mansell, and in a far corner Jones-Evans was laying ten to one on the House in muffins. But a bit of good luck is capable of making a side play in a totally different spirit, and the combined Buller's and Claremont's side started off like a whirlwind. Livingstone kicked off, and the outhouse scrum was on the ball in a minute. For a second the House pack was swept off its feet, and during that second Fitzgerald had dribbled to within ten yards of the line. Foster made a splendid effort to stay the rush, and flung himself on the very feet of the opposing forwards. But the check was only momentary; the forwards rolled on, and it was only on the very line that Lovelace rushed across, and falling on the ball, held it to him, till the House forwards had time to come round. But the rules lay down that a player, as soon as he has fallen on the ball, must get off it at once. Lovelace realized that if he did so, a try would be inevitable. He hung on like grim death, praying that the referee would not see. Before half the House forwards had formed round, the whistle blew.

'Free kick to the School. You mustn't lie on the ball like that, Lovelace.' The referee was not blind.

Anxiously the House lined up and waited for the kick. Livingstone had converted nearly every goal on the Colts' games the term before. It was a trying moment. He seemed to take hours placing the ball correctly. There was an absolute hush as he ran up; then a great sigh, half of relief, half of disappointment, burst from the touch-line. The ball rose hardly six feet from the ground, and sailed harmlessly towards the School House line. And then Turner made a mistake that he cursed himself for ever afterwards. All that was necessary to do was to let the ball bounce, and then touch down. But as the ball sailed towards him, Turner was suddenly possessed with the longing to do something brilliant. He was last man on the list, and had only been put into the side at the last moment, owing to another forward stopping out. It was not unnatural. He caught the ball.

'You blasted fool,' yelled out Richards, 'for God's sake find touch.'

Turner lost his head. He gave a mild punt down field, and before the House had realized what was happening, Wilkinson had caught the ball, and dashed over the line between the posts. This time Livingstone made no mistake. 8–3.

For the next five minutes the House side was entirely demoralized. Nothing went right. The forwards did not keep together. Gordon cursed foully, and only made matters worse. Lovelace's kicks only found touch a few feet down the line. Richards rushed up and down fuming, and upset everyone. It was due only to a miracle and some fine work by Foster that the School did not score at least three times. Foster did everything during those awful minutes. Rush after rush he stopped, just as Fitzgerald was looking dangerous, and he brought down his fly-half every time. Gordon was amazed at his performance; he had always rather looked down on him before. He had never imagined he was so plucky.

But it takes more than two unexpected tries to throw a School House side off its balance for long. Soon the forwards began to reassert themselves. Burgess, the wing three-quarter, a self-satisfied member of Buller's, who was in VI.B, and whose conceit far excelled his performances, got away and began to look dangerous. But Gordon came up behind him. He loathed Burgess, and flinging aside all the Fernhurst traditions about collaring low, he leapt in the air, and crashed on top of him. Burgess collapsed like paper. A great howl went up from the School House. New life seemed to enter into the side. The grovel flocked round, and Collins, heaving Burgess off the ball with a flying kick, dribbled the ball to the half-way line. A scrum formed up and from the heel Richards got the ball to Lovelace, who broke through the defence and with a clear field ahead made for the line.

'Run like hell!' shouted Simonds from the touch-line. He was standing on the masters' side of the ground, just in front of the Chief's wife. But he was past caring about social etiquette. All he wanted was to see the House ahead once more. 'Faster, man, run – oh, damn!'

Just on the line the ubiquitous Livingstone caught him up, and the pair rolled into touch. If, as some say, there is nothing much finer to watch in football than an uphill fight, then the Thirds of 1913 was most certainly the greatest game ever played on the Lower. Lighter and slower than their opponents, the House kept them on the defensive for the rest of the afternoon. Collins was a splendid sight, his hair fell in a cascade over his eyes, his nose was bleeding, his jersey was torn half off his back, but he did not care. His feet were everywhere, and anyone who got in his light was sorry for it. Turner, with the thought that he was the cause of Wilkinson's try, fought heroically. Once when Williamson, a Claremont's forward, began to dribble, he rushed into him sideways and with a 'soccerbarge' knocked him flying into touch, and took the ball back inside the twenty-five. It was a great fight. But no one can strive successfully against the will of the gods, and certainly the stars in their courses fought against the House. Ten minutes before time Livingstone, who had been systematically starved the whole game, got a pass about the half-way line. He was the fastest man in the field. No one could touch him; he made straight for the corner flag, and scored amid the tumultuous applause of Buller's. There could be no doubt about the result now. Before the eyes of Jones-Evans there rose a prospect of eternally treating outhouse men to muffins. Mansell swore violently. 'The Bull' walked up and down the touch-line beaming with delight. Simonds was silent.

'Well, you men,' said Richards, 'we've been beaten, but by heaven we'll shove them the last few minutes. Go for them, tooth and nail.'

The House did so. In hall that night Burgess announced that there was not a single gentleman in the School House, a remark which resulted in a rather unpleasant half-hour with 'the Bull' two days later. For these last minutes produced one of the most glorious charges of the day. From the twenty-five right in to the School half, the ball was carried. Nothing could stop that wild rush. Livingstone and Wilkinson went down before it, but they were passed by. Burgess made a half-hearted attempt to fall on the ball, but did not get up for several seconds, and the House was well in the School half when Gordon kicked a little too hard and the School back, fielding the ball, managed to find touch. But the House was still undaunted. From the line out, the ball was flung to Richards, who, putting his head down, literally fought his way through the scrum and tottered out the other side. He handed off Wilkinson, dodged the fly-half, and made for the centre of the ground. Livingstone came across at him. 'With you, Richards,' yelled Lovelace.

As Livingstone brought Richards crashing to the ground, the ball was safely in Lovelace's hands. Lovelace was about half-way between mid-field and the twenty-five. He ran a few yards, steadied himself, and took a drop.

In deadly silence the School watched the flight of the ball. It sailed high and straight towards the goal. 'It's over,' murmured the Chief excitedly. But as the ball neared the posts it travelled slower, a slight breeze caught it, blew it over to the right. It hit the right post and fell back into play. As the full-back returned it to mid-field the whistle blew for no-side.

From *The Loom of Youth* by Alec Waugh
(Geoffrey Bles, London, 1917)

A Whole New Ball Game

Gareth Williams and David Smith

Two events in the history of Rugby Football stand out above all others. The legendary moment in 1823, when William Webb Ellis first picked up the ball and ran with it during a game at Rugby School, may or may not have actually taken place. It does not really matter, for the legend is now so strong and so fixed in place that no amount of academic querying will displace it from its place in history – the moment of birth of Rugby Football.

The General Meeting of the Rugby Union in the Westminster Palace Hotel in September 1893 which declared the principle of allowing compensation for bona fide loss of time to be 'contrary to the true interest of the Game, and its spirit', is a day of glory or infamy, depending upon which side of the great rugby divide you sit. The declaration led directly to the split between Rugby Union and Rugby League, which continues to the present day.

Gareth Williams and David Smith wrote their magnificent history of Welsh Rugby in 1980, for the first time placing the game in the social context in which it grew. U.A. Titley and Ross McWhirter described the events leading to the split between the codes in their centenary history of the Rugby Football Union, while that distinguished writer and Rugby League devotee, Geoffrey Moorhouse, gives a view of those events from the other side of the fence. It is interesting to note that the two sides remain unable to agree about anything – Titley and McWhirter place the meeting of the Northern clubs in Leeds, Moorhouse (correctly) locates it in Huddersfield!

W.B.B.

The definition of the merits of rugby, as perceived by the chairman of the Llanelli club on the occasion of a wedding presentation to one of the players in 1884, was received with applause by his audience. Rugby, he said, was 'of material aid in the formation of character and it had a great deal to do with the development of those characteristics which have made England a nation – determination and perseverance'. The Welsh ideal was to be recognized as a consequential part of the British political and social structure and for a specific Welsh identity to take its place in the Empire. In 1881 J. Allen Williams of the Llanelli *Guardian* urged his club to greater efforts: '"Onward" be your motto', he cried, 'Play as Britons'. Rugby, after all, was 'the grand old British game'. Or so it was thought . . .

*

Every society seeks to establish links with its past, just as the first act of the parvenu is to invent himself a pedigree. There was no concealing the disconcerting newness of the South Wales society of the last quarter of the nineteenth century, but adjustment to it might be eased by showing that apparent novelty did not necessarily involve a radical break with the past. Rugby football was unknown in Wales before 1870, yet in the 1880s it was often hailed by many of its most active propagandists as 'the grand old game'. In the context of the dramatically expanding industrial South Wales of the last quarter of the nineteenth century, the pretence of maintaining a continuity between past and present may have been psychologically a comfort; historically, it was a distortion.

Bloodhounds roaming the centuries on the scent of the pedigree of Welsh rugby ever since have detected a number of exciting aromas, but they have managed to establish little more than that ball games have been a feature of the Welsh countryside for well over a millennium. We would be ill-advised to attach much credence to the dubious claims of Iolo Morganwg, eighteenth-century Glamorgan's forger extraordinaire, when he regales us with a description of a 'traditional' eisteddfodic olympiad that occurred regularly at Llangyfelach, near Swansea, where football was sandwiched between animal-baiting and old-women's grinning matches. Nor can the twelfth-century testimony of that peripatetic gossip, Gerald of Wales, be regarded as exactly conclusive. He has much to say about many things, but aside from the tantalizing observation that the men of Gwent did not compete at archery because they were concerned not to shoot great distances but to kill people, nothing about sport. Even Romano-Celtic Britain has been ransacked for evidence of football, with laurels being jointly awarded to the Welsh chronicler Nennius's account of a fifth-century ball game between youths of noble birth, and, inevitably, to *harpastum*, the recreation of Roman legionaries as they did violence to an inflated balloon in the Caerleon region, when they were not doing violence to the Silurian tribesmen of the vicinity. The last words on the fatuity of these forays into the past was said as long ago as 1894 by the English International Charles Marriott. 'Football is undoubtedly an ancient pastime,' he wrote. 'Among the carvings on the walls of Egyptian buildings there frequently occurs the representation of one gentleman passing to another in approved fashion what may be a football of the period or a plum pudding. If the former, it proves without a doubt that the early inhabitants of the Nile Valley played under the handling code.'

But when in late-nineteenth century Wales rugby was hailed as 'the grand old game', the game in mind was one that had first been noticed in West Wales under the Tudors, and therefore redolent of Welsh and British associations. This was *cnappan*, brought to life for us even today by George Owen's racy account of it in his *Description of Pembroke-shire* (1603). The cnappan was a ball made of wood boiled in tallow to make it slippery and was the name of the game played between neighbouring parishes on feast days like Shrove Tuesday by anything up to 2,000 men on foot and on horseback. There was no goal as such; the game was won when the ball had been carried so far away that it was beyond return.

These dissimilarities to the rugby game, however, were more than compensated for by some striking similarities. It engendered a vigorous community involvement and fierce inter-village rivalry; it was a game of throwing, tackling and kicking, played in the best spirit of amateurism – 'they contend not', wrote Owen, 'for any wager or valuable thing but strive to the death for glory and fame which they esteem dearer than any worldly wealth'. There were even some technical prefigurations, like the maul which developed when one of the players 'happening on the cnappan clappeth the same against his belly, holding it fast with his hands. Another of his company clappeth him about the middle, they face to face. So then is the cnappan in fastness between both their bodies. And then cometh more of the same side and layeth grips on them, round about them both, so that you shall see a hundred or six score clustered together as bees when they swarm are knit together, the ball being in the midst of them, which the other party seek to open or undo by heaving and pulling.' Nor was traditional Welsh guile at a discount. Twentieth-century tricksters at the base of the scrum – Dickie Owen, Brace, Rowlands, let us say – were the lineal descendants of George Owen's 'young gallant, who not being able to get hold of the *cnappan* started off at a gallop as if he had the ball in his possession. A detachment of horsemen readily taken in followed him in hot pursuit and in time he was overtaken, but alas! the heady youth had not counted on the result . . . ' It required the legal refinements of the late nineteenth century to pronounce those horsemen offside for having been outwitted by the stratagem of the heady youth.

Of course, all ball games will inevitably share some characteristics, and to recognize *cnappan*'s kinship with Cornish hurling and Irish *cad*, French *soule* and plain English *foot-balle*, is not to invalidate the claims made on its behalf: it remains, to a limited extent, Welsh rugby's most plausible forebear. This is not because of its suggestive anticipations of later developments, but because local variants of it were from the seventeenth century sufficiently resilient to survive the successive assaults Puritans, Methodists and enclosing farmers made upon it until well into the nineteenth century. Allowing that the ball was now a bullock's bladder encased in leather, adaptations of *cnappan* were practised as far north as Dolgellau and as far east as Glamorgan. Amazingly, as late as 1884 the town of Neath became a Shrove Tuesday Pamplona as 'all shutters are put up and the principal thoroughfare is given over to the players'.

But if the traditional sports of rural Wales would not meekly yield to the new imperatives of industrial society, what Neath heard in 1884 was the last defiant shout of the old order. Three years previously in the Castle Hotel of the same town the Welsh Rugby Union had been formed to direct the affairs and regulate the expansion of a game that was sweeping South Wales. Sentimental, if calculated, evocations of 'the grand old game' notwithstanding, this was a whole new ball game, tailor-made for and increasingly tailored by the demands of a new society. This game, in intention at least, was shorn of the violent disorderliness of its rural forebears. Thanks to an accumulating complexity of standardizing rules and regulations, it was no longer diffuse and informally organized, its unwritten conventions governed only by local custom without limit of territory, time or participants. This game was subject to formal and elaborately written laws, limited in duration and played in a confined area by a fixed small number of players. In Wales this game was rugby football, and we would do better to seek its origins not in the ritualistic pastimes of the countryside but in the loutish violence of the great public schools of England.

In the first half of the nineteenth century, when the traditional bastions of political power and wealth were being challenged by the profound social changes which were already transforming England into the first industrial nation, the public schools were subjected to agonized re-appraisal. Socially and educationally, they were severely wanting. Indiscipline and disorder, the hallmarks of rural sports which according to contemporary commentators were in retreat in the face of agricultural modernization and urban growth, were to be found alive and kicking in those historic pedagogic institutions which had long since cheerfully disowned their 'public' obligation to provide for poor scholars, and were now narrow enclaves of private privilege. Recreation within their cloistered walls too frequently found expression in organized riot and rebellion.

For a cluster of reasons – anti-aristocratic hostility, genuine concern for moral reform, and the rising demands and expectations of the proliferating commercial and professional bourgeoisie – progressive headmasters like Arnold of Rugby (1828–42) and Thring of Uppingham (1853–87) perceived the advantages that could accrue from harnessing the traditional lawlessness of public school sports. The channelling of athletic energies into organized games would, through instilling self-control, respect for legality and authority, unselfishness and manliness, reinforce the discipline they were seeking to impose on the school community as a whole. Physical recreation was incorporated into the curriculum as an integral component of an enlightened education. Games, especially football, cricket and athletics, became moral correctives, instruments of character formation and social control. Such was the success of Arnold in particular at Rugby School, so insistent the middle-class demand for a greater provision for the proper education of their sons, that old schools took on a new lease of life: new schools from the 1840s – Cheltenham, Marlborough, Wellington, Tonbridge, Llandovery – multiplied; and old endowed grammar schools – Uppingham, Monmouth, Brecon, Cowbridge – transformed themselves into boarding establishments and were remodelled according to Arnoldian civilizing precepts in conscious emulation of the more prestigious public schools.

In the late 1830s Arthur Pell and other Rugbeians at King's College, Cambridge, introduced the game they had learned at school into the university. But other schools, conditioned by different physical environments and traditions longer than Rugby's, played according to different conventions. When Pell and his associates sought to play a group of Old Etonians in 1840, 'the Eton men howled at the Rugby men for handling the ball'. For meaningful fixtures to take place, a common set of rules needed to be agreed upon, and to this end successive attempts were made at the university between 1842 and 1863 to arrive at a consensus. The Cambridge rules of 1863 were adopted as a working basis by the Football Association, which was established later that year, under the aegis of a group of ex-public schoolboys spearheaded by Etonians and Harrovians. The Rugby School faction, whose banner was upheld principally by the Blackheath club, withdrew to form the nucleus of the Rugby Football Union which was established nine years later in a restaurant off Trafalgar Square. But the point at issue between them in 1863 had been 'hacking' – Rugby men regarded the deliberate kicking of an opponent on the shin as character-building, though the R.F.U. would, ironically, abolish it at its formation in 1871 – rather than handling and passing, which were not legitimate till the 1870s.

Whether the evolution of the rugby game owes anything at all to William Webb Ellis must be doubtful. The legend that it was Ellis 'who with a fine disregard for the rules of football as played in his time first took the ball in his arms and ran with it' in 1823, was first circulated in 1880 by a man who had left the school in 1820. Nor is it without significance that the plaque commemorating the alleged exploit was laid in 1895, the year when the rupture between the amateur ex-public schoolboys of the south of England and the non-public school manufacturers who were professionalizing the game in the industrial north became absolute. In the face of repeated attempts to outlaw it by law-makers at the universities, Rugby School's stubborn adherence to 'running in' with the ball instead of kicking it back to the opposition, owed less to the insubordination of a day-boy than the school's search for some identifying characteristic. For whatever Ellis did or did not do in 1823, being a day-boy he was of inferior social status and more likely to have been punished for his contravention of the rules than praised as an inspired innovator; in any case, 'running in' was not legalized even at Rugby till 1841. Far more crucial in the context of the times is that Rugby School was a relatively recent foundation and anxious to assert itself at the public school high table. Because of its middle-class sympathies it lacked the impeccable aristocratic credentials of Eton and Winchester, who could incorporate the old kicking game into their reformed football without any qualms. Middle-class Rugby could not afford the risk of being contaminated by the lower orders, and carrying the ball became its distinctive feature.

From *Fields of Praise* by Gareth Williams and David Smith
(University of Wales Press, Cardiff, 1980)

The Spectre of Professionalism

U.A. Titley and Ross McWhirter

The northerners came down in two special trains, to make sure of maximum possible representation, but some of them got lost in the metropolis as country bumpkins used to do even in those days. But they were up against the brilliant organizing genius of H.E. Steed (Lennox FC), who saw to it that there was a full poll of all the clubs who were to oppose the motion, and found proxies for 120 of those who for various reasons could not attend the meeting. His plans were ready days beforehand, and were certain to succeed. The Northern Union subsequently said that instead of Oxford and Cambridge Universities having a single vote each, the individual colleges from both Universities voted.

The 418 votes cast constituted a record attendance, and the 120 proxies were probably decisive. At the opening there was a strange and uncanny silence which often comes before the settlement of great issues by ordeal of battle. Everybody now knew that a decisive engagement was at hand. No possibility of compromise obscured the prospect of a fight to the finish. Feelings ran higher than ever before or after. When the chairman announced the result there was a loud, contrasting burst of applause.

Thus was laid the spectre of professionalism in the Rugby Union game, and a special General Meeting of the Union was held immediately after the close of the main one, when careful and significant revision was made of some of the by-laws, altering the system of election of Members to the Committee and officers of the Union, and laying down new lines of procedure for general meetings. These were carefully prepared and served their immediate purpose – 'to crush any attempt to establish professional cells within the Government machine'.

That famous occasion saved the Union, but it remained to drive out professionals, so the Committee prepared a draft of proposed new laws against professionalism, which contained exceedingly wide definitions and drastic punitive clauses. These were introduced and passed at a general meeting on 19 September 1895, and at the same time the revised by-laws were adopted which tightened the Union's hold upon leagues.

These happenings produced exactly the result expected and desired by the Committee. On 29 August 1895 (only three weeks before the General Meeting of the Rugby Union) there was a meeting of twenty-two clubs at the Mitre Hotel, Leeds, at which it was decided to form what was then described as a 'Northern Football Union', to be established 'on the principle of payment for *bona fide* broken time'. Following this meeting all the clubs involved resigned from the Rugby Union.

From *The Centenary History of the Rugby Football Union*
by U.A. Titley and Ross McWhirter
(RFU, London, 1971)

Broken Time

Geoffrey Moorhouse

What happened that day in Huddersfield was, with smaller repercussions, as much of a social, economic and political insurrection as the resistance of half a dozen farmworkers at Tolpuddle, sixty-one years earlier, to a reduction in their wages. It, too, was fundamentally about artisans and labourers making ends meet.

The game which gave rise to the dispute, although the result of a popular evolution across centuries, had been systematically organized in the nineteenth century by the upper and middle classes, who played a similar role at approximately the same time in the development of golf, soccer, athletics and cricket. William Webb Ellis's famous handling of the football at Rugby School is supposed to have occurred in 1823, but it was not until 1871 that the Rugby Football Union was founded, to be followed within a few years by the formation of similar bodies in Scotland, Ireland and Wales. By then, rugby was no longer the sole preserve of the well-to-do, as it had originally been. It had become the people's game as well, most notably in South Wales and in the North of England, for reasons connected with the great industrialization of these areas in the nineteenth century. 'Sport provided pleasure where work did not, and the more strenuous the physical labour the more strenuous the physical release it demanded.'

In time, the majority of rugby clubs in the North drew their playing strength from the mills, the foundries and the coal-mines of the region, and these footballers were not often from the salaried management: they were wage-earners of the rank and file. Such were the men who started to play rugby in Huddersfield in 1878, when the local team was formed.

The five-day week was still two or three generations away and Saturday was no different from Monday, whether you were labouring on piece-work or on shifts. If you wanted to play football or otherwise pleasure yourself on the seventh day, you forfeited that part of your wage. There was the rub. Many of the finest rugby footballers in the land simply couldn't afford to. These were rules codified by men who could take time off from their properties, their businesses and professions whenever they had a mind to play games, to go fishing, to hunt fox, to shoot birds. But gradually a number of northern clubs sought to revise them, and it is likely that they were impelled by a desire to maintain their success on the field as much as by any considerations of equity off it. For the North had become the English stronghold of rugby.

The RFU, for reasons which are understandable enough, has always chosen to represent 1895 as no more than a hiccup in an otherwise stately advance along the years: 'its progress was impeded for a while', according to one chronicler of the Union code. The reality was more uncomfortable than that. The England XV, weakened by the withdrawals from the North, began to lose international matches at an unheard-of rate, and when Wales crushed them 26–3 at Swansea four years after the great schism, the defeat was specifically attributed by many observers to the loss of Yorkshire and Lancashire forwards who had traditionally provided the backbone of the pack. A correspondent of the *Morning Leader*, a London newspaper, smarting in the aftermath of the Welsh victory, saw a more fundamental reason for England's humiliation that day.

> For many years the Rugby Union has been a closed corporation, composed of men with the mistaken idea that only public schoolboys and University men could play the game. The middle-class and working-man footballer was barely tolerated. And yet it is the latter class rather than the University player that furnishes the majority of the best footballers today.

The point about the closed corporation was to remain valid for many a year, with lasting effect. One consequence of 1895 was that the Rugby Union's version of football ceased to be a working-class game in England except in a few margins of the realm: the Celtic fringe of Cornwall, the secluded Forest of Dean, the fastnesses of Cumbria; scarcely anywhere else. The lost ground has never been recovered. Another consequence was a sourness in the air between the old guard and the renegades which has not yet disappeared, so that we are still from time to time obliged to behold the patronizing figure of Homo Twickiens, as well as his natural adversary, the aggrieved belt-and-braces character from the North.

From *At The George* by Geoffrey Moorhouse
(Hodder & Stoughton, Sevenoaks, 1989)

A Story

Dylan Thomas

There is another great tradition in Rugby Football, which it would be remiss of me not to include here. It is the great tradition of rugby men taking a glass or two after a game, and a glass or two more when on tour. Rugby players and supporters alike will empathize with Dylan Thomas's story of an epic trip by a group of Welsh rugby men.

W.B.B.

Closing time meant nothing to the members of that outing. Behind locked doors, they hymned and rumpused all the beautiful afternoon. And, when a policeman entered the Druid's Tap by the back door, and found them all choral with beer, 'Sssh!' said Noah Bowen, 'the pub is shut!'

'Where do you come from?' he said in his buttoned, blue voice.

They told him.

'I got a auntie there,' the policeman said. And very soon he was singing Asleep in the Deep.

Off we drove again at last, the charabanc bouncing with tenors and flagons, and came to a river that rushed along among willows.

'Water,' they shouted.

'Porthcawl!' sang my uncle.

'Where's the donkeys?' said Mr Weasley.

And out they lurched, to paddle and whoop in the cool, white, winding water. Mr Franklin, trying to polka on the slippery stones, fell in twice. 'Nothing is simple' he said with dignity as he oozed up the bank.

'It's cold!' they cried.

'It's lovely.'

'It's smooth as a moth's nose!'

'It's *better* than Porthcawl!'

And dusk came down warm and gentle on thirty wild, wet, pickled, splashing men without a care in the world at the end of the world in the west of Wales. And, 'Who goes there?' cried Will Sentry to a wild duck flying.

They stopped at the Hermit's Nest for a rum to keep out the cold. 'I played for Aberavon in 1898' said a stranger to Enoch Davies.

'Liar' said Enoch Davies.

'I can show you the photos' said the stranger.

'Forged' said Enoch Davies.

'And I'll show you my cap at home.'

'Stolen.'

'I got friends to prove it' the stranger said in a fury.

'Bribed' said Enoch Davies.

On the way home, through the simmering moon-splashed dark, old O Jones began to cook his supper on a primus stove in the middle of the charabanc. Mr Weasley coughed himself blue in the smoke. 'Stop the bus' he cried 'I'm dying of breath!' We all climbed down into the moonlight. There was not a public house in sight. So they carried out the remaining cases, and the primus stove, and old O Jones himself, and took them into a field, and sat down in a circle in the field and drank and sang while old O Jones cooked sausage and mash and the moon flew above us. And there I drifted to sleep against my uncle's mountainous waistcoat, and, as I slept, 'Who goes there?' called out Will Sentry to the flying moon.

From *A Prospect of the Sea* by Dylan Thomas
(J.M. Dent, London, 1955)

2
GREAT TRIES

A Definitive Statement

John Reason

The purpose of rugby is to score tries. Over the years there must have been millions –
I even managed the odd one myself – but a handful of tries have been so exceptional
that they have lived in the memory to be recalled with pleasure years and even decades
later.

Ask any rugby fan to name the greatest try he has ever seen and the odds are better
than evens that the reply will be 'Gareth Edwards' try for the Barbarians against the All
Blacks in 1973'. John Reason describes the background to that celebrated match and
that extraordinary try.

W.B.B.

Some of the uglier aspects of nationalism in sport had spread to Rugby football and
nowhere was this unhealthy development more apparent than in the relations between
New Zealand and Wales. Since 1953, the All Blacks had enjoyed an unbroken run of
success in their matches against Wales, and it was a run which was to continue. Justifiably,
the All Blacks will look back on their international victories in 1972–73 with pride. They
were gained in the face of internal dissension and considerable local hostility, but ironically,
their tour will be remembered for their match against the Barbarians at the end. It was a
match which the All Blacks lost but as hundreds of millions of ecstatic television viewers
will testify, it was a match which could lay fair claim to being the greatest ever played in
the history of the game and it went a long way towards redeeming the less attractive
features of the tour.

The only sadness was that Barry John was not a part of it, because the team chosen by
the Barbarians was essentially the team that had represented the British Lions in New
Zealand in 1971. John Dawes, captain of the Lions and the Barbarians, asked Carwyn
James to coach the team in a training session on the Thursday before the match at Cardiff
Arms Park. The Lions' coach said that he felt that it would not be appropriate for him to
do so, but after discussing the matter with Geoff Windsor-Lewis, the secretary of the
Barbarians, he agreed to give the team a talk on the morning of the match.

Apart from a game against Oxford University the previous autumn, the team had not
played since it left New Zealand in 1971. A certain rustiness seemed inevitable, and
perhaps a lack of familiarity, because Barry John's place at fly-half had been taken by

Phil Bennett, and Bob Wilkinson and Tom David had been chosen as uncapped players in the pack. Gerald Davies had to withdraw, too, because of indisposition on the eve of the match so David Duckham switched to the right wing and John Bevan came in on the left.

Carwyn James reminded the players of what they had achieved, and what they could achieve. He told them not to be inhibited and to enjoy themselves. He turned on Phil Bennett, his club fly-half at Llanelli, whom he had known and nurtured since he was a schoolboy. 'Now what are you going to do, Phil?' he asked. 'You've got a great side-step, but I don't suppose you will use it. Yet these All Blacks are made to be side-stepped!'

It was not possible for Carwyn James to do more than encourage his players; to re-assure them; to stimulate them; even, in the case of one or two like Phil Bennett, to goad them a little. Even so, Carwyn James felt optimistic. Barry John, Gerald Davies, Mervyn Davies and Peter Dixon were missing from his team, but Phil Bennett had played for his own Llanelli club team that had staggered the All Blacks by beating them at the beginning of their tour, and so had Tom David. That was the day the pubs had run dry in Llanelli. It was a day immortalized in song by Max Boyce, who was becoming as much a part of Welsh Rugby as Grenville Jones who, under the name of Gren, had drawn an intensely amusing world of cartoon characters straight from the gut of Rugby humour. With their troubadour to sing of their deeds, and their court painter to add to the legends, Bennett and David knew what it was like to beat the All Blacks, and they would not be afraid of doing so again.

Carwyn James tried to imbue his players with confidence. J.P.R. Williams said, 'When we went into the meeting, we were all a little bit hesitant, a bit uncertain. It had been a long time since we had played together. But as Carwyn spoke, suddenly it seemed all right. We knew we could do it.'

Indeed they could. They went out on to the Arms Park and played the game of their lives, and extraordinarily enough, they began with a breathtaking try scored from a sweeping counter-attack which had its origins in three staccato bursts of side-stepping by Phil Bennett from a position deep in defence.

From the moment that Bennett kicked off for the Barbarians, there was a feeling of tension and last-night drama in the air, probably because most people considered that it was the fifth test match between the All Blacks and the 1971 Lions. The first scrum went to the All Blacks; the first line-out to the Barbarians. There were a couple of exploratory kicks, and then Sid Going caught a high ball from J.P.R. Williams and went probing forward. Going linked with his forwards and Ian Kirkpatrick put Bryan Williams away on the right.

Williams cross-kicked when he was squeezed towards the touch-line and what happened thereafter must have stunned him as much as it delighted the crowd. Bennett had to chase the kick deep in his own 25 and looked over his shoulder to see Kirkpatrick and Scown bearing down on him. When he picked up the ball, though, he did not kick for touch. Instead, he turned sharply back and cut the first wave of All Blacks to pieces with his side-steps before passing to J.P.R. Williams. The Barbarians' full-back was almost garrotted by a high tackle but Pullin supported him and made room for Dawes near the left touch-line. Dawes sold the sweetest of little dummies before passing inside to David who gave a low, one-handed scoop of a pass which Quinnell somehow took from down round his knees.

Quinnell recovered his balance and the Barbarians were in full cry near the half-way line. Quinnell went to pass to Bevan on the left wing but Edwards came snorting through to intercept the pass and beat the despairing New Zealand cover in a ferocious forty-yard sprint to the line. It was one of the most exhilarating tries ever scored in top-class Rugby and the rhythm of the passing and the running was as definitive a statement of a theme as the opening of Beethoven's Fifth Symphony.

From *The World of Rugby* by John Reason
(BBC, London, 1979)

What a Score!

Gareth Edwards

Gareth Edwards is one of the greatest scrum-halves I have ever seen and that great try showed many of the facets of Edwards' peerless game, his vision, his power, his pace and above all his fierce determination – a great competitor, scoring a great try. Here is his own description of the move that ensured his rugby immortality.

W.B.B.

It was a beautiful day. The crowd were in an exceptional mood, as if they sensed something was going to happen. The first two minutes quickly vanished and my mouth was dry with the nervousness which overcomes everyone in such circumstances. I was forced to challenge Bryan Williams, who received a pass from Ian Kirkpatrick following a blind side break. Williams hooked the ball down towards our posts and I thought: 'What did he want to do that for?' I was already feeling the pace and had to force my legs to run backwards to cover when I saw Phil Bennett scampering back towards our posts, being chased by three All Blacks.

I thought he was bound to kick the ball for touch, but for no apparent reason he side-stepped back inside, beating all three men. On the film you see me covering back, as Phil is coming forward infield towards the south stand. By then I was somewhere between the 25 and the half-way line. Surprised that he hadn't kicked, I didn't really know what to do. On film movements appear to be fast but during the game they are slower, unfolding in front of you. Phil passed the ball to J.P.R. Williams, who rode a tackle before passing to John Pullin. As Pullin is unaccustomed to such a situation, everyone expected him to kick to touch and kill the ball there and then. Instead he passed on to John Dawes, who ran past me as I was going in the other direction. Everything was now happening behind me.

As I turned round to attempt to join the move my legs felt like lead. I was breathing hard and my mouth was dry. All I wanted somebody to do was put the ball to touch so the game could settle down. I was frightened we would do something daft early in the game. I saw Dawes side-step two men and break infield passing to Tommy David. I still could not understand what was going on fifteen yards ahead, but then I thought something could happen and decided to chase. The crowd were beginning to sense something momentous was about to take place. They had been lifted by Phil Bennett not having killed the ball, by his failure to conform.

Four Barbarians had handled the ball within our 25. So everything everybody had hoped for had already begun to happen within two minutes of the kick-off. Tommy David now brought off a superb one-handed pass to Derek Quinnell, who somehow managed to take the ball below his knees. I only remained with the play because it is the scrum-half's job to be up for any breakdown. I was frightened what would happen if the ball went loose and I was not there to pick it up. It's funny looking back on it that I was there running in support mainly because I didn't want to make a fool of myself. Most of what happened in the closing stages of that try are a blur. I remember Quinnell being tackled and just throwing the ball to his left. I managed to take it and had the sensation I was running faster than ever before in my life. Although I was oblivious to the crowd I could hear the background murmur. There were still thirty yards to go to the line, but as I went past the first defender I knew nobody was going to catch me. It didn't matter if I had to run to Newport, I was not going to be caught. I just had to score.

From *How the Lions Won* edited by Terry O'Connor
(Collins, London, 1975)

Tries Which Thrilled 70,000

H.B.T. Wakelam

Englishmen have scored their share of memorable tries too, whatever our detractors in the Valleys may say! To mention the name of Obolensky is enough to produce a response, even from those not born until long after 'Obolensky's Match'. The Russian prince, a student at Oxford University, scored two exceptional tries 'which perhaps no other man of today could have scored' in the words of the *Morning Post*'s formidable correspondent H.B.T. Wakelam.

Perhaps those tries, scored at Twickenham in 1936, might have faded from memory, but they led to England's first-ever victory against the All Blacks. It had been a long, thirty-year wait, and Obolensky's part in the victory will not be forgotten as long as rugby is played.

W.B.B.

Perfect football weather and a crowd of over 70,000 greeted the New Zealanders at Twickenham for the last match of their tour – a match which was to prove historic, for England, playing really remarkable football, avenged her defeats of 1905 and 1925 in no uncertain style, and registered a magnificent and genuinely gained victory. Before the kick-off the Prince of Wales, with a keen regard for the muscles and nerves of the participants, visited each team in turn in their dressing-rooms, afterwards to sit, with the Crown Prince of Egypt, in the Royal Box, and to follow each move of the game with the keenest interest.

And what a game it was! Probably not even the most fervid English supporter could have hoped for such a decisive result; indeed, one has to go back to the days of Wakefield and Davies to find any kind of a parallel to the display of the Englishmen. From trials and previous reportations, the general impression had been that the fifteen chosen were a sound but not too convincing sort of a team, but that impression was utterly mistaken, for with each man striking the top of his form, there was a zest and fire about their work throughout which have been rather lacking of late years.

Moreover, there was team-work, a virtue so often conspicuous by its absence in our Home International fifteens. In fact, had a complete stranger made his way into the ground, he might very reasonably have thought that it was the men in white who had played so often together. Naturally, one seeks for the reasons for such a display, and just as naturally, perhaps, the name of Obolensky comes straight to mind, for undoubtedly, his two first-half tries, which perhaps no other man of today could have scored, had a tremendous bearing on the result; but all the same, one fancies that the real decisive factor was the truly remarkable midfield defence, and the really deadly marking and tackling of Caughey, Oliver and Co. by Candler, Gerrard and Cranmer.

After all was over, a very knowledgeable observer who stood on the South Mound, thereby being able to watch the tactics of the game, remarked that only once throughout the whole eighty minutes did the New Zealand attack bear straight towards the English goal-line – this occasion being the strong midfield dash by Gilbert in the first half, which so nearly led to a try by Reid. Only once, too, did Oliver 'shake' his man, this time in the second half.

Here, then, is the complete proof of that marking-down, and just to quote one outstanding instance of it, one recalls the adventures of Caughey in a likely-looking New Zealand attack not long after the start. Sent off beautifully by Corner and Tindill, he seemed almost through with one of those deadly short bursts of his, but crack! crack!! crack!!! and Candler had him round the neck, Cranmer round the waist, and Gerrard round the ankles. And that, very definitely, was that.

To continue on this defence topic, nothing could have been finer than the spoiling work of Gadney and the ever vigilant Weston round the blind side, whilst Hamilton-Hill, in his first international, fairly covered himself with glory by the way in which he helped Candler to keep Tindill in complete subjection. Sever, too, tackled splendidly, but, perhaps, the most prominent individual was Obolensky, whose deadly grassing of the dangerous Ball was almost as great a delight to the crowd as his phenomenal attacking stride.

And then there was Owen-Smith, ever at hand, ever ready to take a sudden pass back from a harassed brother defender, cool and calm throughout, and a most consistent touch finder. Once or twice he may have slipped or fumbled, but that was only a proof of the treacherous going after the recent frosts and rains. The short smother-tackling of the forwards was another very prominent feature, and altogether the whole defensive plan of the team was extremely well devised and carried out.

When it comes to the attacking side of things, we saw everything. The sudden, strong Gadney break, with Hamilton-Hill invariably up – the well-judged and well-timed Candler pass to the man behind him – the brilliant Cranmer cut-through, which incidentally led to two tries – the steady and reliable Gerrard always in the right place – the strong, 'never-say-die' Sever full out on any and every occasion – and last, but not least, the amazing pace and running genius of young Obolensky.

Runners we have seen before, but since the days of C.N. Lowe (at the moment, no doubt, a very, very proud selector) never such a runner with such an innate idea of where to go and how to get there. His double swerve to gain his first try was remarkable enough, but the extraordinary turn in and diagonal right-to-left run which won him his second, and which drew forth that great Twickenham rarity, a double roar of applause, will never be forgotten by anyone who saw it.

After almost half an hour of even play, with England playing from the South end, the ball came to Obolensky on the half-way line. Half-tackled, he went down on one knee, to spring up again like a flash, and to make off down the wing. Beating first his own man, and then Gilbert with a lightning swerve, amidst a roar that must have been audible miles away, he crossed just by the touch-flag, and, hunted home by Corner, grounded the ball half-way out. Dunkley's kick hit the cross-bar and rebounded.

Three minutes before half-time, Peter Cranmer shot straight and hard through the centre to give to Candler at the twenty-five, with Obolensky on Candler's right. Seeing his direct way apparently barred, Obolensky suddenly dashed behind Candler, to take a perfect inside pass, and to spreadeagle the New Zealanders with a most remarkable diagonal run towards the left-hand corner flag. Mitchell dived gallantly at him, but his pace carried him safely round, and he slid to rest well over the line as the surprised coverers converged on him.

From the *Morning Post*, 6 January 1936

Oboe Obbligato

The editorial in the *Morning Post* on the following day struck exactly 'the right note of English modesty'.

W.B.B.

It would not be right to boast about England's decisive defeat of the All Blacks in the final match of a tiring tour. The victory was utterly unexpected, and the vast crowd were wildly enthusiastic. For the first time in the annals of the Twickenham arena we saw hats being hurled high in the air by staid stout Englishmen of outsize physique who might have been second-row forwards in a previous generation. But the right note of English modesty was struck by a small middle-aged spectator, formerly a well-known scrum-half, who thought the game a blessed exception to Mr Dooley's ironical ruling: 'The English are good losers – they lose every time.' Let us leave it at that and congratulate the two sides, and also the referee, on collaborating in as glorious a display of Rugby football as was ever seen in an international match. There were very few penalty kicks, not too much use of the whistle, and every player lived up to the exhilarating maxim that the best form of defence is attack. And a new hero of the game appeared in the flying wing three-quarter affectionately styled 'Oboe', whose running, as befits his Russian origin, had the speed and urge of music by Tchaikowsky. Even the 'Flying Scotsman', Ian Smith, never did anything to surpass the two tries he scored in the first half. His first triumphant sprint left the New Zealand defence standing, and his second, when he crossed to score in the wrong corner, was a stroke of genius. May we live to see many another Obolensky try!

From an Editorial in the Morning Post, 6 January 1936

Jackson's Try

Peter Robbins

For sheer drama it would be hard to beat the try scored by Peter Jackson for England against Australia in 1958. Jackson crossed in the dying seconds to seize a victory that had seemed lost. Peter Robbins, a make shift centre in that England team, recalls Jackson's genius.

W.B.B.

The Wallabies were very anxious to beat England and would have earned at least a draw but for Jackson's dramatic try. Neither do I use the word dramatic loosely, for the situation had been building up wherein only a stroke of genius could rescue England.

Consider the fact that Horrocks-Taylor had been carried off fifteen minutes before half-time with Butterfield moving into his position. Australia had led at half-time through a penalty by Lenehan which Phillips cancelled out by a brilliant try in the second half. But then, six minutes before full time, Curley, the Australian full-back, kicked a beautiful drop-goal for what looked like the winning score.

Critically at this point both teams became desperate, but their desperation took two entirely different forms. England began to pass the ball on every occasion. Marques, Thompson and Jackson were all just held on the line. Australia showed their panic by some blatant late tackling on the England three-quarters, especially on Butterfield. In addition Thompson had been brutally and needlessly kicked when on the ground, and these incidents incensed the crowd. According to Jackson, this heightened the tension and thus made his try even more sensational since the crowd were now without shame part of the England struggle.

With time running out, England launched a series of frenzied attacks. I was playing in the centre in the second half and had only one thought: that was to give Jackson the ball whenever and as soon as possible. Marques won the line-out on the Australian twenty-five, and on the left playing towards the south terrace. The ball sped from Jeeps along the line to Jackson, who received it just outside the Australian twenty-five with Phelps, Curley and the cover to beat.

Jackson says that Phelps did not come in cleanly enough to tackle him, and so he was able to hand off, using Phelps's head as a lever. This left Curley, who knew Jackson's liking for coming inside. Jackson vividly remembers that Curley shaped up to expect this inside jink, and he says that this was all he needed. To use his own words, he did a double shuffle to the right, and I believe that only he could have left such a vital decision to this last moment. Curley got a hand to him, and incredibly Phelps got back to retackle, but Jackson had already launched himself at the line.

I asked Peter Jackson what had been going through his mind in this hectic period. His prime thought was that, under Evans's encouragement and fine leadership, there must be a chink with so much pressure. When he got the ball his reaction was, 'At last I have space and time. Here is a golden chance.' He quickly erased any other thoughts from his mind and his brilliant rugby brain turned its attention to the local and away from the general situation.

Had Phelps not been so psychologically afraid, the game might have ended in a draw. Yet it was this very paralysing effect that Jackson had on defenders, coupled with his own genius, that gave England victory.

When the try was given the scenes were extraordinary. Cushions flew sky high. The crowd cheered in joy, excitement and relief. Jackson walked back to the halfway line feeling nothing but complete numbness, so drained was he emotionally and physically. We all felt numb in the dressing-room afterwards. There was total silence until our wonderful skipper, Eric Evans, said in that chirpy voice of his, 'Well, we beat 'em.'

From *Touchdown*
(RFU, London, 1958)

Sharp's Try

Cliff Morgan

Cliff Morgan, one of the great fly-halves of any era, is perhaps as good a man as any to judge one of the great fly-half's tries – that scored by Richard Sharp for England in the 1963 Calcutta Cup against Scotland at Twickenham. Some dispute Sharp's right to be included in a selection of great tries, claiming that he was selfish and should have been tackled, but Morgan, who should know, will have none of this.

W.B.B.

Richard Sharp said, 'Mike Weston really made that try. You see, the critical man in a scissors move is *not* the man carrying the ball. Just as in soccer, it's the player running *off* the ball who does the damage. That's what Mike did – causing the defence to hesitate a fraction and so give me the space I needed.'

Richard Sharp was not being modest. His assessment of that never-to-be-forgotten twenty-two seconds of magic was realistic.

It will come as a surprise to many that this move had been pre-planned. England had scored an almost identical try against France the season before, and Sharp and Weston believed in the scissors. Working on the hard facts that in a period when, more often than not, the defensive formation was flat, they decided that there were only a limited number of possibilities of attack from a set scrummage (from the line-out, attack was almost impossible).

It was the age of the selective and discriminating player. The fly-half could do one of four things: a high punt to catch the opposition full-back in possession; the long, rolling ball to the corner flag; the short chip over the heads of the advancing three-quarters – or the scissors. Sharp's effort against Scotland has become the classic example of that.

From the moment he received the ball the try was on. A flat Jeeps pass taken at speed put Sharp a yard outside the back-row cover. He was immediately moving faster, for Sharp's real advantage was that he was even quicker over the second ten yards than he was over the vital first ten. At this moment his direction was somewhere along a line from the twenty-five yards mark on the right-hand touch-line, to a point fifteen yards in from the other side.

Mike Weston ran wide with Sharp for several yards – and here is the secret of a perfect scissors. The supporting player has first to run with the carrier of the ball before switching inside. Weston's move inside and his call were perfection, and they brought confusion in the Scottish centre. That moment of hesitation gave Sharp only a split second, but that's all a great player needs.

Sharp didn't stop to ask the time of day, and he found his wing, Jim Roberts, up in support at his left elbow. Only one Scot was in the area – the full-back, Colin Blakie – so it was a two-to-one situation and a certain score. It was at this point, with Blakie in his sights, that Sharp straightened and leaned away from Roberts, in classical style, as he offered a pass. For a fraction of a second, Blakie moved towards Roberts – a glorious dummy – and Richard Sharp had crossed the Scottish line.

Some who saw that try still claim that Sharp should have passed to Roberts, but to the trained eye it was plain. Sharp simply had to go it alone . . . 'I had no choice, for my mind was made up for me. Blakie committed the cardinal sin of not going for the man in possession. I was almost on top of him when I realized that although he was physically in front of me, his mind was on Jim Roberts. The memory of that moment is still vivid. I know I did the right thing.'

So many things could have ruined that moment – had Sharp decided to pass to Roberts. The angle at which Roberts was forced to run to get up with Sharp might well have meant a forward pass. The pass could have been a bad one. Equally, Roberts could have put it down. But these things are conjecture, and the hard fact is that Sharp scored a winning try.

The real test of greatness is in adversity, and this try is proof. It was scored from a set scrummage in a period when it was virtually impossible to move from a set-piece. And it was scored when England trailed by eight points to five.

In this glorious flourish Richard Sharp, like all the great professionals at a craft – like Sophie Tucker and Bob Hope – revealed a perfect sense of timing. This one move bore the hallmark of Sharp's class. From the moment he fastened on to that low, flat pass from Dickie Jeeps until he touched down – near enough to make the conversion by John Wilcox a formality – it was all grace, pace and co-ordination. For a fly-half watching a fly-half, this try was the ultimate.

From *Touchdown*
(RFU, London, 1970)

The Finest Match I've Ever Seen

Stephen Jones

If the 1973 Barbarians versus All Blacks game was one of the greatest games ever seen, the 1987 World Cup produced one to rank alongside it: the semi-final between Australia and France at the Concord Oval in Sydney. It was a humble venue for a great occasion, but as *Sunday Times* correspondent Stephen Jones reported, it ' . . . gave a passable imitation of a cathedral of the game. The rugby came from up above too.' A match almost lost by an error by Serge Blanco was retrieved by a typical piece of flair from the great man, one of the giants of world rugby carrying his team to the final of the World Cup.

W.B.B.

My immediate reaction when the final whistle blew on a stunning match was that this was the greatest rugby international of all. After more sober reflection, the reaction was just the same.

In Sydney yesterday, France thundered into the World Cup final when everyone had mentally reserved it for New Zealand and Australia. They did it with a performance of such wondrous commitment and skill that the Australian crowd stood to them. Even so, they won it only in the last seconds as Australia superbly defended their supposed divine right to the final.

Serge Blanco, the French full-back, made a terrible error with the match at 21–21 and inside the last three minutes of normal time. He tried to beat one man too many in his own twenty-two. He was caught and shipped out a hospital pass to Didier Camberabero, who in turn was engulfed by what looked like half the Australian nation underneath his own posts. Camberabero infringed in the depths of a frightening ruck and Mike Lynagh kicked the penalty as Blanco held his head in his hands. Australia led 24–21.

Soon afterwards, Didier made his mate Serge feel a lot better. Camberabero kicked a fine goal – the pressure kick of his life – after a late tackle. And deep, deep into injury time, Serge Blanco came again.

The move began with Australia in possession and Lynagh and Campese ready to surge. But Lynagh was crunched by two Frenchmen and Lagisquet kicked the ball on. After it, running like a wounded stag, went Lorieux, the French lock who played a game of staggering intensity.

Lorieux reached it first and play moved to the right. Charvet was caught, the ball was switched. Lagisquet made ground and Rodriguez fed Blanco with the loose ball. Blanco set off with twenty-five metres to go and, though he was hammered by the cover defence, he forced the ball down in the corner. Camberabero kicked a huge conversion and the whistle blew.

When Blanco touched down the rest of the players were strewn all over the place. There were two Frenchmen and one Australian prostrate on the field and the others were scattered along the sinuous route of the final movement. Indeed, a long pass by Berbizier to Lagisquet came within a foot of being intercepted, and therefore within a foot of a winning try at the other end.

This climax sat perfectly on the rest of the match. There were some sweeping movements, breathless, elongated passages of play involving the electric Blanco or Campese.

The forward play, given the circumstances and all that was at stake, kept remarkably within the laws, except for a crude lunge by Tony McIntyre which would have ended Lorieux's prospects of having much fun in his later life had it connected.

Everything else was marvellous to watch. The final couldn't possibly be better, but so what. This match can be treasured for years. What a pity it was not networked live on the BBC television screens.

The pre-match propaganda from the French headquarters suggested that they were tired after their long, long season. They should play tired more often. Rodriguez led so many charges in the loose, and Garuet and his front five packed such a shove in the scrum, that the Australian pack hardly figured – and all week, Australian forwards had been appearing in the media telling everyone how fearsome they were.

Admittedly, they were hampered in the line-out when Bill Campbell, their 6ft 8in lock, went off with a knee injury, but David Codey, his replacement, was the outstanding Australian player.

Australia held on through Cutler's telescopic arm in the line-outs and through the fearless, hungry scrabbling of Miller. Lynagh played a fine game and Campese, described by his coach as the Bradman of rugby, had another typical match. One minute he was spilling easy passes, the next he was goose-stepping off through the heart of the French defence.

Indeed, it was Campese who steadied Australia when they were three points down well into the second half. Just before half-time Lorieux had scored a try by wrenching the ball free from Tony Coker at a line-out and driving over down the blindside.

Just after the interval, Champ and Lorieux had set up a chance for Sella, who cut diagonally across the grain of the defence to take it superbly. Thus France, who had made a nervous start, led 12–9.

Then Lynagh made a break close to a ruck and Grigg sent Campese on his way to the try – his twenty-fifth in international rugby and a new world record. That set up a breathless rat-tat-tat.

Blanco carved out an opening for Lagisquet to score and Camberabero kicked a penalty. Just into the third quarter, the referee allowed Australia a try almost as controversial as the one Campese was awarded against England three weeks ago.

Mr Anderson allowed Australia to throw the ball in two yards crooked at the line-out. Australia knocked on when they tried to clean up, then Codey seized the ball and stormed over.

Blanco summoned up every English word known to him and probably tried to add a bit of a Scottish accent for Mr Anderson's benefit. But the try stood and Lynagh's kick made it 21–21. Extra time beckoned; then came Blanco's moments of pain and elation.

To their credit the crowd swallowed their disappointment at finding that the invincible were beatable. For the French there was an added bonus: their prime minister, Jacques Chirac, had promised the team that he would personally finance a holiday in Tahiti if they reached the final.

Practically the only drawback on the day was that bungling by the marketing agents for the tournament had taken the match away from the Sydney Cricket Ground and into the smaller, suburban Concorde Oval. Yet as the French team returned to the pitch in the dusk to sing for their supporters and their TV cameras, the Oval gave a passable imitation of a cathedral of the game. The rugby came straight from up above too.

From the *Sunday Times*, 14 June 1987

Did Deans Score?

Cliff Morgan

There is one 'try' that is still discussed with passion, and occasionally fury, though well over eighty years have passed. Wales' 3–0 victory against the First All Blacks at Cardiff Arms Park in 1905 laid the foundations of an intense rugby rivalry between the two countries that continues to this day. Like Deans, New Zealanders will go to their graves claiming that he did score; like Gabe, Welshmen will just as vehemently argue that he did not. As a Welshman, Cliff Morgan can have only one answer to the question, 'Did Deans Score?'

W.B.B.

When Mr W.J. Dallas disallowed a 'try' that R.G. (Bob) Deans of New Zealand claimed he had scored, the Scottish referee could have had no idea that the rights and wrongs of his decision would be talked about eighty-five years later.

It is said that children on their mother's knee in New Zealand learn, not nursery rhymes, but the fact that Deans did score at Cardiff. I know for a fact that every Welsh schoolboy is taught the opposite. Whatever the truth, one thing is certain: the most controversial and talked about moment in rugby history is in its way as significant as the moment when William Webb Ellis first picked up a ball and ran. New Zealanders make pilgrimages to Cardiff Arms Park to take away some blades of grass . . . 'from the spot where Deans scored in 1905'. The first thing you're shown when you join the Cardiff Rugby Club, is the 'spot' where Deans didn't score.

The referee, Mr Dallas, was never in any doubt that Deans was tackled short of the Welsh line – as you see from his testament which his widow donated, with his whistle, to Mr Hubert Johnson for the Rugby Museum at the Cardiff Athletic Club.

Teddy Morgan claimed he'd tackled Deans and twenty years later wrote a message on a menu card which confirmed that Deans had scored. Meanwhile R.T. (Rhys) Gabe, another of the Welsh backs, claimed he had tackled Deans. In fact, only a few days before Mr Gabe died, he told me, during a radio interview, that Deans had not made the line. 'I tackled Deans about 6–12 inches from the line. Now if he was over the line as he claimed, why did he try to struggle forward? That's proof he hadn't made it.'

In New Zealand it has been reported that Bob Deans, with his last breath claimed . . . 'I did score at Cardiff.'

Fable or fact? It doesn't really matter, for that disallowed 'try' – which cost Dave Gallacher's team its only defeat of the tour – has been a stimulating talking point for generations.

From *Touchdown*
(RFU, London, 1970)

3
GREAT OCCASIONS

The Greatest Match

J.B.G. Thomas

The controversy over the Deans 'try' was only one of the factors that made the clash between the First All Blacks and Wales in 1905 a game to live in the memory. The unbeaten All Blacks, facing a powerful Welsh side as the last hurdle on a hitherto unbeaten tour, a packed Arms Park, a superb Welsh try, the Deans incident and eighty minutes of incredible tension, made it a match the spectators would never forget, even if J.B.G. Thomas's estimate of the size of the crowd is a little high!

W.B.B.

The conquering march of the first 'All-Blacks', as they traversed the Home Countries, grew into a majestic challenge for these proud Welshmen. Never before had 'foreign' invaders reached these shores and beaten our leading teams at Rugby Football, but here in 1905 the 'All-Blacks' not only won their matches, but won them with consummate ease, scattering the opposition to the four corners of the field. Yet, wherever they went, exiled Welshmen would utter the cry, 'Wait till you meet Wales!'

The morning of the match produced tremendous scenes of excitement in the City of Cardiff. The New Zealanders had been royally entertained by the first Lord Mayor of the City on the Friday, and had been shown around the City and the Docks, and all had reported fit except their flying wing, George Smith. Referee John Dallas had arrived from Scotland, and although presented with a new silver whistle for the occasion by the secretary of the Welsh Rugby Union, Capt. Walter Rees, he decided he would use his own favourite whistle, which, incidentally, he bequeathed in his will to the Welsh Rugby Union, together with the explanation of what took place in this controversial match, and which ends for all time, in my opinion, the New Zealand claim to have scored an equalizing try.

Nearly twenty minutes had gone and there was little chance of either side breaking out of each other's defensive grip. Virtually, it was stalemate, and then, suddenly, Gwyn Nicholls gave the signal for the special movement to be carried out, when a scrum was formed nearer to the half-way line than the New Zealand twenty-five, just to the right of the New Zealand posts.

It was the Welsh ball, and Owen put it in. They heeled quickly, and Owen whipped around the scrum to gather and move towards the right, with Bush outside him and Nicholls coming up as centre. Owen went three or four yards to complete the impression that the attack would come from the right. Then he swung his body and sent a reverse pass across the scrummage, which was now breaking up, to the 'rover', Cliff Pritchard, running up on the left-hand side of the scrum. Taking the pass perfectly, Pritchard moved hard to his left, where Rhys Gabe and Teddy Morgan were racing up at top speed in support. This really confused the 'All-Blacks', and they had only Deans, at centre, and McGregor to stop the movement. Naturally, Pritchard drew Deans, and Gabe, handling perfectly, caused the right wing, McGregor, to turn inside, before sending Teddy Morgan away. The little wing went like lightning down the left wing to outstrip Gillett, the 'All-Blacks' full-back, who failed to cut him off, and Morgan went diving over in the corner to score. It was a superb try and the crowd became hysterical in their appreciation of its magnificence. To this day everyone who was alive at the time of the try, and who followed Welsh Rugby, claimed they saw it scored. By quick reckoning this would reveal at least 220,000 spectators watching the match at the Arms Park!

Winfield did not convert the try, but the valuable lead of three points gave Wales great courage and confidence, although Rhys Gabe admits now that it would probably have been better had the Welsh side continued attacking with greater freedom than being content to sit upon their valuable lead. The New Zealanders were disturbed by the success of the Welsh manoeuvre, and they decided that they must equalize before the Welshmen produced another surprise movement to make their victory safe. But they could not find a way through the determined Welsh defence. All the backs tackled and saved magnificently, but none better than the diminutive Owen, who was frequently knocked out in bringing much larger opponents down, and in falling before the flying feet of 'All-Blacks' as they rushed the ball from end to end. However, the Welsh defence survived until the interval.

Early in the second half the 'All-Blacks' almost equalized when Wallace made a dangerous dash. However, he was held up short of the line, and the Welshmen hung on desperately as the time moved on steadily, with the 'All-Blacks' becoming more frustrated. Bush had a second shot at dropped goal, but failed to get the ball between the posts. Then McGregor was sent running for the Welsh line through a good pass from Deans, and when faced by full-back Winfield, kicked high instead of attempting to swerve past the defender. Soon afterwards came the much-disputed 'try'. There was a movement which ended in Wallace racing into midfield, gathering the ball and moving away upfield to deceive Welsh defenders. He found Deans supporting him, and when challenged by Willie Llewellyn, sent the ball inside to the centre, and Deans made a brilliant burst for the Welsh line. Everyone present felt he must score, only for Rhys Gabe to dive on to his back and bring him down inches short of the line. As Gabe said: 'I knew it was touch and go as to whether or not he had scored. But as he kept struggling to move forward, I knew that he had not reached his objective. Other players by this time had joined the maul, and then I heard referee Dallas blow his whistle and order a scrummage.'

Obviously it was a near thing, but the fact that the ball was in Deans' possession when the referee arrived on the scene, and not on or over the line, was proof enough that the 'All-Blacks' had not scored. Gabe maintains that there was no argument about the score on the field of play, but only in the pavilion after the match, and that hearing of the discussion, a newspaper correspondent sent a telegram to London quoting Deans as saying: 'I grounded the ball six inches over the line, but was pulled back by the Welshman before the referee arrived.' Deans continued to maintain that he had scored right up until the time of his early and untimely death. After this narrow escape, the Welshmen defended more vigorously than ever before, and eventually the final whistle went for time. The 'invincible' New Zealanders had been defeated, and hats and sticks were thrown high into the air as the crowd gave vent to its feelings with continuous cheering as the players left the field.

Several of the Welshmen were carried off shoulder-high, and then the Pressmen present, after subduing their own personal excitement, sat down to send the reports of the most famous match in Rugby history. It was not, perhaps, a great match, considering that two such wonderful sides were in opposition, but it was a hard match. The New Zealand backs did not play as well as they should have done, but they were marked more closely than at any other time during the Tour. The forwards found the Welshmen equal to them in ideas and courage, and Winfield, the Welsh full-back, gave an outstanding performance as a touch-line kicker in support of his forwards. The fact that the Welsh backs did not execute a large number of attacking movements leads one to believe that, even in those far-off days, sides could play the 'tight' game in times of emergency!

The New Zealanders were naturally disappointed at losing their wonderful record, and perhaps it was a good thing for the Game's development and history, that this greatest-ever Rugby Test left in its wake a long controversy, which still has not subsided. Because of the incident, Wales and New Zealand have remained great and friendly rivals, and even now in New Zealand, whenever the surviving members of the 1905 'All-Blacks' side meet, they discuss in detail what they claim to be 'Bobby Deans' try'.

From *Great Rugger Matches* by J.B.G. Thomas
(Stanley Paul, London, 1959)

Blanco in at the Kill

Clem Thomas

The greatest occasion of them all in the world of rugby is now, of course, the Rugby World Cup. Each tournament has produced one game that has left even the most hyperbolic commentators lost for superlatives. In 1987 it was the Australia versus France semi-final. It was one of the greatest spectacles of running rugby ever seen, but to the disappointment of expectant television viewers around the world, it was followed by a final that was as dour as the French semi-final had been enthralling.

W.B.B.

This match was a complete vindication of the concept of the World Cup, without question one of the greatest Test matches ever played. The lead changed hands a palpitating six times and was level twice before France, the Five Nations champions, squeezed through to the final in the dying minutes.

For those privileged 17,768 spectators at the Concord Oval in Sydney, which can hold some 20,000 people, it was a pleasure to have seen a match of such physical tempestuousness and intensity, of such marvellous versatility and style, and such enormous endeavour.

In short, as Australia's disappointed coach Alan Jones said afterwards: 'It was the game which the World Cup was looking for.'

The French coach, Jacques Fouroux, told us: 'We have been told that we were only kings in our garden in the northern hemisphere.' Stunningly, France proved to the world that this was a false jibe which probably provoked them to this glittering performance, so full of character and classic French skills and flair that at the end one was left marvelling and drained by the experience.

One should not underestimate the gutsy Australian performance, for they too played bravely and handsomely, and there was more than one turning point when they might have won the game.

Nevertheless the Wallabies were left floundering by the wit and genius of the French attack. They were like a clumsy bull against the grace of a matador.

There was a complete contrast of style with Australia playing percentage rugby, kicking high or to the diagonal to create the platform in their opponents' twenty-two, while France employed the elegance of hand-to-hand forward attack and sprayed passes about with the runners darting and wriggling through like trout.

Australia paid the price for not having a play-maker in midfield, for they had almost as much ball as France, winning the line-outs by twenty-five to nineteen, but losing the rucks and mauls by thirty-two to twenty. They were also unlucky to lose their star centre Brett Papworth after ten minutes, and then ten minutes later, their big lock and experienced line-out man Bill Campbell, both with bad knee injuries.

However, they had no forwards to match the piercing drives and extraordinary power of the French number eight, Laurent Rodriguez, playing the game of his life to create havoc with his plunges into the Australian pack, or the vitality of the big second row, Alain Lorieux. These two were easily the pick of the French forwards who were rampant in the loose.

Behind the French scrum it was once again the mercurial Serge Blanco who was their genie, popping up all over the place to work his magic. It was typical of this great player that, after making a disastrous mistake, three minutes from the end of ordinary time which gave Australia the lead after Camberabero had levelled the score with a penalty, it was his try which brought the winning score two minutes from the end.

There were other fine performances by both backs and forwards. Patrice Lagisquet on the left wing had a tremendous match, and so did that master centre Philippe Sella while Didier Camberabero, after a shaky start, weighed in with clever play and four conversions and two penalties. But then the whole French team are worthy of the *Légion d'Honneur* when they get home to France.

France began nervously and although they constantly created more scoring opportunities, uncharacteristically they spilt too much ball. This allowed the Australians to pressure them with high kicks to create a platform which ominously resulted in Australia forging into a nine-point lead in the first thirty minutes from a drop goal and two penalty goals from the dependable boot of Michael Lynagh.

Remarkably the French kept their composure, even when the referee failed to play the advantage when Erbani seemed about to score and instead gave France a penalty which Camberabero missed.

Critically France put in a delightful attack at the end of the half, with Lagisquet and Blanco, as ever, leading the way. From the line-out which followed Lorieux ripped the ball from Coker to smash his way over for a try, converted superbly from the touch-line by Camberabero. France were back in the game.

Four minutes into the second half, Lorieux put in another fine drive and laid the ball back for Berbizier to work the narrow side for Sella to cut inside for a try under the posts which was converted by Camberabero.

Australia responded instantly when Lynagh, with a neat side-step, broke the defence. He gave the ball to Grigg, who flicked it back inside to Campese, whose score, converted by Lynagh, broke the world record of twenty-five tries in Test matches set by Ian Smith of Scotland before the war.

France regained the lead with a magical piece of ghosting by Blanco who put Lagisquet over for Camberabero to convert. Camberabero then kicked a penalty, but again Australia gallantly replied with a try by Codey, the replacement forward, when he picked up in a ruck to crash over for Lynagh to convert once again.

Blanco then made what seemed a fatal mistake three minutes from the end of ordinary time when instead of clearing he passed inside to put Camberabero and Lagisquet under pressure. From the ruck France conceded a penalty which Lynagh kicked. However, Camberabero again levelled the score after eighty minutes with a penalty for a late tackle.

Finally, two minutes from the end of six minutes of injury time came the French kill. A kick ahead by Lagisquet saw Lorieux burying Campese with a tackle and Ondarts and Garuet were up to carry the ball right.

Berbizier again changed the direction by going left to Lagisquet, who had much to do before giving the ball to Rodriguez who put Blanco over in the corner. Camberabero then sent over another terrific conversion to end one of the best games of rugby I have ever seen.

From the *Observer*, 14 June 1987

Captain Kirk's All-powerful All Blacks

Stephen Jones

For this rugby match to have lived up to the rest of the tournament it would have needed a 67–66 win for one team or the other, achieved with a dramatic and controversial try in the last second and a conversion bouncing off both posts before it went over. I think we can say that the World Cup final never began to measure up.

New Zealand kept up a steady momentum, accelerated briefly in the second half, and David Kirk's right to have his mitts on the cup was utterly beyond question. But it was never a stirring match.

For France, it was one game too many. They have been playing or in training non-stop for nearly three years, and they looked drained. They were more ambitious than New Zealand, but the crackle of electricity had left Blanco and Charvet, and the legs of Rodriguez and Lorieux, pounding in the brilliant semi-final, were reduced to plodding.

Two men who should never have been on the field had contrasting afternoons. Wayne Shelford, the ferocious New Zealand No. 8, had another high-octane game. But last Sunday he laid out a Welsh player with a nasty punch from behind under the eyes of the referee and he stayed on the field. The New Zealand selectors, with video replays graphically available, should have dropped him.

The man who should have sent off Shelford was Kerry Fitzgerald. Astonishingly, he was back for the final yesterday. My argument is not just that he failed to send Shelford off. It is that Fitzgerald is not in the same class as Clive Norling, David Burnett or Fred Howard, or other referees I could mention; even his peers believe Norling is the best.

Of course, New Zealand were delighted with his appointment. 'He lets it flow,' they said. What they meant was that he lets too much go. Yesterday, he was alarmingly hard on France. At the same time he missed far too many important things; he allowed New Zealand to hack away for long seconds at Eric Champ on the floor, then he penalized Pascal Ondarts in the same ruck for one foot out of place. If his performance yesterday was 'letting it flow', then I don't want to watch the game he keeps on a tight rein.

The All Blacks back row, Shelford included, were a massive influence. France held on well in the line-outs, and the New Zealand scrummage was creaking. Shamefully, they were once allowed to collapse a scrum without penalty when France were driving for the line with the ball in control.

However, in the loose New Zealand were in a different class.

Michael Jones came into the All Blacks squad because Brewer and Hobbs, the usual open-side flankers, were injured, and had a magnificent final. He made killing tackles everywhere, scored one try and set up another. New Zealand produce men like Jones with the monotonous regularity that the West Indies produce fast bowlers. Just as well for them, because yesterday, and throughout the tournament, the All Blacks backs produced all the skill of cart-horses, all the spectacle of paint drying.

Basically, New Zealand's three-quarter line consists of four refugee flankers who run straight and hard and long to find the shelter of the closed spaces. Grant Fox is a marvellous goal-kicker, but as a fly-half, as a conjuror, he is a non-starter. Still, with the commitment and the passion of the All Blacks, who needs flair? But more than once in the final and the rest of the tournament, I wondered if the All Black machine was actually having any fun.

France held the All Blacks to 9–0 against the wind in the first half, and New Zealand were fortunate to be that far ahead. Fox kicked a dropped goal and the conversion, but the try was lucky, so lucky. Fox tried to drop a goal with four men outside him, and mis-hit the ball completely. It squirted away in disgrace, but bounced wickedly as Lagisquet tried to grab it. Jones arrived in the confusion and scored.

Yet it never bothered New Zealand that they were against the wind in the second half, or that rain fell for practically the first time in the tournament. Fox drip-drip-dripped the life out of France with four penalties and, in between, New Zealand wrapped it up with two tries.

Midway through the half, Jones took an inside pass from Fox, burst through and set up a try for Kirk. A few minutes later, Kirk broke splendidly down the blindside of a ruck, made sixty yards and looked back for the inevitable support. Shelford arrived first at the tackle and gave Kirwan a try in the corner.

Berbizier, France's best player, appeared four times in the same move to score with the last throw of the match, but the crowd had known for a long time that there was to be no explosion by the French.

The presentation was an important moment for this beautiful country. Rugby split the nation by entertaining the Springboks in 1981, and by making last summer's sneaky, squalid Cavaliers tour of South Africa. Now the instrument of the split has been the catalyst for the rejoining.

And the events surrounding the final – the warmth pouring into the All Blacks headquarters, the excited news stories that yet another African or Far Eastern or South American country was taking the final live on television, proved that we may have been 12,000 miles from the birth of rugby, but we were still in the capital of the rugby world. The World Cup, the meteor, is over.

From the *Sunday Times*, 21 June 1987

Lynagh's Try Ends Heroic Irish Effort

Edmund van Esbeck

In 1991 it was the quarter-final stage that produced the match to savour – Australia's last-gasp victory over the Irish. This time, if the final lacked some of the exuberance of that game, none could complain about the excitement and tension of a game that went right to the wire.

W.B.B.

'Of all sad words of tongue or pen the saddest are, it might have been.' With just three minutes to go at Lansdowne Road yesterday, Ireland had defied the odds and stood three points clear of Australia. A place in the World Cup semi-final beckoned and the crowd was in a frenzy. And then, in a dramatic moment that will be etched in memory for ever, Australia struck and scored a try, to turn their perilous position of a three-point deficit into a precious one-point lead. That was enough to see them to victory. For Ireland, a glorious dream died.

All around was silent stillness afterwards as one sought to collect one's thoughts and if there could be consolation in a defeat of this nature, and, of course there was in many respects, the primary one was that we had been privileged to witness one of the greatest rugby matches ever to take place on this famous old ground.

A complex analysis is not necessary: in the end, the Australians had the composure and the confidence to get the vital try and it came from a back movement of simplistic beauty.

Australia won the ball wide on the left, it was moved to the right. The Ireland defence was stretched to breaking point and as the tackle went in on David Campese, he laid the ball back and outside-half Michael Lynagh got over for a try close to the right corner flag. His conversion attempt failed narrowly, so there was still hope, tenuous hope that somehow Ireland might contrive a score of some kind in the few meagre minutes that remained. But it was not to be and Australia had prevailed as most had expected they would, but surely, few if any could have visualized that it would be such an almighty close run thing.

As the crowd turned to go their diverse ways in the immediate aftermath of a match that lifted this World Cup to a new level, all around the words were said as one. 'We should have won.' Perhaps, but most certainly we *could* have won. In the end, victory was denied by our failure to clear our lines after the Australians had been stunned by a great Ireland try, scored with six minutes to go by one of the game's outstanding players, flanker Gordon Hamilton.

With the game in the seventy-fifth minute, Ireland started an attack inside their own half. Jim Staples kicked the ball on, Jack Clarke was up to gather it and passed inside to Hamilton charging up in support. He had the pace and the will to make it to the Australian line and to a thunderous roar got a try to set beside some of the best I have seen. Ralph Keyes took the conversion from wide on the left and, with unerring accuracy, he kicked a magnificent conversion.

Ireland led for the first time in the match 18–15 and now the ingredients were there to write a story of what would have been unquestionably one of the greatest victories in the history of the game in this land.

Then the Australians struck and all credit to them for it. Ireland did not lift the pressure after the kick-off. Rob Saunders, the Ireland scrum-half, failed to get touch with his kick out of defence, the ball was readily dispatched to the Irish right-hand corner and the Australians had got a footing in a key area and at a crucial time. They won a scrum, and as they had often done throughout the afternoon, their back line went into top gear. The Irish defence was in trouble and what would have been one of the greatest of victories was instead turned into the bitter taste of defeat.

There is no doubt that Campese had a profound part to play in getting his country to the semi-final, for he scored two tries, both beautiful in creation and telling in execution. The Australians, in fact, scored their tries from set piece possession and they mingled orthodox attack with shrewd kicking from Lynagh.

It was a match marked by unforgettable moments of dramatic nature. And we did not have long to wait for the first, an unedifying punch-up in the first minute as fists flew between the forwards after one initial fracas between Philip Matthews and Villiame Otah-engane. But that died down, fortunately, and we did not again have anything to soil a marvellous occasion.

Ireland played with the wind in the first half and for twenty minutes could scarcely get out of their own half. But they defended with great resolution and effect until the sixteenth minute when the dancing master on the Australian right wing Campese waltzed his way through the Irish defence after Australia won a line-out. Lynagh kicked the conversion. Ireland stood six points down now – could they reveal the necessary level of character and application? They answered the call with courage.

The Irish pack set about their opponents. Australia won more possession in the line-out, but Ireland disrupted it very effectively and when Nick Farr-Jones had to leave the field just after his side's opening try, his replacement Peter Slattery was set for a torrid time.

All the Irish forwards deserve great credit, but the play of the back-row trio of Matthews, Robinson and Hamilton was awesome in effect. The Irish scrum was rock solid. In the loose the Irish revealed a tenacity that had the Australians clearly disconcerted.

Keyes kicked a penalty for Ireland in the twenty-fourth minute and then added a second in the thirty-first minute. Thus it was 6–6 and that was how it stood at the interval.

Ireland had played with the benefit of the wind in the first half, so Australia had reason to feel reasonably pleased, even if surprised by the nature of the Irish challenge. But, even better was to come in a second half that will live in the memory.

Lynagh struck the first blow of the second period when he kicked a penalty, but after a great high kick to the Australian posts by Keyes, the Australians had to concede a scrum and Keyes dropped a goal, the ball going in off an upright. Now it was 9–9 and suddenly there was an awareness on the field and off it that here we could be witness to a match of immense proportions. And so we were.

Then Campese struck again in the fifty-second minute. Australia won a scrum on the left; the ball was moved outside. Marty Roebuck came up from full-back, the Irish defence was broken and Campese scored a try to the right of the Irish posts. Lynagh converted and so Australia led again by six points.

But heads did not drop on the Ireland side. The pack continued to play with heroism and to such effect that they left us under no illusions that the match was not over yet.

Now, too, the Irish backs were running at their opponents and, had Jack Clarke not elected to cut inside instead of going for the left corner, Ireland might have scored a try. But Keyes kicked a penalty midway through the second half to leave just three points in it.

Simon Geoghegan came in from the right wing to join in attacks going left. Again the Australian defence was stretched but Clarke could not make it. He just did not have the pace of the man he replaced, Keith Crossan. Those were the kinds of chances on which Crossan prospered.

Then, with the match entering its closing phase, came Hamilton's try and Keyes's conversion and all Ireland wished that the five minutes that remained could somehow just fly by.

To the Australians' great credit, they kept their composure and then came the thunderbolt to Ireland's hopes in the form of Lynagh's try. A gallant effort had failed but a team had won a nation's heart.

Keyes scored fourteen points to bring his World Cup total to sixty-eight and he again played splendidly. The Irish backs did all in their power to respond to the magnificent forward effort and it was a pity that those movements that saw Clarke foiled twice near the line had not gone the other way for surely Geoghegan would have made it. Yet Clarke, like all his teammates, gave his all and played a major role in Hamilton's try.

Never for a moment did the Irish challenge wilt and as the drama unfolded one was reminded of those beautiful words that sum up courage and bravery, 'to strive, to seek, to find, and not to yield'.

In the final analysis, Ireland did yield, but the message went out loud and clear that the heart of Irish rugby still has a strong beat. For the Australians it was a day of some alarm; for the Irish players an effort to be proud of; they left the scene signed with their honour.

From the *Irish Times*, 21 October 1991

England Swing Low as the Dream Dies

Hugh McIlvanny

The wheels certainly did not come off the sweet chariot of England's World Cup dreams yesterday, but the superior rugby skills of Australia forced it into the ditch some way short of the promised land, leaving the host country honourable losers by twelve points to six after an unremittingly tense final at Twickenham.

English supporters had no trouble finding the heart to sing the old spiritual that has become their rallying hymn when their players stepped disconsolately up to the Royal Box to receive runners-up medals from the Queen, who was smiling sympathetically behind her glasses.

Understandably, decorum fought a losing battle with exultation as the Australians thanked Her Majesty for a better brand of trinket. Some of the winners were spinning away to salute their huge contingent of fans almost before the regal handshake had been completed.

Their captain, the scrum-half Nick Farr-Jones, summed up the mood when he said: 'I am going to have a good night with my team and my family. Whatever is ahead, it will be good.'

In their dejected state, England were still able to recognize the justice of the result, and the warmth of neutral condolences was increased by the fact that on the biggest day in the history of rugby they had abandoned their previous emphasis on grinding forward power and attempted bold passing attacks.

Many, however, agreed with David Kirk, who captained the New Zealand All Blacks to victory on their own soil in the inaugural World Cup four years ago, when he said that yesterday's final was hardly the time to start practising passing.

Kirk thought England should have accustomed themselves to more open rugby earlier in the tournament. Many spectators had made a similar plea over the past month, suggesting sourly that Will Carling and his men often performed as if the ball were a necessary evil, concentrating so much on the bruising strength of their pack that it almost seemed they were intent on tunnelling to the Webb Ellis Trophy.

At times, said their critics, there was the impression that the most creative attackers, Guscott, Underwood and Carling, might have to apply in writing for a touch of the ball.

The claim that they were applying the methods best calculated to defeat specific opponents was partially justified yesterday by the dramatic change of tactics they carried into their final with Australia. Unfortunately, all those earlier occasions when the ball saw less daylight than Mrs Rochester exacted a price and, while England's surges gave them more than sufficient possession to swing the game their way, the ultimate pass was frequently wayward. With a swirling, frustrating wind mainly against them in the second half, they never appeared likely to win.

Australia's confidence began to build in the first half when they were narrowly thwarted after David Campese, who is rated the finest talent now playing the game, kicked towards the English line and set off in exhilarating pursuit. Campese came back upfield smiling to himself, like a man who had confirmed his account was in order and knew the bank would open any minute.

However, though a converted penalty kick and a try from a drive at a line-out put Australia 9–0 ahead at the interval, they were soon disabused of any assumption that they could cruise into an unassailable lead.

Two penalties kept England at their heels and in the end the Wallabies, who had come to Europe with the reputation of being the best attacking team in the world, won the supreme championship because of the spirit and discipline of their defence.

From the *Observer*, 3 November 1991

The last three Great Occasions are also great highlights from my own career. The Second Test at Lancaster Park in 1977 was one of the most violent I have ever played in, but we kept our heads and our discipline, despite the provocation, to earn a famous victory for the Lions. Two years later, I had the great pleasure of leading the Northern Division to an equally famous victory against the All Blacks, this time in the homely surroundings of Otley's ground. The greatest moment of my rugby career came the following year, however, on 15 March 1980, when I led England to their first Grand Slam in thirteen years. I wrote ten years ago that I wanted my jersey bespattered with mud as it was, stuck on my study wall for ever. It's still there.

W.B.B.

The Lions Walk with Pride from the Battlefield

John Hopkins

Minutes before the Lions took the field at Lancaster Park for the second Test, the pack leader Terry Cobner called his seven other forwards together.

They moved across the changing room, their studs ringing out on the stone floor, went into the lavatory and shut the door. Cobner was pithy and adjectival. He appealed to their emotions. He pleaded with them. He said he wanted his wife to be able to walk down the street in Pontypool with her head held high.

An hour and a half later the scene in the same changing room was one of jubilation. Players wandered round in a daze of happiness. Terry Cobner, naked save for a towel around his waist, sat staring at the floor. Periodically he raised his right hand, his fist clenched, in a gesture of silent superiority. He was clearly near to tears.

The Lions had just won what for most of them was the most important Test match they had ever played in. And much of the credit was due to Cobner's leadership of the pack and his thoroughness in preparation for the Test. The forwards were his choice, the tactics were his. He organized a forty-minute line-out practice the day before the Test and then he quietly told Englishman Billy Beaumont, Scotsman Gordon Brown and Irishman Willie Duggan: 'If we win this game it will be because of you and the line-out ball you win. If we lose you will be blamed.'

It was an emotional moment when the final whistle went, not only for the players but for the few hundred British spectators. They had seen the Lions keep the series alive despite a rash of savage attacks on them by the All Blacks.

The New Zealanders unquestionably started the violence. From the stand it looked as though they were determined to injure Phil Bennett at any price. Early on the Lions captain slipped and was badly done over by the All Black forwards. He rose to his feet, his mouth cut and bleeding, his confidence shaken. Later he was caught again by the opposition forwards and he was being punched long after the ball had gone.

Worst of all, soon after half-time Bennett fielded a kick from behind his own goal-line, and had returned the ball into touch when All Black flanker Kevin Eveleigh flew at him in an atrociously late tackle. Bennett went down, the Lions rushed back to help their man, and fighting broke out and continued for twenty seconds or so.

Faced by such aggression the Lions were lucky to have a man of Cobner's character and attitude leading the forwards. He knew what to do when attacked. His men – rightly or wrongly – didn't turn the other cheek. I must say I saw a boot going into an All Black forward; the brilliant New Zealand wing Bryan Williams was late tackled. But the actions of the Lions seemed to be in defence whereas the All Blacks' overt attacks on Bennett can only be described as premeditated.

As pack leaders go, Cobner ranks high. 'There are two ways to lead men,' he says. 'One is by example, to earn their respect that way. The other is to frighten players. I always go for the easier, the first, and only use the second if I have to.' With the Lions Cobner has had to earn his spurs, there having been some doubts – outside Wales – at the start of the tour about his playing ability.

Now he commands everyone's respect for the way he improved the forward play after the first Test, starting with the game at Timaru, and for his leadership in the second Test. 'When I come off the field I want to be able to look Cob in the eye and know I did OK,' says Gordon Brown, the big Scots lock forward. 'I don't want to look at him and see him turn away. I want that moment of respect from him. It means so much to me. After the Test I said to him: "I can look you in the eye tonight," and he replied, "Broonie, you can look into my eyes all night if you like." '

Cobner is barely six foot tall, and despite being one of the smallest forwards on the field he is an excellent motivator. His vocabulary is limited. He talks a language in keeping with the cold, bare stone floors of most rugby changing rooms.

In the last minutes before a game he likes to talk about home. It may sound maudlin in print, to describe seven grown men surrounding Cobner as he asks them to remember the people of Pontypool sitting up listening to their radios in the small hours of the morning, and how lights are flickering in homes all over Britain, but the results prove his approach to be right.

Much of Cobner's success with the Lions has come from his natural pride in his family, his home village of Abersychan, his rugby club Pontypool and his country. He does not speak Welsh yet he is so strongly Welsh that he has named his daughters Rhiannon, Sian and Bethan 'so it's quite clear where they come from'.

When letters arrive from home he rips them open, showering the floor with pieces of envelope in his hurry to find out the latest news of the family he began to miss when he left Wales for London last May. I shan't forget the photo he showed me last week. 'Just got this from home, John,' he said, thrusting a colour snap of his three-year-old daughter peeing on a lawn. 'It's the middle Cob watering the grass.'

Cobner's mentor is Ray Prosser, the jovial Pickwickian figure who coaches Pontypool. The two are as close as father and son, and before the tour Prosser told his young friend what to expect in New Zealand based on his own experiences with the Lions in 1959.

Nothing however could have prepared Cobner or the rest of the Lions for the level of hostility that has been aimed at them and now seems to be endemic to rugby in this rugby-mad country.

A simple analysis is that rugby crowds in New Zealand, influenced by telecasts from English soccer games, are starting to behave like British soccer crowds. Why and what can be done about it is difficult to know.

Frankly the Lions are fearful, as are many New Zealanders, of what the future may hold. 'I wouldn't want my kid to play rugby over here,' one Lion told me last week. 'It's too rough. If my nipper ever kicked someone on the ground I'd give him such a roasting he'd never do it again.'

From the *Sunday Times*, 17 July 1977

The Roof Fell In

John Hopkins

The roof fell in before the start of this game, showering wood, and corrugated from on top to the stand below. By half-time, New Zealand's world had caved in too. Despite the help of the slope and a strong wind behind them, the All Blacks trailed 0–7 at the interval, out-thought and out-played.

The Northern Division were a team picked for a particular style of rugby. Their play pivoted around the back row and half-backs. They drove from line-outs, and even – Hallelujah! – ran the ball from rucks. A magnificent game was played to their tactics and at their speed. Little wonder that in their first defeat in England for six years, the All Blacks were out-scored by four tries to one.

The speed of thought and action, the sense of purpose and tactical appreciation, that these All Blacks have shown on their better days were gone. Instead, those qualities belonged to the men in the red shirts, a team that hummed as smoothly as a Yorkshire weaving mill.

Uttley, as slim as a spear, Dixon, his hair newly trimmed, and Neary played the games of their lives with their tackling, covering, and sense of direction. It was only near the end when they and some of the other greybeards in this pack found that these spring-heeled youngsters, Mark Donaldson, Stu Wilson and Eddie Dunn, were moving a little too fast that ominous gaps opened up in defence. Once New Zealand's inevitable attack at the start of the second half had been contained, they looked beaten men.

As is nearly always the case, the Northern Division's forward superiority won them the day. Big Jim Syddall was brilliant in his line-out work in the first half, eclipsing Andy Haden, and Neary and Uttley both blocked the loose holes and controlled the effervescence that Mourie and Mexted are normally allowed to display.

Mike Slemen deserves a medal for valiant defence in the opening thirty minutes, when he safely fielded at least four high attacking kicks. And some of the tackling by Bond, Wright and Neary was exemplary.

New Zealand's cause was not helped when Richard Wilson failed with five penalty attempts and was mortified to see a drop goal rebound off a post in the first half.

Two telling tries by Bond in the space of ten minutes in the second half took the home side to a lead of fourteen points. Stu Wilson lit a flickering flame with an opportunist try nine minutes from the end, but then that Northern sage, Alan Old, rounded off an extremely competent afternoon by scoring himself.

Optimists will now hope that the enthusiasm and skills of a number of this team will be displayed again at Twickenham on Saturday, preferably with the same result.

From the *Sunday Times*, 18 November 1979

Where England's Plan Succeeded

David Frost

'We decided to tire out the England forwards by making them chase about the field,' Andy Irvine, captaining Scotland for the first time, said after the 30–18 defeat at Murrayfield on Saturday.

'We did this but we had given them too much of a lead,' he said.

The strength, technique, experience and control of their forwards brought England a lead of 19–3 at half-time and eventually won them the Calcutta Cup, the championship, the triple crown and the Grand Slam for the first time since 1957. But the refusal of the Scotts to lie down meant that the second half was more lively and challenging than anyone had any right to expect.

Well before half-time England's pack were in such command at the scrums and in the loose that many opponents would have resigned themselves to their fate. But, Scotland decided to run everything and they were rewarded with two stirring tries and fifteen points in the second half.

England's triumph was not due entirely to their forwards. In this match the half-backs kicked well and the elusive running of Woodward fashioned the first two tries for Carleton and Slemen. Hare's conversion of both these tries, the second from near the left touch-line, had an important psychological value, and Carleton ended up with a hat-trick of tries. The England three-quarters were brought into the game and they did not let the side down.

The basis of England's victory on Saturday – as indeed of their hearteningly successful season – was their thorough organization, given life and purpose by the inspiration of Billy Beaumont. The richly experienced players around him knew what to do, and Beaumont, like Eric Evans before him in 1957, led them into action with zest and relish.

Another important factor in the current England revival has been the presence, behind Beaumont, of two intelligent optimists, Mike Davis and Budge Rogers. Davis, as coach, has seen to it that England's preparations at squad sessions have been thorough and apposite.

Rogers, as chairman of selectors, has seen the value of experience and a settled team, and his enthusiasm and planning have given momentum to the whole campaign.

It seems an age ago that Davis conducted his first England coaching session on an echoing grassless, suburban pitch in Tokyo. Yet it was on that tour last May and June that Davis laid the foundations of Saturday's triumph and that Beaumont grew up as a captain.

England's third try at Murrayfield showed them at their best. At a scrum in the right-hand corner they drove the Scots backwards with perfectly timed and controlled shoves until a pushover try seemed on the cards. Instead, they let the ball out on the blind side and Scott and Smith put Carleton over, giving England a lead of 16–0 after thirty-one minutes.

Two penalty goals by Irvine and one by Hare made the score 19-6 and then, eight minutes after the interval the England forwards struck again, retaining possession through ruck after consecutive ruck until Smith was able to get over for a try, making it 23–6.

From the stand it never looked as if Scotland would make up that deficit, but their daring running brought them a combined try by Tomes and an individual one by Rutherford, both converted by Irvine.

There was point in the remark after the match of Scotland's coach, Nairn MacEwen: 'If we could do all that running without forward strength, what cannot be achieved with forward strength?' For England, Hare kicked another penalty goal, and Carleton got his third try, from a kick ahead by Dodge.

Rutherford's individual try was a gem, but it is difficult to believe that Saturday's game will force the Lions selectors, who will today announce the team for the tour of South Africa, to alter their opinions. Slemen and Carleton were always likely to be taken on tour, and all four of Saturday's centres have been on the fringes of selection. At least Woodward proved on Saturday that he now has the confidence to show his true form on the big occasion.

Apart from an even further strengthening of Beaumont's claim to the Lions captaincy, the forwards who probably did most for their cause were Colclough and Blakeway. Colclough, in particular, played a most effective all-round game. In the Scotland pack Beattie was already more or less assured of a place in the Lions' party, while Tomes had one of his most impressive games for Scotland.

Something like eight or nine of Saturday's England team should be in the tour party, together with four or five Scots. But all of Saturday's thirty-one players – Jim Gossman (West of Scotland) came on in the second half for Hay who had a rib injury – deserve credit for providing a memorable match played in a spirit almost of chivalry.

Beaumont said afterwards: 'Ireland, the first match, was make or break for us. Then, when we won in Paris, everything became possible. Wales was the hardest game physically – ignoring the aggro. On Saturday we played some of the best rugby seen on an international field.'

'I am a bit resentful that some people have labelled us a poor side,' Beaumont said. 'It seems like sour grapes to me. Any team that wins both away matches by scoring heavily must deserve the sort of rewards we have earned.'

From the *Guardian*, 17 March 1980

Grand Slam

Bill Beaumont

As I battled my way back to our changing room through a throng of exultant English supporters, someone thrust a beautiful pure wool sweater into my hand. When I got back to the relative safety of our team room, I looked at the sweater and saw it had the bright red rose of England and a huge emblem which read: GRAND SLAM CHAMPIONS – 1980. It was somewhat precocious but one of the boys said, 'Put it on.' 'No,' I replied, 'I'm not going to wear it. Remember the words of John Burgess – "always show humility and grace both in defeat and in victory".'

The team climbed aboard the coach and at that moment it was probably the happiest place on earth. The general feeling was one of excitement and relief. When we reached our hotel it was bustling with activity. I was delighted to be greeted by members of the Fylde Rugby Club. Fylde had played against Gala in Scotland that morning and were there to share our triumph.

The team were mobbed all night by ecstatic supporters and the champagne flowed freely until the early hours of the morning. At one stage early in the evening though, Fran, Nero and I slipped away to a bar for a quiet drink. There we recalled the black days of 1976 when we lost every game and no one wanted to know us. We also talked about the ups and downs in between. We all savoured that day because we knew it was a once-in-a-lifetime experience – 'Like the snow upon the river, a moment white then gone for ever'.

I have one other memory of that glorious afternoon. Only the fifteen England players who took part will ever really know what it felt like when the final whistle went. Only they will ever be able to understand it fully. All the press, who had written millions of cutting, damning words about English rugby between 1957 and 1980, all the former England international players, all the spectators, all the experts and all the ordinary punters could only guess what that moment of ecstasy actually felt like. I was one of the fifteen and I shall never forget it. Alan Tomes came up to me in the tunnel and asked to swap jerseys with me. In the past I had always exchanged my jersey with my opponent, but on this special occasion I declined as politely as I could. I explained that I had waited all my life for that one moment of triumph and I doubted I would ever be fortunate enough to enjoy a repeat performance. I wanted to keep and treasure that particular jersey with its unique memories and associations until the day I died. I wanted it, bespattered with mud as it was, stuck on my study wall for ever as a perpetual reminder of 15 March

1980. Alan could see that I was glowing with pride and, slapping me on the back, he smiled. He knew exactly what I meant and how I felt.

From *Thanks to Rugby* by Bill Beaumont
(Stanley Paul, London, 1982)

4
GREAT LAUGHS

Rugby has given me some great moments; I've also had some great laughs too, even if a few times the joke has been on me. If there was a Five Nations Championship for wit, however, the Irish would do the Grand Slam every year.

W.B.B.

The Oval Art of Self-Defence

Tony O'Reilly

George Bernard Shaw once said that Ireland's complexes towards Great Britain manifest themselves either in militant nationalism or in a touch-of-the-forelock, I'll-leave-it-to-yerself-sur mentality. It is a curiously accurate assessment of those of us who live in 'the Celtic twilight'. W. John Morgan immortalizes these emotions in a classic pre-match conversation between two Welshmen and an Englishman in Piccadilly the night before an England–Wales game. 'Ah, well', said the Englishman, his red face glowing with centuries of successes, 'I hope the best side wins – after all, it's only a game.' His Welsh compatriots stared at him, their features hard and unyielding. His smile faded. 'I was only joking,' he muttered sheepishly, and slunk away into the well-lit darkness.

To the Welsh the pulse of the year for good or evil is struck by their rugby fortunes. The Irish are not quite as formally attached to the successes of their team as their Celtic cousins. None the less, Twickenham on the day sees every Irishman for ten generations back swathed in green and impregnated with the 'hard stuff', determined that this time Oliver Cromwell and the fourteen other members of the English team will have justice done them. Shoulder to shoulder they stand, Wimpey navvies, the entire staff, male and female, of the National Health Service; salesmen, and soldiers from Montgomery to Private Rafferty, unified by the only cause that can really unify Irishmen – Englishmen!

Inside the dressing-room the atmosphere is a compound of fear, frivolity and determination. Twickenham exercises a peculiar influence on all the Celts, but more particularly on the Irish. The fear is bred of an inferiority complex, the frivolity of a complex mixture of apprehension and confidence, and the determination, although expressed by all, is felt by few, and these mainly the more experienced. There is a well-worn phrase testifying to England starting with a five-point advantage at home. Against Ireland this may be an underestimate. The chatter and babble, so loud two hours before kick-off, diminishes as the decisive hour approaches. 'Pass me the swerving oil!' says a Northern voice. 'Who's got the strapping?' shouts a gnarled Western forward. 'Begobs, it costs more to put you on the field every year!' counters a squat Southern prop already mummified in five yards of Elastoplast wrapped round his head. Four of the forwards wearing headbands look like convalescents from brain surgery. A fifth forward goes round sprinkling holy water on his team-mates. Three Northern brethren recipients of his thoughtfulness have religious doubts as to whether this is in the Lodge or not. The door opens – 'Ireland captain, will you toss?' Seven voices advocate heads and the remainder tails as he trots forth, calls wrongly. We face a strong sun and gale-force winds for both halves.

The England dressing-room presents a different scene, as I once discovered. Being forgetful by nature, I turned up for an international without either shorts or laces. The kindness of the Rugby Union supplied the former, the latter apparently were no longer in stock. Ten minutes before the Off I entered enemy territory to find Eric Evans, the England captain, standing on a large table in the centre of the room, his face matching the red rose on his chest.

For a moment I was unseen. 'Remember Dunkirk!' he shouted, 'and Alamein! Discipline, that's where we can lick these b . . . Irish – all fire and fury, but irresponsible.' 'Excuse me,' I said politely, 'but has anyone got some hairy twine for my boots?'

When Churchill said in the dark days of 1941 that the position in England was serious but not hopeless, was it not an Irishman who replied that the position in Ireland was always hopeless but happily never serious?

From *The Wit of Rugby* edited by L.H.W. Paul
(Leslie Frewin, London, 1972)

This is What the Game is All About

Alan Watkins

'Good afternoon, Bill.'

'Good afternoon, Nigel.'

'Well, here we are at the Cardiff Arms Park or rather, I should say, the National Stadium. What was it called in your playing days, Bill?'

'It's interesting you should ask me that, Nigel, because, blow me, it's so long ago I can't remember.'

'Ha, ha.'

'But what I do remember is that after eighty minutes out there you knew you'd been in a match and no mistake.'

'It's certainly a veritable cauldron of emotion still. Anyway here is Jonathan Davies, the brilliant young Neath stand-off half, whom many shrewd observers have compared to the late Barry John, with the kick off. He's following the modern fashion and booting it over the dead ball line. Any comments on that, Bill?'

'That's an interesting point, Nigel, because England have to drop out and concede possession and territorial advantage. But I think you can overdo these new-fangled notions.'

'Thank you, Bill. The England forwards are certainly piling in. They want to show that their inspiring performance against the French at Twickenham two weeks ago was no flash in the pan. As you will be able to see when the camera gets round, there are already three Welsh forwards flat on their backs.'

'England, have served notice, Nigel, that they're not going to be messed around by anyone.'

'As the old Duke of Wellington put it, they're getting their retaliation in first.'

'I always thought it was Field Marshal Montgomery, Nigel, before the battle of Alamein, but we won't argue about that.'

'Certainly not when Gareth Chilcott, the uncompromising Bath prop, has been laid out, or so it seems, in an unprovoked assault by Stuart Evans, the uncompromising Neath prop. Clearly a penalty, Bill.'

'I agree, Nigel. Marcus Rose has kicked more penalties at this distance than I've had hot dinners.'

'And he's done it. Any advice to England at this stage, Bill?'

'Richard Hill should be saying: Look, lads, cool it a bit. Settle down. Let's get the ball off the park, safe in touch. Then hopefully Marcus Rose will be able to slot some more penalties.'

'It looks as if Hill isn't taking your advice, Bill. He's actually running with the ball and he's giving it to Ieuan Evans. Is Evans offside, Bill? Anyway no one's going to stop him now. Chilcott, the only man in pursuit, will never catch him from this distance.'

'A very lucky score, Nigel. I think that Ieuan Evans was morally offside although the laws don't agree with me. And what made it more unfair still was that Rory Underwood, the RAF flyer, who would have given the gifted young Llanelli three-quarter a run for his money, was stuck on the other side of the field.'

'It would have been against the run of play if that conversion had gone over. As it is, England can still salvage this match. And a penalty. What was that for, Bill?'

'I'm fairly sure it was for dangerous play by Stuart Evans, the uncompromising young Neath prop, Nigel.'

'This should present Marcus Rose with no difficulty. And the Harlequins and former Cambridge University full-back, restored to favour after six years in the wilderness, has done it again. Any advice to England in the second half, Bill?'

'I think Richard Hill should be saying to the lads: Look, lads, let's control the pace of this match. Settle down a bit. Get the ball off the park out of harm's way, that's what this game of rugby's all about.'

'Thank you, Bill. In the meantime, a ruck-situation has developed just outside the English twenty-two-metre line. Jonathan Davies seems to have dropped a goal. The referee certainly appears to think so because he's pointing at the centre spot.'

'It wasn't one of young Jonathan's better efforts, Nigel. That ball lurched through those posts as if it would fail the breathalyser, no trouble.'

'My own feeling was that it was a straight toe punt by the gifted young Welsh half-back. But England have everything to play for still. Oh, a penalty to England, thank goodness, I mean thoroughly justified. What was it for, Bill?'

'Some nonsense between Stuart Evans and Gareth Chilcott, Nigel. Marcus Rose should have no difficulty.'

'Well done, Marcus. And there goes the final whistle with English pride restored. They didn't score any tries but it's what's on the board that counts. Many congratulations to Martin Green, who's taken a lot of stick and who's restored English pride.'

'Good afternoon, Nigel.'

'Good afternoon, Bill.'

From *The Independent*, February 1987

Coup de Grass

Myles na Gopaleen

It happened a good few years ago. It was about noon on a rather dirty day when I was relaxing in a restaurant, smoking a cigarette and toying with a cup of coffee which I had laced with angostura and benzole – the latter a coal-tar derivative and an excellent man for the kidneys. I was casually watching a very large chap at a nearby table who apparently was trying to eat a cow. Ah, well – wasn't I smoking a camel myself? Finally, very tired, he desisted and called for coffee. When this arrived, I took a phial of sinister blue glass from my pocket, held it aloft and called to him in a cultured tone:

'Benzole?'

'Bonjour,' he replied, picking up his coffee and joining me.

'That's a rough class of a day,' he said. 'We will have plenty of muck. I suppose you are going to the match?'

'Easy now,' I said mildly. 'One has heard of the Fechner-Weber experiments. We have a considerable corpus of quantitative results on liminal determinations. For the theoretical objective the constant method with weights, lifted by the hand, has been most favoured. The psycho-physical methods, however, are *au fond* behind all quantitative techniques of experimental psychology, especially those dealing with sensation. You would be soaked and frozen above in the Park today, man.'

'The Park?'

'Sairtintly. Cricket is a summer game. Cricket is my own game, of course.'

'*Cricket?* Oh!'

'What is *your* game? Handball? Snooker? Lacrosse, perhaps?'

'I suppose you could call it handball of a kind. It is usually called rugby.'

'Well, by domm! And whom are you playing? Bective Seconds? Now don't tell me you are in the Schools Senior Cup team?'

'I am not. *We are playing France.*'

'Ah, la belle! Daladier. Maginot. Laval. Baudelaire. Rabelais. Jeanne d'Arc. Monsieur Sam Beckett. Did you ever hear Madame Kirby-Lunn sing *Printemps qui commence*?'

'I have not.'

'Superb. She is long dead, of course. Allow me to order another pot of coffee.'

The Old Times

I found my friend eyeing me rather closely without revealing clearly whether he was pleased or annoyed.

'You will permit me,' I ventured, 'to have the diffidence to enquire your name?'

'Clinch. They call me "Jammie" Clinch.'

'Ah. So? Then you must know my pupils Farrell, Sugden, Davy, Pike, Stephenson? Promising lads one and all. I, too, have played, of course.'

'Rugby? For Ireland? Well . . . by gob!'

'Ah, yes. I turned out in the first game against France in 1909. Odd, isn't it, that the 1959 match will be the fiftieth encounter. France had some very clever men in those days. Jauréguy, for instance, or Cassayet. Glad to see you are turning out yourself. I suppose you know what a rugby ball is?'

'A *what*? It's an oval affair.'

'No. Oval connotes a plane configuration; you could never pick anything oval up, or kick it. You might, perhaps do something with an *ovoid*. In fact a rugby ball is a prolate spheroid.'

'I never knew *that* was what I scored with.'

'Well, it was. Most rugby players are very ignorant about the game. Quite a few don't know even the rules and are offended when whistled up. Most of them know the game was invented at Rugby school in 1823 by a chap named William Webb Ellis who got fed up with a scoreless encounter in what we now call soccer and who, picking up the ball, ran with it. Soccer is the granny of rugby. Notice the sinister duplication of a letter in each of that fellow's names. They look like tall goal posts.'

'Yes. This coffee's all right, but I think I'll have a pint. Will you join me?'

'Of course. I'm not eccentric. Let us drink a toast to my old friend C. B. Fry.'

'All right. Is he the cocoa man?'

The Great C.B.

The pints arrived and we attacked while pondering this most offensive query. I decided it was unintended and persuaded myself not to take offence.

'No,' I replied, 'he was not the cocoa man. He, myself and Dr. W. G. Grace were top men at the Test Match in Nottingham in 1899, the doctor's last Test, Fry's first. Heavens, I drove, hooked and cut the bowling that time, and developed a sort of a cricket Garryowen. Make no mistake about Fry. He was a grand soccer player and when at Oxford in 1893, he won the world championship for the long jump with a lep of 23 feet 6½ inches. A lovely man. I will tell you another thing. There is in London a man named Stephen Potter who made a reputation with books bearing such names as *Gamesmanship, Lifemanship, One-upmanship* and others. I have read none of them because, decent men as they are, no Englishmen can write anything funny. But I did read a scolding review of the latest thing in that series saying that Mr Potter should stop leaning so heavily on his witty title formula. Fair enough, but at the turn of the century my friend C. B. Fry wrote a book named *Batsmanship*. You see? Nothing new in the world. Ever hear of the

Springboks? Do you know anything of the new rugby mystique invented by Dr Danny Craven and presented to the world in that book by Bob Scott. Ever hear of "the box"? (I didn't say the Boks.) That crowd decided that, after a scrum, there was no future in passing the ball to a string of centres and wings but to get it to the blind side of the scrum and get it to 'the box', an area practically devoid of defence. The result of this conspiracy was a plethorium of scoretown. Ah, but shure I might as well be talking to the wall. *Mick, two more pints!*'

That 1909 Job

The pints were brought and we tested them. As a man who is ageing but not old (I dandled Jackie Kyle on my knee in Belfast and gave him a wee bar of sugarstick when I was up there in 1913), find it hard to prevent my mind running backwards, to stop remembering the old days. I rooted in my pocket, produced a battered wallet and handed Jammie a few bits of dog-eared paper.

'That's from *Le Matin* of January, 1909,' I said. 'Never mind the clipping at the back. Read the translation on top. Gob, we were divils in those days. I was having tea and Madeira cake in the old Hammam Hotel one Saturday when a chap wearing maybe ten mufflers and four overcoats came in and asked me to turn out for Ireland against France. I thought it was opera or ballet or something like that and immediately said I would help out. Let me quote the translation of the *Le Matin* report:

"'Startled cries of *cherchez la femme, quelle farce* and *parbleu* came from our box when the Irish team took the field, led by a young and very beautiful lady. That, at least, was our first impression, for the slim figure seemed quite out of place in the stubble of forwards. But even sex was forgotten when it was noticed that this strange player was carrying *un crosse*, or what the English call a cricket bat. He (for indeed it was a man) was almost immediately engaged in a heated altercation with the referee, a dour Scotsman, who motioned that cricketer repeatedly to the line. We understand that the latter kept insisting that there was nothing in the rules to forbid a player carrying a cricket bat, and at one stage he seemed to be threatening the referee with the bat. But when the Irish captain intervened, this strange young man from Santry ran to the touchline, threw the bat into a group of frightened spectators and went back to engage in that game wherein his crash-tackles and shots at goal have become a fable.'"

After Jammie had read this, he gave me a rather suspicious look and said:

'You're not playing today, are you?'

'No. Wasn't asked.'

'Right. Must get going. Who do you think will win?'

'Ireland, of course. Five nine.'

'I hope you're right. Cheers.'

From the *Irish RFU programme: Ireland v. France*, 18 April 1959

Up for the Big Game

Michael Green

There is just a touch of hysterical relief about the way in which players from junior teams watch an international match. Firstly, it is a treat for them not to have to spend a Saturday afternoon panting aimlessly around a manure-covered field miles from anywhere; and secondly, it is even more of a treat to watch someone else undergoing the intense physical discomfort that playing a game of rugby involves. At least, it always used to involve me in intense discomfort, perhaps because I was usually sick at half-time, and judging from the expression of the rest of our side, they weren't in much better condition.

There is also the rare pleasure of being able to make up for one's own ghastly sense of inferiority by hurling abuse at famous players. I never cease to be fascinated at the sight of men whom I know from bitter experience to be incapable either of holding a pass or running more than six feet without a rest, shrieking insults at an international winger who has had the bad luck to be tackled on the line after a seventy-five-yard sprint. If anyone shouts 'You're just not fit enough, Ireland' this afternoon, ten-to-one it will be a fat pimply specimen, reeking of stout, who only gets into his local third team because they're so short of players. Or he may not even be a player at all, like those insipid youths who were throwing toilet rolls around at Twickenham during the Varsity game. The Rugby Union is rightly concerned over their behaviour. So am I. I got a mouthful of wet toilet paper at half-time.

From all this it is possible to formulate the Second Law of Coarse Rugby (the first being that neither side has fifteen men): 'The amount of noise made is in inverse ratio to the playing ability.' This applies both on and off the field. The worst players usually have the most to say for themselves.

A further pleasure which an international gives a junior player, is that of letting himself go on Saturday mornings. The only training I ever did was to stop smoking Saturday mornings, and it was very pleasant to sit smoking and drinking at lunch-time, thinking of the thirty internationals shivering with nerves in their hotel, and chewing glucose frantically. At least, that is the popular conception, but I know one England forward of ten years ago who felt so dry on the morning of the big match that he sneaked into the hotel bar and ordered a pint of bitter. Just as he lifted it to his lips one of the Rugby Union committee walked in. With commendable presence of mind the player handed the beer to the committee man and ordered an orange juice for himself. Despite this precaution he never played for England again.

The growing habit among junior sides of playing a game on the morning of an international, however, is tending to spoil the day for the junior player. The last Saturday morning game in which I played was particularly unfortunate. To start with it was teeming with rain, with the result that halfway through the match the goalposts at one end sank into the earth and finally fell down. This did not stop the game as we were used to this sort of thing. We simply took all the kicks at one end of the field, so that most of the match was spent marching up and down to place the ball. Then we had a little trouble with the referee, who objected when one of our players asked him for a light. It turned out afterwards that he didn't mind the player smoking during a conversion, but he had not called him 'sir'. Finally, I couldn't get washed. We changed in someone's garage and both teams had to share two small domestic baths, one of which fell off the bricks on which it was balanced, and overturned, so there just wasn't time to clean up. I scraped off what mud I could and spent the afternoon with my knees caked in dried earth, feeling as if I was in a plaster cast. What I smelt like, I shudder to think, but as my prevailing scent was that of beer and rum perhaps any other odours went unnoticed.

The worst thing, however, was that our visitors battened on us for the rest of the day. They were one of those gallant sides carrying the rugby flag aloft in some remote part of the country and to come to London for an international was the highspot of their season. They were a rather unsophisticated crowd. In fact two of them were genuine gypsies, who had been recruited to play while pulling sugar beet from a field near the ground. I managed to avoid the gypsies (whom I later learned were arrested for being sick in Trafalgar Square) but found myself landed with a shaven-headed yokel who kept going up to women and laughing in their faces, and a large Irishman named, not unnaturally, Pat. Being convinced that the streets of London were littered with scarlet women and gold they demanded to be taken to the West End.

It was rather embarrassing. Pat, who was full of Guinness, insisted on walking up Oxford Street singing 'The One-Eyed Reilly' while our shaven-headed friend shambled along behind women, like a great ape, giving that vacant laugh every so often. After a while he got tired of that and repeated monotonously, 'I want to see the girls.'

I took him to a dreadful club, along with Pat, who was now on 'The Rose of Tralee'. Their desire to see the girls was immediately gratified. Two hostesses appeared instantly and suggested to the lads that they all had a drink. Ignoring my signals, the boys ordered.

Half an hour later the girls simply got up and went, and a man came along with a large bill.

'That's all right,' said Pat, 'those girls very kindly asked us to have a drink with them.'

The waiter explained that the girls were hostesses.

'And very fine hostesses too,' said Pat, 'they kept buying us drinks.'

The waiter fetched the manager who asked Pat what he was going to do about it.

'I'll tell ye what I'm going to do,' said Pat, who had at last grasped the situation. 'I shall now sing the first verse of "The Rose of Tralee".'

After one ear-splitting line the manager gave in, grasped me by the arm, and said fiercely, 'Get your two lunatic friends out of here.'

I led Pat out, still singing. I am thankful to say that later in the evening we became separated in Piccadilly. Next year I told the team secretary that in future I wasn't available to play on the morning of an international.

From the *Irish RFU programme: Ireland v. England*, 9 February 1963

Turn the Other Cheek

Andrew Mulligan

The England–Wales match in 1965 wasn't exactly a friendly. Geoff Frankcom, the English centre, complained bitterly that he was unable to recognize the Welsh forward who had not merely bitten but half eaten him in a loose scrum.

At the after-match banquet Frankcom was suddenly heard pointing an accusing finger at a Welsh second-row foward. 'It's him. It's him. He's just refused a third helping of beef because of what he ate this afternoon.'

Rabies, I thought. We'll have to give him the injections. Geoff had clearly been bitten during the game, for he bore the marks of an attack on his arm – as neat a circle of incisor marks as you ever saw. He was very indignant at being bitten, but by the time he had freed his arm the urge to kill had faded.

The Kav didn't agrèe. He says reprisal is the only thing the Welsh understand and he regretted the new fashion of biting – not because it was sinful but merely because it doesn't get you anywhere.

But the Kav always preferred a good rib tickling 'lurry' or kidney kick, though he draws a careful line between a fully escalated war and guerrilla raids against an aggressor. For him it's a private war ('Is dis a private fight or can anybody join?' goes the old Irish saying) any self-respecting forward accepts as an occupational hazard.

But the hard man can't understand why the spectators get mad at the punchers. After all, they are at least honest and declare their fists to all and sundry, including Action Replay on the Box. It takes a lot of skill to land a worthwhile KO, which is why pro boxing fights keep going the distance. And it takes a consummate ability and a real sense of occasion to lay on a royal punch-up for the Prince of Wales at Cardiff Arms Park.

Any hard man will tell you that the real clutchings, the rakings and trampling, hair-pulling, eye-gouging and nostril-splitting are done with surgical precision by specialists in the murky twilight of the loose rucks. The noise in there is frightful – rather like a stereo-psychedelic Chamber of Horrors. And there is total discretion that even Action Replay can't penetrate unless the rumour is true that the BBC have ordered infra-red cameras for Action Replay to capture the provocation as well as the reprisal.

The fact is that the fellows in the scrum couldn't live without their intimate savagery, and it's discourteous to pry into their masonic world.

From *Heard in the Line-out* edited by Robert Anderson
(Stanley Paul, London, 1969)

All Dr Kildares at Heart

Tony Lewis

It was the sight of Pontypridd's masseur hot-footing to the scene of many disasters last Monday evening at Bridgend which made me think that this was a good moment to wish him and all his voluntary brethren a happy and not too eventful New Year.

Legends have built up around the game's great spongemen. They are not just the repairers of broken bodies on a Saturday afternoon. The masseur's manual is extensive.

Only a long apprenticeship can provide the knowledge that, of the twelve fish and chip shops open on the South Circular on a Saturday night only one has space for a coach to park outside; that there is only one free house within three miles of the M5; that the bus has to leave Northampton by 7 o'clock if you are to get your feet under the bar in the Newport club house by 10.25. His information on the location of steak bars is unchallenged.

Excuses for delaying the bus always come easily to his mind if the club's skipper is chatting up the barmaid and promising her a summer of fidelity before returning to her next winter.

Committee men have to be 'buttered up' so he baffles them with medical language which neither of them understands . . . 'Yes, John's lateral meniscus is more serious than Fred's super spinatus' – is usually a certain conversation stopper.

In dressing-rooms he provides tie-ups for socks, speed-oil for tired legs, vaseline, gum-shields and sheaths of plaster to bind together the wobbly limbs of those who are afraid to cry off in case the reserve plays well.

On the field, if you have ever been booted in the nose, dropped on the spot, and prayed that death would scoop you up out of your misery, the first sight as the eyes eventually clear, is the feet of your Florence Nightingale. If you move he rubs you, if you do not then he douses you in cold water – either way it works.

At least, that is how it used to be. Nowadays, a new sophistication has come to the job. The first reserve or the spare committee man is no longer entrusted with the job of trainer. Similarly the plastic bag containing water is outmoded equipment.

Still, it was never very comforting to see the trainer jog on to the field looking as if he had just won a goldfish at the fairground. 'You all right, old man?' Why the answer never came back, 'Of course not, I am bleeding like a pig, aren't I?' I shall never know. British stoicism.

Pontypridd's trainer is now a veteran, but no one over the years has raced to the wounded faster than he. These days two heavy bags immobilize his arm, so his legs have to move like pistons. All that is missing from the silent movie action is the honky-tonk music. His black track suit, with the white strips along the side, adds to the Chaplinesque aura he creates. Often he is moving so fast he overruns his target.

I have seen a modern masseur dressed in white medical Dr Kildare coat to rub in the wintergreen. He loves waving to doctors in the grandstand to indicate that he has recognized, or rather diagnosed, a serious injury. At heart they are probably all medics *manqués*, or, perhaps players who never made it.

They frequently get worked up and involved on the touch-line, engaging in cross-talk with away crowds. Was it not Swansea's man who became distressed by the habit of the vast and feared second-row forward of taking a nibble at his players' flesh?

Thomas, of Neath, is reputed to have been led off by his own trainer with blood gushing from a split lip all over his chin and chest. The Swansea man could contain his fear no longer as Thomas passed by for treatment; 'Count Swansea ref! I think he's eaten one of us.'

Yes, a Happy New Year to them all.

From the *Daily Telegraph*, 27 December 1975

Tom Kiernan's Advice to the Irish XV

P.J.H

(as Overheard and Reported by Larry Flynn, dressing room attendant)
(With apologies to Percy French)

'See here, me men,' sez he.
'We're here again,' sez he.
'A match to play,' sez he.
'At three to-day,' sez he.
'So I want yez all,' sez he.
'Both big and small,' sez he.
'To listen well,' sez he.
'To what I've to tell,' sez he.

'There are some that said,' sez he.
'They're livin' in dread,' sez he.
'Of what England will do,' sez he.
'To me an' you,' sez he.
'After our mischance,' sez he.
'At the hands of France.' sez he.
'Oh! Yes we were bet,' sez he.
'But we're not dead yet.' sez he.
'These English chaps,' sez he.
'Are good, perhaps,' sez he.
'But they're only human,' sez he.
'Or so I'm assumin'.' sez he.

'So right from the start,' sez he.
'We'll frighten the heart,' sez he.
'Out of Dicky Sharp,' sez he.
'Till he sees that the harp,' sez he.
'Is playing once more,' sez he.
'As never before.' sez he.
'An' we'll give our socks,' sez he.

'To John Wilcox,' sez he.
'Till he's sorry that he,' sez he.
'Ever crossed the sea.' sez he.
'Peter Jackson, I've heard,' sez he.
'Is an ikey bird,' sez he.
'Don't give him a yard,' sez he.
'But put him down hard,' sez he.
'And tell the same tale,' sez he.
'To Roberts from Sale.' sez he.

'Now Phillips and Weston,' sez he.
'Will take some bestin',' sez he.
'So Jerry and Pat,' sez he.
'Look after that,' sez he.
'And make them see,' sez he.
'By ten past three,' sez he.
'The best thing to do,' sez he.
'Is to keep clear of you.' sez he.
'About young Clarke,' sez he.
'I'm in the dark,' sez he.
'But I expect you, Jim,' sez he.
'To put paid to him.' sez he.
'When before yeh met,' sez he.
'Ye had him bet,' sez he.
'So keep him subdued,' sez he.
'Without bein' rude,' sez he.

'Now about their pack,' sez he.
'Every man Jack,' sez he.

'Must go for his man,' sez he.
'As hard as he can,' sez he.
'And Mulcahy and McBride,' sez he.
'Must quickly decide,' sez he.
'How to be over throwin',' sez he.
'Alec Davis and Owen.' sez he.
'The hooker Thorne,' sez he.
'Don't treat him with scorn,' sez he.
'But let him see,' sez he.
'With Dovey and Lee,' sez he.
'They've bitten off, too,' sez he.
'More than they can chew.' sez he.
'Hanley, Wightman and Rogers,' sez he.
'Are artful dodgers,' sez he.
'Especially the last,' sez he.
'He's big and fast,' sez he.
'So yous two and Dick,' sez he.

'Just bury them quick,' sez he.

'Now that's about all,' sez he.
'Go after that ball,' sez he.
'With all you've got,' sez he.
'And we'll whack that lot.' sez he.
'I've finished me oration,' sez he.
'And for inspiration,' sez he.
'Remember our fate,' sez he.
'In ninety-eight,' sez he.
'And Cromwell, too,' sez he.
'In sixteen forty-two,' sez he.
'And yez needn't frown,' sez he.
'Becos we're one down,' sez he.
'We'll can still go to town,' sez he.
'And win the Triple Crown.' sez he.

From the *Irish RFU programme: Ireland/Scotland v. England/Wales*, 31 December 1955

Coarse Rugby

Michael Green

'I don't know what effect these men will have upon the enemy, but by God, they terrify me.'—*Duke of Wellington, after reviewing his troops.*

The object of the game of Coarse Rugby is to *win*. Let there be no mistake about that. It is fashionable to refer to the object of a sport as to have a good time and a clean open game. Nothing could be further from the thoughts of a Coarse Rugby player. He knows it is extremely doubtful if he will have a good time, as only eleven will turn up and he is not really fit enough to play these days. He prays fervently that it won't be an open game, as this means running about. And it is most unlikely to be a clean game.

No, if he can win, that is enough.

Coarse Rugby players are not alone in this attitude. Even rugger players remember best those games that were won. One does not hear first-class players saying, 'Do you remember that smashing 44–nil defeat by Cardiff?' So don't be hard on the coarse player.

It is also the object of a coarse player to win *with the least possible exertion*. Strenuous exercise can be dangerous to the average Extra B man. Besides, any fool can win by running faster and tackling harder than the opposition. It takes brains to win without over-indulging yourself physically. Anything that can be done to win without actually picking up the ball and running with it should be done. Running is a last resort.

Preparations for winning begin long before the kick-off, at the annual meeting in fact. Many a club has given its coarser teams a wonderful time by skilfully renaming them. It is easy to take advantage of the euphemistic system of calling lower sides by letters, by which the seventh side becomes the Extra C. This system is not standardized. Some clubs call their second team the 'A', while others call it the Extra First, and the 'A' is their third team.

By juggling with the name of the second team it is possible to push all the others down a grade, e.g. the Extra B will become the C and so on. In this way the Extra B can take over some of the C's fixtures. There is no need to arrange the whole fixture list like this, just give the lads a break about once a month.

Even better is to give the lower sides names such as Undesirables or Vandals. Then nobody knows whether the Vandals are the third or the seventh team and they can be matched with anyone.

I have had some glorious games in which the third team were pitted against someone else's fifth side. We all scored tries, even the full-back, and won about 70–nil. That's my idea of a game of rugby. Not every week, perhaps, but about once a month. It makes up for all the miserable matches when it rains and you are kicked on the knee.

More preparations can be made in the week before a match, when it is customary to send the other side a card giving directions as to how to reach the ground.

This card should be as vague and misleading as possible without actually giving the wrong directions. This is not difficult, because coarse pitches are usually miles from anywhere. London is easily the finest place in the country for losing your opponents, and here is a typically misleading London card:

SUBURBITON R.F.C.

BY RAIL TO ACTON. TURN LEFT OUTSIDE STATION, TURN LEFT AGAIN AT TOP OF ROAD, THEN BUS TO FIFTH TRAFFIC LIGHTS ON RIGHT, GO DOWN ROAD BY ROW OF SHOPS (IGNORE CRICKET GROUND SIGN), TURN SHARP LEFT BY GROCER'S, AND GROUND IS FIFTEEN MINUTES' WALK UP LANE AT END OF STREET.

If possible a little map should be enclosed. Like this:

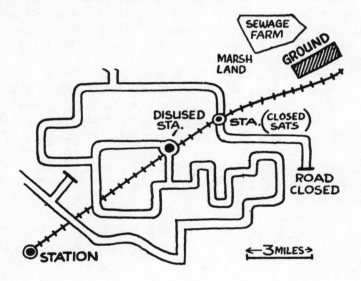

This is a beauty. The first direction, 'By rail to Acton', should flummox them for a start, as there are at least six stations in Acton. Even if by some miracle they should hit the right station, no firm address is given for the ground. They cannot ask the way to such-and-such a road. They must follow this rigmarole of leaping on and off buses and deciding which are the fifth set of traffic lights.

If they ask the way it is certain that they will receive nothing but lunatic replies. Nobody ever knows the way to a rugby club. The most you can hope for is to land up on a hockey pitch. (The public lump all games together. Whether you ask for the rugby ground or the soccer field, you'll still be directed to the hockey pitch. The only way to find the rugby ground is to ask for the cricket ground.)

Of course, if a club plays on two or three widely separated pitches, the task is even easier. Just send no directions at all, and all the opposition will go to the First XV pitch.

Ideally, one should work these schemes so that just nine or ten opponents find the ground. If none of the other side turns up the game will be cancelled and you won't be able to win. Fortunately, there are usually enough opponents who have played there before to ensure that they don't all get lost.

Let there be no doubt as to the success of this splendid wheeze. One London suburban fourth team went through a season unbeaten simply because they changed their pitch. Good heavens, there are *still* chaps wandering around West London trying to find the ground. If you ever meet a man carrying rugby kit and wandering aimlessly around Middlesex, just tell him the game's over, will you? And tell him they lost.

This scheme can recoil on your own side, however. We lost several of our own men because of these direction cards. They joined the club and were picked for the C and were sent a direction card and we never saw them again. A pity, but they had all paid their subs so we didn't worry too much. I often wonder what became of them. One of them might have been some good. He said he used to play for Rosslyn Park.

An alternative to this scheme involves the exact opposite. Instead of trying to keep the other side away from the ground, give them an embarrassing welcome. At least one London college has employed this technique (I won't name it, but the words 'desiccated calculating machine' may ring a bell).

When their opponents arrived all the way from Oxford they were greeted by a dozen students, and wined and dined heavily. Normally they would have carefully refused, but they could see the opposition tucking in, so they did the same. When the meal was over, and they were all thoroughly blown out and quite unfit to play rugby, their skipper said to one of the college men: 'How do you chaps manage to play after eating and drinking like this?'

'Oh, we don't have to play,' came the reply. 'We're just the reception committee.'

It only remains to say that the home team, who had carefully starved themselves all morning, won easily.

From *The Art of Coarse Rugby* by Michael Green
(Hutchinson, London, 1960)

A Bloody Good and Healthy Game

Spike Milligan

I was in Nairobi when England played Wales at Twickenham last season. I couldn't get a thing on the radio. I went mad, tearing at the knobs, twiddling the dials – nothing. The frustration was unbearable. That was the moment I realized how much the game means to me.

When I was talked into playing rugby in the Army, I had very little idea. I'd played football, and had a couple of games of rugby in Rangoon where they had a side which was half Burmese and half European. But I couldn't really rate rugby. I was a sort of peaceful boy, you know, and my first taste really shook me. This sudden collision of flesh against flesh, it disturbed me. But in the back of my mind there was something nagging. Running with the ball in your hands seemed more exciting than kicking it on the full.

When I joined the Artillery we had a Welsh sergeant – Sgt Griffiths. I can't remember his first name, but we used to call him Griff. I'd only been in about three weeks when Griff came around asking for names for football and rugby. I put my name down for football, which filled up in no time, but they had a pretty hard time with the rugby.

A pal of mine who used to play coaxed me to join in. 'It's a bloody good and healthy game,' he said. Griff took us to the Bexhill grounds and gave us a rough briefing. It looked all very good when he was explaining, but he didn't mention the bloody agonies that were to come. I played wing three-quarter – I don't know why except he said to play there.

I remember one tremendous game we had against Sussex Regiment on a muddy day in September. Up to that point we had been fairly evenly matched in weight and size with other teams we had played. But then these 'things' came on the field.

They got off a three-ton lorry, and my first instinct was to say to Griff, 'I'm not going to play with those things unless I hear them talk first.' Griff told us that it was going to be a hard game and much rougher than we had been used to. 'You've got to tackle harder,' he said, 'and don't be too worried about taking them by the legs. Get 'em round the head if that's the only way you'll get 'em down.' Honestly, they were like monsters looming on the horizon.

Well, the game started and the first loose maul – which I can only describe as a pile of creatures – and there was Griff shouting, 'Jump on, or pull the buggers off. Jump on, or pull the buggers off.' So I jumped on and landed on something that was strong and big, and suddenly an elbow caught me between the eyes.

When I came to, I was lying in a sort of shallow grave and play was up the other end of the field. I'd just lifted my head and seen them – all of them – charging back towards me when Griff shouted, 'For God's sake don't get up or you'll put us all off-side.'

I got old, and after the war I started watching to see how the game really should be played. At a match I play every point. Against Ireland last year I nearly got to Hiller when he kicked those two wonderful dropped goals. I could have brought him down, I know it. I thought I could have caught Hancock in his long run.

Cardiff, though, is the place for getting you in the throat. Walking in is like going into chapel. My wife, who's a singer, had never been there before and she looked at me in amazement. What's this all about? Are we really in Great Britain? You know, rugby is near to music for me. Great.

From *Touchdown*
(RFU, London, 1970)

5

HEROES AND VILLAINS

All Black and Blue

Willie John MacBride

When I was serving my rugby apprenticeship, I looked to two second-row forwards as supreme examples that I should try to emulate. Willie John MacBride is a hero as both a player and a leader, a man who gave his all himself and expected no less from the players around him. Colin Meads is another hero as a great, perhaps the greatest, second-rower, though he is also a villain for the infamous incident that saw him sent off in a Test match at Murrayfield.

    Willie John experienced both the misery of defeat with the 1966 Lions in New Zealand and the joy of victory five years later, with the all-conquering 1971 Lions.

W.B.B.

One thing that stands out in my mind was a remark from a New Zealander shortly after we arrived in the country. 'You had a great record in Australia and I saw you play there,' he said, 'but you will see what rugby is about from now on'. He was right. When the pressure came on us, we did not have the qualities required to meet it.

    There was a lack of commitment from some players and I attribute that primarily to a breakdown in management. Players broke up into groups with national boundaries often the demarcation line. Many players felt that they had not been given a fair chance to stake a claim for a Test place and it was hard to argue against some of them. Mike Campbell-Lamerton was asked to bear a tremendous burden, far too great for any one man to carry.

    There is often talk on tour about Wednesday teams and Saturday teams, with the Saturday men the recognized stars. Never had this been more obvious, and the final straw came when shortly before the first Test, it was decided that a Test panel would be taken away for special preparation with the rest of the players left to fend for themselves. My selection for the panel did not diminish my disagreement with such an action. A touring squad is a team or nothing. We even had the ludicrous rule of a ten o'clock curfew being put on players. To treat grown men in this way and expect commitment from them shows just how sad the whole scene had become.

    Not surprisingly, we were devastated in the first Test, New Zealand winning by twenty points to three. But for the displays of Dewi Bebb and Mike Gibson in the backs and Ronnie Lamont and a few other forwards who were outstanding in the pack, the score would probably have reached record proportions. Roger Young the scrum-half was playing in his first Test match and he got a real gruelling yet he stood up to everything thrown at him.

After the humiliation by a New Zealand team that showed the true greatness of All Black forward play, a few of the players got together with Mike Campbell-Lamerton. Noel Murphy, who knew more than any of us about New Zealand rugby, spoke frankly, as did Ray McLoughlin and a few others. Campbell-Lamerton took the courageous decision to drop himself from the second Test side, and Delme Thomas and myself formed the second row. We did reasonably well in that game and in fact led for quite a while before the All Blacks pulled away to win by four points. At least there had been marked improvement from the humiliation of Dunedin, but things had gone too far to hope for a recovery against a country that had so many great forwards and backs who did not make mistakes, even if they did not exactly set the world alight with their spirit of adventure.

Despite all our troubles on that tour, there were some of our backs who showed the All Blacks what flair behind the scrum was all about. Gibson was brilliant and Colin McFadyean, Stuart Wilson, Dewi Bebb and David Watkins showed a willingness and ability that was markedly absent in the play of the New Zealand backs. The irony of the whole affair was that despite the fact that New Zealand won all four Tests and in fact became the first country to achieve such a feat in a four-match Test series anywhere, there was a lot of soul-searching in New Zealand. Many were not satisfied with the play of the New Zealand backs. They were either limited or not prepared to take any chances in attack. Certainly they were at best stereotyped in attack and the backs did not in general respond to the work of their brilliant forwards. And how brilliant some of them were! Colin Meads, his brother Stan, Brian Lochore, Ken Gray, Kel Tremain, Wacka Nathan – there was not one in any of the Test packs the All Blacks fielded who was other than thoroughly well versed in the needs and totally competent in carrying out his brief. Not only were there no weak links, the whole chain was incredibly strong.

We lost the third Test and then the whitewash was completed in the fourth Test in Auckland. That final game took place on 10 September, so by then we had been away from home well over four months. Furthermore we were scheduled to play in Canada on the homeward journey. Like much else on that unfortunate tour, it was far too long and contributed to the catalogue of disaster.

I was certainly convinced that the attitude and approach which Ray McLoughlin had tried to instil into his players for Ireland was more than ever right. He spoke an immense amount of sense on that tour and so also did Noel Murphy. Regrettably, too few were prepared to listen to them. Too many had opted out long before the tour was over and I felt especially sorry for Mike Campbell-Lamerton who, I believe, lost over three stone on the tour, not surprisingly.

The apportionment of blame may be easy in retrospect, but basically I think the whole approach was wrong. The truth was that we were light-years behind the All Blacks in method and application. Their game was developing through good organization and coaching, and those aspects allied to the tremendous physical strength and natural ability of their forwards, was opening up a gap even wider than had obtained in the past.

From *Willie John* by W.J. MacBride
(Gill & Macmillan, Dublin, 1976)

A Long Hard Road

Willie John MacBride

From the moment we assembled at Eastbourne to prepare before the journey to Australia, it was plain that James, Smith and Dawes believed that we could win the Test series. They transmitted that confidence to the whole playing party. It was obvious that Smith and James had done their homework down to the most minute detail. I remember before the team was picked being approached by the two men and asked about New Zealand and what kind of players I thought would be suitable. I do not know whether they heeded my advice, but they sought it and that was typical of the men and their attitude, and it never varied from start to finish of that great tour.

Carwyn James had time for everybody. His is not alone a fine rugby mind, he is also a great psychologist. He knew the personalities of every player and he knew how to deal with every player in every circumstance. I have not come across a better combination in the art of man-management than the manager and coach of the 1971 Lions. James would seek everyone's point of view and listened to it with respect. Doubtless he did what he thought best, irrespective of advice offered to him, but you left him feeling here is a man who respects me and wants to hear what I think. His analysis of opponents was nothing short of brilliant and his reading of the game astonishing.

Doug Smith had that great facility for gaining respect without the use of the heavy hand and at no time on the tour did he make a wrong move. That is the best tribute I can pay to the man I would unhesitatingly name as the greatest manager under whom it was my privilege to play. Quite apart from his qualities of leadership, Dawes was a great player, yet he was the most underrated of my era. He was not a flamboyant centre, but none did the basics better than Dawes. His passing was perfect; he always did the right thing at the right time and his leadership was nothing less than superb.

I bracket Ray McLoughlin with the management trio because although he did not play in a Test, his contribution was immense. He did a great deal of coaching on the forwards and I remember in particular one stage of the tour when he set about building up our physical strength. 'They are supposed to be physically stronger than us,' he told the players, 'so we will get stronger.' He was as good as his word.

When we lost the first of our two games in Australia against Queensland, the knockers were in quickly to say that for all our preparations we had hardly shown that we were going to do any better than some of our predecessors. It was a rash judgement as things turned out. We beat New South Wales in the second game and then it was on to New Zealand.

We reached the first Test in Dunedin with ten wins out of ten; the rugby world had by now sat up and taken notice. I shall not forget the build-up for the first Test and Carwyn's assessment of what he wanted from us. We did not let him down and won by nine points to three. It was the proverbial cliff-hanger but a win of incalculable benefit.

In the early stages of that game, the All Blacks came on us in waves. Gareth Edwards went into the game with a hamstring injury and had to be replaced by Chico Hopkins after ten minutes; and how well the Llanelli man played when his hour came! We led 4–3 at half-time, Ian McLauchlan got a try for us after charging down an attempted clearance. Fergie McCormick kicked a penalty for the All Blacks and then in the second half Barry John kicked two penalty goals and we were home. McLauchlan and Sean Lynch were the props that afternoon and were to be together in all four Tests. It was during the tour that the diminutive Scot earned the title 'Mighty Mouse' for his exploits. Mighty he was, but no mouse; a Lion in every sense of the word if not in stature, his heart provided all that was required to meet the physical demands.

John's two penalty goals were just two of the many great and invaluable scores he got on the tour and the title 'King John' that he earned was a title of which he was worthy. But he was just one of a great bunch of players.

We might have lost that first Test, but we did not. This time we were able to stand up to the pressures put on us by the All Blacks. It was not until three minutes from time that John sealed it for us with his second penalty. We had matched them forward and we knew we were better than them behind the scrum. Events were to prove that assessment to be right. Colin Meads who had led the All Blacks that day was gracious enough when it was all over to say, 'The better team won on the day'. Maybe only just better, but we were better nevertheless.

I shall never forget how I felt after that match; I have seldom known a prouder moment in my life. I had endured the humiliations of 1966, so to win a Test in New Zealand gave me indescribable pleasure. Now we knew Carwyn was right, we really could take this series, but it would be a long, hard road.

From *Willie John* by W.J. MacBride
(Gill & Macmillan, Dublin, 1976)

I'm No Angel

Alex Veysey

Some people in Britain may remember Colin Meads only as the All Black sent off at Murrayfield in 1967. If so, that is a harsh judgement on one of the greatest second-row forwards of all time and a man devoted to the game of rugby football. Two of New Zealand's finest sportswriters present a more balanced view of 'Pine Tree' Meads.

W.B.B.

If New Zealand rugby suffers more painfully from one sickness than from any other at this time it is a sickness of spirit. It seems that a black jersey bearing the silver fern might just as well be any old jersey for all it achieves in lifting good players into great ones – great, if not in quality then in the searing spirit with which they play the game. Pride is the name of this game. The sort of pride which makes a man vow to himself he will lie down and die rather than submit while he is wearing the colour of his country. In more recent years any All Black who had, in fact, made that silent promise would have succumbed an unhealthy number of times. But pride is what Meads experienced when he shrugged into his black jersey; it was what his great contemporaries experienced. It does not mean that when wearing that jersey he did not perform some acts on the field which were outside the laws and, perhaps more importantly, outside the spirit of the game. He has struck fierce blows, some in anger, some probably in that quaint form of forceful psychology which only the players of rugby understand.

When the writing of this book was about to be started one journalist extended his sympathy because, he said, it could not be written without a thorough exposure of the Meads warts. It would be a pointless exercise to present Meads as what he is not. He is not, for instance, of such an angelic disposition that a place above is reserved for him between such gentle souls as St Francis of Assisi and St John. He himself would react with dismay at any such injustice. 'I'm no angel,' he says. 'He's no angel,' says his wife. So we can assume it is readily accepted that an angel is what he is not. But no fiercer pride burned in any All Black or any representative of any sport for any country. If some of his acts on the field suggest there are double standards in that pride let them be judged in the context in which they will be discussed in this book. He had great pride as an All Black, great pride as a King Country representative, great pride as a player for his tiny Te Kuiti club, Waitete.

He grew, too, to have pride in himself through a system which has been maligned probably more than praised, bandied about the political highways and byways, exploited as an electioneering plank, yet which was to Meads simply the greatest thing that ever happened. He says it without qualification, which is puzzling at first hearing because leaving school to farm, playing for the All Blacks, getting married, having his own family seem to be more in the line of great things which have happened to him. But, unquestionably, on deeper reading the Compulsory Military Training scheme for eighteen-year-olds was greater than any because it gave him the discipline and the self-respect which were the cornerstones without which these other great things could not have been so successfully constructed. His three months of training saw him grow from a 13½-stoner at 6ft 4in. to a 15-stoner at 6ft 4in. He found out what C.B. was all about because he spent a lot of time in that undesirable state, but when he had learned he could not, indeed, buck the Army he revelled in the life it gave him.

Rugby still dominated and he knew he had to have rugby early in the season to hope to qualify for selection in the Northern King Country team, the first stepping-stone toward King Country representation. So he broke camp. Again. It was a simple piece of logic. He wanted to play for King Country. He could not play for King Country unless he played for his club. He could not play for his club in Papakura Military Camp because his club was in Te Kuiti, well over a hundred miles south. He could not get leave to play for his club. Solution: go without leave. Which is what he did; although he returned to more C.B. He *had* been seen by the selectors, and he *was* chosen for the Northern King Country team. From there it was another step into the King Country representatives and his first first-class game as a lock against Counties. To hear Meads tell it, a chapter of accidents in that game led to his selection for a North Island Colts' trial which was to be played at Palmerston North a couple of weeks afterward. The ultimate was a dropped goal . . . 'a scoury drop-kick from fifteen yards in front of the posts; it scraped over the bar . . . I had been so late getting to a ruck that I was where the first five-eighth should have been when the ball came clear . . . I didn't know what the hell to do so I had a drop at goal,' says the man who drop-kicked his way to fame.

Watching that game was a wise man named Jack Finlay, a magnificent loose forward himself, one of the finest players with the New Zealand Army team, the Kiwis, beloved of British and French rugby people at the end of World War II. Finlay sent a message off to Jack Sullivan, then a New Zealand selector, earlier a most brilliant three-quarter for the All Blacks, later to be chairman of the New Zealand Rugby Union in its most difficult days. 'There's a boy Meads up there with a ton of potential,' said Jack Finlay. And suddenly the boy Meads was named out of the blue for the trial. The King Country selector Eddie Walker wrapped his reluctant star in cotton-wool for a match against New Zealand Maoris the week before the trial but Meads was far less careful about his future in a club match a few days later. He was to be in Palmerston North for the trial on a Monday. Come Saturday he played for Waitete and, for the first time, found himself in a situation which as his career developed was to become, if not common, then not exactly unfamiliar to him. He was ordered off. Consternation. The cause was a comradely sort of act, really. In the opposing forwards was a bloke with whom Meads had become great mates in military camp . . . 'He was giving me a hell of a time in the line-outs. I told him I'd get him. He came through a line-out. I leg-tripped him and pushed him into the deck.' Just a gesture of affection, no more. But the referee saw it as an act of grotesque violence and ordered the apple of the selector's eye from the paddock. Meads was summoned with great urgency and no lack of ceremony before the sub-union judicial committee. Sitting on it was Eddie Walker looking grim and forbidding. He confronted his golden-haired boy with a withering full frontal attack, raked him mercilessly. This was no way to play the game of rugby, he said and then demanded to see Meads outside. There he grabbed the bemused young man by the arm and said, 'Look. Take no bloody notice of what I said in there. Get down there and get stuck into that Colts' match.'

And this Meads did, to such effect that he was selected for the New Zealand Colts' team to tour Ceylon – though that is not as Meads tells it . . . 'I was the biggest there; a former King Country boy writing in the local Press gave me a great write-up . . . just a case of having the right guy in the right place at the right time . . . and that's how I got to Ceylon in 1955.'

The truth is that Meads was becoming a very good player of rugby. He was athletic and hard physically and he was adventurous and hard mentally. Without consciously deciding that this is what he would do, he committed himself to total rugby, total involvement. There was in him already the element which takes some men beyond others in many fields, whether in soldiering, in music, in commerce, in sport. Its ingredients are several, involving, among others, courage, dedication, an aggressive response to challenge, an obsession with succeeding, a strange, powerful sort of love. They are all there in one measure or another and they were all ripening in Meads.

His pursuit, though, was not of greatness but of playing rugby as well as he could and as often as he could at the highest level that he could. It was one of his greatest fears after being sent from the field at Murrayfield that this, for him, catastrophic experience would bedevil the rest of life, would shroud from the recognition of those who followed the simple fact that he was an All Black. He said, 'I do not want to be remembered as Colin Meads, the man who was sent off in the test at Murrayfield. I want to be remembered as Colin Meads, the man who was an All Black. Just that.' Perhaps there was with him the knowledge that Cyril Brownlie, stricken as Meads had been by being ordered off in a test match on one of the great sporting stadiums of the world, lived the rest of his life in that shadow. It was never 'Cyril Brownlie; ah, what a great player he was.' It was 'Cyril Brownlie, who was ordered off at Twickenham in 1924.' Perhaps it is a measure of Meads' grip on the New Zealand rugby public that within three years of that event in Edinburgh, the ordering-off was something long since gone, a fleeting incident rarely mentioned in the pubs and clubs where rugby is always top of the bill.

From *Colin Meads: All Black* by Alex Veysey
(Collins, London, 1975)

Pine Tree

Terry McLean

You get some idea of what Colin Meads means to the rugby folk of New Zealand from the account that Bruce McLeod, the All Blacks' hooker of recent years, gives of the events attending his first cap. When the announcement of the team was made over the radio one Sunday evening, McLeod's neighbours in their quiet suburban street invaded his home. There were millions of telephone calls, the Press was kind and McLeod, rather emotional by nature because he was orphaned at an early age, shed a tear or two of pride. All was joy. But the supreme moment occurred a few days later when the All Blacks were assembled in their hotel at Wellington. McLeod, the new boy, was walking up the stairs as Meads, *le grand seigneur*, was coming down. They met at the landing. Meads put out his hand. 'Congratulations, Bruce,' he said.

The awe has never left McLeod's voice. 'That was,' he says, 'the greatest moment of my life.'

For all that vast experience, including something like forty-seven caps and more than 300 games at first-class level, a great many of them for New Zealand, the Meads who comes to an international match is, oddly enough, still as nervous and as proud as was the young McLeod. The oddity is that in all outward aspects he is a mature and contained breadwinner. He farms 700 acres of hill country extremely well. In due time, if he wishes it, his will be an important voice in farming affairs.

His family life may be thrice blessed because his wife understands his passion for rugby better than anybody. But it is otherwise entirely normal and notable principally for a son who is tending to look more like Colin Meads than Colin Meads, if that is possible. From a great deal of touring – twice to the British Isles, France and Canada, thrice to Australia, once to South Africa and Lord knows how many times up and down New Zealand – he has acquired a poise which apparently, though not really, covers up the formidable shyness he developed as an adolescent of limited education. He is thirty-four, tolerably well circumstanced. He has, as he is aware, a peculiar place in New Zealand as a folk-hero comparable with Arnold Palmer in the United States and Sir Stanley Matthews in Britain. One could assume that everything in his outward life would cause him to regard the black jersey and the silver fern as incidentals.

On the contrary. Every time Meads plays for New Zealand, he feels joy and pride and humility as keenly as at his first cap, away back in 1957. His lean yet powerful body, 16 stones in weight year in and year out, his ice-cold brain which so acutely dissects the technicalities of Rugby, his massive hands which grip a rugby ball as if it were no larger than an orange, his legs which in shape and proportion were once ecstatically compared, by none other than John Reason, with the celebrated understrappings of Miss Betty Grable – all these have been paramount factors in the man's development and in the consistency of his astounding career.

But the first explanation of his greatness, I say without reservation, has been that curious compound of fear and ardour and immense pride which he has felt every time he has pulled on the jersey. The emotion may be a part of that atavistic streak whose other facets have at times – too many times in so good a player – bewildered and daunted those who, at the technical level, would be prepared to say rugby has not produced a finer forward.

For an insight into Meads's attitude, come with me to Cardiff Arms while the All Blacks of 1967 are playing East Wales in the penultimate match of their tour. Because of *that* incident at Murrayfield ten days before, Meads perforce is among the non-participants. There has been much snow on the ground. It is cold, so bloody cold that two or three other All Blacks, also non-participants, have provided themselves with whisky. Meads dourly spurns their offer of a nip. East Wales have the lead, three to nil. There are howls and yowls when the referee does not award Keri Jones a penalty try after he has been shouldered by Fergie McCormick. Then Tony Steel, given the ball, skips and side-steps and speeds, and with his famous try saves the unbeaten record of the team. For all New Zealanders, it is a moment of ecstasy. 'Here,' Meads commands gruffly. 'Give us that bottle.' He takes a swig.

Now, these years later, he cannot speak of that reflex action without conveying that he still feels ashamed of himself. He has, in fact, never forgiven himself for taking a drink in public while wearing All Black uniform. He never will forgive himself. His feeling is that he dishonoured both his uniform and his country.

Incidents like this provide the inexplicable paradox about Meads. He would not wilfully do anything to harm the New Zealand game. Yet he has been execrated beyond all other leading players of his time – except, perhaps, several Frenchmen who kick men much more scientifically, and brutally, than they kick a ball – because of the vigour of his methods. Meads disarms one because he does not deny that he has been vigorous. His test is whether the vigour will give his team a legitimate advantage. If he feels so, he will use it – 'I like to put something across my man,' he says. But if the vigour will not serve his team, if it is only a personal satisfaction, Meads claims he will not be tempted.

He does not carry me all the way with the sophistry of this argument. And there have been times, as when he tried to scalp Tony O'Reilly in New Zealand in 1959, knocked down Michael Campbell-Lamerton in the London Counties game in 1963, and stopped the Welsh hooker, Jeff Young, cold in New Zealand in 1969, when I have despaired and had many others with me feeling the same. But, in rugby, there is always another side to the question. The other side of this aspect of Meads is the tendency for opposing teams, not forgetting internationals, to put two and even three men against him, to harry him and goad him. Some of these teams, not least the Welsh, have excelled in their nefarious activities. Yet Wilson Whineray, as a prime example, could always persuade 'Pine Tree' to attend to the main job. The man can be tamed. It really is a question who is doing the taming.

Meads's shyness enveloped him when he and his younger brother, Stanley, after a brief venture into scholarship, roamed their farming district as shearers, roustabouts, anything that would bring money into the home. Theirs was a hard life which offered little contact with ease and none with elegance. By eighteen, when he was called on to do Army training, Colin was a lean, reclusive young man of 13½ stones. Three months of military training enlarged his frame by twenty-eight pounds.

He was a loose forward, a Number 8, when he tried out for a Colts' team which was to tour Ceylon, the players putting up some of the expense. For no sensible reason that he can recall, he dropkicked at goal during a qualifying match and so amazed a senior selector who happened to be present that all thorns were removed from the path which led him into the team. He was still a loose forward of the All Black team, his first, which toured Australia in 1957, but because of casualties was put to lock in the second test with the Wallabies. There he has stayed, to the joy of teammates and the despair of countless opponents. With each passing year, his reputation as a player has grown more extensive. In his own country district, he is, in all things, Superman, Batman and Miracle Man wrapped in one. He reacts with instinctive shyness to this adoration. Yet he will go anywhere, at pretty well any time, to help a club, or a team, or a friend, so long as the cause is rugger.

It may be that Meads is the greatest player, day in and day out, in rugby at the moment. (As a modest man, he would never dream of suggesting this.) The question is, can New Zealand hope to produce another Meads? My answer would be yes – so long as the rural life of New Zealand, as it has done for almost a hundred years, takes its keenest sporting and social pleasure from the game. There are many other physical Meadses in New Zealand, men who work long hours at demanding physical jobs and who develop prodigious strength and stamina. Meads is exceptional because his physical qualities have been refined by a keen, natural intelligence, vast playing experience and contact with many great opponents, among whom he rates Rhys Williams, of Wales, and Johan Claassen, of South Africa, very high. But the raw material which could shape into other 'Pine Trees' is still fairly abundant in New Zealand.

Whether there will be another as good cannot be foretold. The man who is to emulate or supplant him must have many qualities – hands, head, strength, stamina, speed. Above all, he must have love – a true, abiding love of rugby as the greatest of all games.

From *Touchdown*
(RFU, London, 1970)

A Blow for Australia

Steve Finnane

If Colin Meads is both hero and villain to me, there is no doubt in which category I would place the Australian Steve Finnane. Like Meads he was sent off in an international, but while I have got a great deal of time for Colin Meads, I can find little to say in mitigation for Finnane, whose own version of events just leaves an even nastier taste in my mouth.

W.B.B.

If you ever worked for years for something and then faced one last hurdle before the final achievement, you will be able to appreciate the depth of emotion that enveloped the dank, old-fashioned changing rooms at the Sydney Cricket Ground at 2.45 p.m. on Saturday, 17 June 1978.

A coach, a team manager, fifteen players and six reserves, in the gold jerseys and green shorts of Australia, sat tensely on wooden slat benches or shuffled restlessly about the stuffy room, boot studs clattering on concrete floor to create the only sounds in a cell of silence.

Fifteen minutes to the moment of truth.

I finished bandaging my right hand which had been stamped on the previous Saturday in Brisbane as we beat Wales, the champions of Europe and, in their own eyes, of the world, in the first of two Tests in their initial rugby tour of Australia. I flexed the hand and it felt solid and secure in its binding. Just as well. If the Welshmen went into today's game in the way they had their others on tour, that right hand would be needed.

Coach Daryl Haberecht had finished his talk and the room was quiet as we digested his thoughts and did our own private mental preparation. We had come a long way. Twelve of the fifteen Test men had been in Britain with the Wallabies in 1975 when the brilliant Welshmen demolished Australia 28–3 before 55,000 of their singing, wildly cheering countrymen at Cardiff Arms Park. The night after that defeat a group of us vowed we would even the score. We would learn from the Welshmen and the other international top dogs in the sport, we would improve our technique, and we would make Australia a force again in world rugby. The next time we met the self-confident boyos of Wales we would know what we were up against. And when they piled in boots and all we wouldn't step backwards.

Now the time had come. The noise of the crowd floated in from the remote sunlit world outside. There were nearly 42,000 of them waiting impatiently to share in a great moment for Australia and we must not let them down the way Australian rugby had been let down so often in the past.

Apart from their first Test defeat, the Welshmen had lost to Sydney and the Australian Capital Territory and their party was decimated by injury, but we had no illusion that misfortune would make them easy prey. Welsh pride was at stake today and they would play like fanatics. The cornerstone of their team, the famous Pontypool front row of Graham Price, Bobby Windsor and Charlie Faulkner, was intact and I had heard along the grapevine that they were gunning for me. They were said to be the toughest front-row trio in the world and although I had played against them before there had never been quite as much at stake as today.

Nerves twisted inside my stomach and I had to go to a cubicle to retch, knowing I was not the only Wallaby to be affected that way. At last the referee's whistle shrilled. The call to combat.

It was a relief to be out in the middle with the din of the big crowd pouring down. We flicked a football around as we waited for the kick-off, then the ball was in the air and it was time to let the nervous energy pour out.

My guard was up. I had taken plenty from the Welshmen in the previous two weeks and I wasn't prepared to spend another seven days in a daze wondering whether my brains had been scrambled.

After five minutes, Graham Price bored in at a scrum and a fight followed as the two packs separated. I stepped into him and threw a short right.

The impact sent my name hurtling around the world with a label attached that said – often in 72-point type – 'thug'.

Price fell, his jaw broken in two places, and I parried counter-attacks from second-rower Clive Davis and acting flank forward J.P.R. Williams, until the referee arrived to calm things down and allow Price to be led from the field, one hand cupped under his shattered jaw.

I have never regretted throwing that punch. I only wish it had done no more than I intended it to do – to show Price and the other Welshmen that Australians would not bow to standover tactics.

Price is a brave and uncomplaining opponent whose only public comment on the incident was to tell Welsh reporters when he got home: 'It wasn't a particularly tough tour. You give some and you take some.' But his manager Clive Rowlands desperately needed something to distract attention from Wales' disastrous showing in Australia. At the reception that night to celebrate our victory he made the first public accusation about 'thuggery'. The word was soon rumbling around the world with the British Press having a picnic at my expense, New Zealand newspapers calling on their government to ban me from the country, and the Australian media laying a three-week siege on my front door and telephone.

One of the stories that circulated at the time was that Price had kneed me in the groin before I struck him. That wasn't true. He simply lost out in the ritual of intimidation and counter-intimidation that has become part of modern international rugby. Not that violence is uniquely modern. The practice of props testing each other with an exploratory punch or two, just to establish mutual respect, is as old as the game itself. Rugby is a tough sport and anybody who is not willing to take and give a little should play something else. But the international scene in the 1970s has become pretty intense and such teams as Wales play for big stakes in terms of their standing in their own community and the reputation of their country internationally. Defeat to some of them is not far removed from treason.

On scores of occasions during the tour Welshmen swung their boots and fists at Australians. But I became a scapegoat because my punch was a good one – much more effective, in fact, than I had intended. There are many people in rugby who encourage their players to get in first and get on top of the other fellow, but when things go too far and a jaw or a cheek-bone gets broken they throw up their hands and cry 'thuggery'. Their double standards make you laugh.

The Price incident was not the first to bring outrage on my head. The English reacted rather sourly when I played for Sydney against their touring side in 1975 and met fire with fire – to the discomfort of three of their forwards. The following year there were moves to have me banned from Australian teams after a player's jaw was broken in a game between Sydney and NSW Country. By then the Sydney Press had created the legend of the Phantom Puncher complete with a little cartoon of a hooded rugby executioner.

People began to talk about me as an enforcer – a term borrowed from rugby league and usually used to describe a player who was in a team for his fistic rather than his football ability. I can only say that I never went on to a football field with anything except playing and winning the game as my number one priority. The times I did use my fists, with one exception, were in retaliation or during the exchanges that develop out of the ancient forward code of confrontation, when two packs square off like dogs in the street and you either teach the opposition respect or you slink off with your tail between your legs. One of my old sparring partners, Tony Miller, summed it up when he defended me over the Price incident. He said: 'You just cannot allow rival footballers to ride roughshod over you without retaliating. The front row is a fraternity all its own. There's no way you are going to cop things without hitting back. If you fold, the whole team goes.'

The last sentence is the key. A team cannot afford any member to buckle under, but if a front-rower surrenders everything is lost. That's a responsibility you carry into every match and you become particularly aware of it when the match is a Test for your country. I always played with this in mind and if refusing to step back was being an enforcer, I'll accept the title.

From *The Game They Play in Heaven* by Steve Finnane
(McGraw Hill, Maidenhead, 1979)

Referee Fatigue

J.A. Buttery

Referees are the villains that we all love to hate. J.A. Buttery's piece written after the All Blacks had beaten Surrey 11–0 in a match refereed by the founder of Twickenham, Billy Williams, shows that as far back as 1905 no one loved the referee.

One referee who is widely admired and respected, except no doubt, by World Cup committees and those he has just penalized, is Clive Norling. Not afraid to send players off when their offences merit it, Norling has the wisdom to see that the crowd have come to see rugby played, not to endure a trumpet voluntary on the referee's whistle. If only there were more like him!

W.B.B.

In the face of lowering clouds which threatened every minute to burst – which in fact did eventually drench the great majority of spectators – over 10,000 people, many of them ladies, made their way from various parts of the metropolis to see the All Blacks side that everybody is talking about. They expected to see some wonderful football, but they had reckoned without one factor – the referee.

This gentleman – a Londoner and a member of the Rugby Union committee – was evidently under the impression that everybody had come to hear him perform on the whistle, and as he was in charge of the stage so to speak, he was enabled to indulge his fancy to his heart's content.

The finest artists are said to shut their eyes when whistling their hardest and, judged on this hypothesis, the referee must have had his eyes closed on and off for the greater part of the game. The fantasia commenced in the first minute and continued, with brief intervals for respiration, throughout the game.

As one of the rules of rugby is that you may not kick or handle the ball while the whistle is blowing, it is obvious that there was very little actual football. Directly someone got the ball and there was the prospect of a bit of play worth seeing, the referee would recommence his fascinating solo.

A Scottish lady, whose first football match this was, and evidently with literary recollections of the efficacy of the pibroch in clan warfare, asked her escort after one particularly dangerous All Black movement had been stopped at the referee's musical behest, 'Why aren't the New Zealanders allowed to have a man whistle for them, too?'

The rain came down in torrents, and between the bars of the referee's interminable selection, the players flipped and flopped about the slippery ground like seals on an ice floe. A confused entangled mass of legs and arms and black and red and white jerseys danced in rhythm to the referee in various corners of the field, but there was no football. 'When are they going to begin?' enquired a soccer enthusiast who had come many miles because a rugby friend had assured him that he would see something in the way of football he would remember all his life.

It was then closely approaching half-time. Twenty-five minutes from the start, however, the referee showed signs of fatigue, whereupon the All Blacks, quickly seizing their opportunity and the ball, crossed the Surrey line and kicked a goal.

Several explanations were advanced for the referee's extraordinary lapse, but the two most generally accepted were that he had either dropped his whistle or that the pea in it had stuck. Unabashed by this temporary eclipse, however, he blew harder than ever, and for the remainder of the first half football was again out of the question.

During the interval the referee was the recipient of many congratulations from musical friends on his magnificently sustained effort, though fears were expressed that the severe exertions he had undergone would tell on him in the second half.

And this proved to be only too true. His whistle failed him on at least two occasions. The line was crossed twice more. To their credit be it said, the crowd by this time realized the mistake they had made in supposing that the affair would be an athletic display. Some, stung to emulation, whistled obbligatos to the shrill music that rose from the middle of the field. Others, with their sodden coats over their heads and their dripping umbrellas in front of their faces, beat time to the pulsating notes that indicated the whereabouts of the referee's triumphant march. 'What an awful day for an open-air concert,' shivered a young lady in the grandstand as she gathered up her skirts to depart. As for the game – there was no game. It was an exposition of the power of music to tame even the New Zealand rugby footballer.

Though unnoticed by the crowd there were some highly interesting interludes to some of the referee's most brilliant flights. The All Black captain, who evidently had no ear for music, desired enlightenment on more than one, to him, discordant passage. He is still pondering over the answers. It is understood that Mr Dixon, the New Zealand manager, is also dubious as to the correctness of many of the notes, and that he intends to take the earliest opportunity of interviewing the President of the English Musical Union on the matter. Everyone went away whistling – except the New Zealanders. 'No wonder it rained,' they said.

At the end of these games there is usually a rush for the jersey of the man who has scored, so that it may be kept as a trophy. Yesterday there was a wild scramble for the referee's whistle.

From the *Daily Mail*, 1905

Taking Norling for Granted

Steve Bale

He was only twenty-three when he dismissed Eddie Meredith, a Metropolitan Policeman, against Bristol in the 1973 RFU quarter-final.

It was one incident among several which established Norling's reputation as a disciplinarian. Another came after he had returned to Wales when he sent off Ian Eidman of Cardiff and Bridgend's Ian Stephens, both international props, for persistently collapsing.

But Norling is better known for his uncompromising attitude to foul play. He had the temerity to dismiss Jean-Pierre Garuet, the prop, in front of 55,000 baying Frenchmen in Paris – one of forty-nine players on whom he has imposed the ultimate sanction in his twenty-two years of refereeing.

'As time has gone by I've had to send off fewer players, because they are fully aware that if they want to step out of line I'll come down on them as heavily as I can. I don't hold reputations in any esteem; I've sent off at international level and all the way down the scale.' Last season there were only two; in the three months of this season, none.

Norling's refereeing has by its quality provoked a fierce debate over the way Test matches are allocated. The Buggins's turn by which appointments are shared out meant that he was excluded from last season's Five Nations' Championship apart from running the Ireland v. England line.

Through the old invitational system – the best referees in charge of the best players in the best games – Gwynne Walters (the last man to be invited annually by Oxbridge) and Kevin Kelleher reached their joint record, twenty-three Tests. Had he had the same advantage, Norling might by now have reached his half century, and would also in all probability have taken the inaugural World Cup final in 1987.

Instead, his services were dispensed with after he had refereed two of the first-round group matches. 'I wasn't in the least surprised,' Norling said. 'I'd looked at the composition of the referees' committee – chaired by an Australian, sitting with two others from the southern hemisphere, a Scot and a Frenchman.

'The numbers were always against me. I'm delighted that for the next World Cup they're going outside International Board committee men and have active refereeing assessors. This is a great advance and should do a lot to ensure the best man gets the job.

'I'm always ambitious and for a referee there couldn't be a higher ambition than that match. But first of all I have to be re-elected to the Welsh international referees' panel and be selected as a Welsh referee at the World Cup. I've never taken anything for granted and I'm not going to start now.' The rest of us, though, have been taking Norling for granted for a long time.

From *The Independent*, 1987

Not the Good Ref Guide

Alan Watkins

A few weeks ago I suggested to a colleague in the sports department of this paper that I might write a column, to be entitled provisionally 'The Good Ref Guide'. 'That will be a very short column,' he replied. Nevertheless, I have been following the controversy about British referees in the World Cup, particularly Clive Norling, with a certain detached interest. It is detached both because I was several thousand miles away at the time and because I tend to judge my countrymen with perhaps too much severity. To adapt Dr Johnson: 'The Welsh are a fair people; they never speak well of one another.'

Norling still seems to be the best referee not only in these islands but also, from the evidence of television, in the world. There was a marked decline in the standard when either of the Australian referees, Fordham and Fitzgerald, was in charge. I think Roger Quittenton of England was shabbily treated too. I do not share the prejudice of my fellow countrymen against Quittenton. His trouble is not that he is an incompetent referee but that he is too pleased with himself, or anyway appears to be so. While most of his colleagues resemble suet puddings, he gives the impression of being a West End actor who has seen better times, and is now spending the autumn of his days playing in rep in Richmond.

Norling is no suet pudding either. Indeed, I would describe him as a fine figure of a man. But the reason given for sending him home early was that he was 'too fat' to referee in the concluding stages. If referees are to be judged in this way, what about players? Gareth Chilcott of Bath would be permanently barred on aesthetic grounds. Incidentally, I have a friend who takes his two small sons to matches. They are at the age when other people's physical characteristics are a subject for much mirth. When they become bored with the game, they scan the crowd for generously proportioned ladies, saying ungallantly: 'Look, Dad, there's Chilcott's sister.'

However, there is something faintly depressing about boasting that we produce the best referees. It is rather like claiming, as it is often claimed, that we are the leading nation for company liquidators and trustees in bankruptcy. We should certainly not be complacent. From my observation this season, our referees have several failings. They are over-strict about some things and overindulgent about others.

Forward passes are now allowed regularly, particularly where there is a traditional, flowing movement ending with a try or with the player's being forced into touch near the line. It is as if the referee is reluctant to spoil the fun. This is an excellent principle, as the best of all post-war referees, D. Gwynne Walters, fully realized. But it should be applied by an imaginative use of the advantage law and by a reluctance to niggle. A forward pass is not a niggle.

Again, throws into the line-out are now usually successful exercises in deceiving the referee. The deception is rendered easier by their habit of standing several yards to one side of the 90-degree line along which the hooker (usually) is meant to be throwing. The reason is supposed to be that, by so positioning himself, the referee avoids being in the way. A moment's thought will show that the chance of being in the way is unchanged, even increased, because the action takes place on one side or the other, rarely in the middle.

On the other hand, referees penalize dangerous tackles when they are not dangerous at all, but merely on the high side. . . . Much more serious, however, are the penalties for being over the top, killing the ball, failing to release. John Griffiths' *Phoenix Book of International Rugby Records* tells part of the story.

The record points-scorers, the Ollie Campbells and Dusty Hares, are all kickers of recent years. Even comparative newcomers, such as Gavin Hastings, Paul Thorburn and Rob Andrew, are already statistical immortals owing to their feats with the boot. The great try-scorers, by contrast, are from the past. But for a change, we will have to alter the laws, not the scoring system.

From *The Independent*, November 1987

Referees Who Are Losing Face

Steve Bale

When Stephen Hilditch sent off Grégoire Lascubé and Vincent Moscato at Parc des Princes, it seemed to be the two Frenchmen – one dismissed for stamping, the other for butting – who threatened public order.

When David Bishop was assailed in the players' tunnel at the Parc by Daniel Dubroca after an earlier France–England game, the World Cup quarter-final, was it not the French coach, bellowing 'cheat' and manhandling the referee, who threatened public order?

Mais non. Eventually Dubroca resigned but as anyone would realize who subscribed to French conspiracy theories, on each occasion it was the referee who was to blame. And the French, well some Frenchmen anyway, are not letting them get away with it.

In one tiny corner of rugby's south-western heartland Hilditch and Bishop have had the full weight of municipal sanction brought down on them. They have been banned, as undesirable and a threat to public order, from Moncrabeau (population 792) and will not be permitted to stand in the annual election of the 'king of the liars', nor the triennial world championship of making faces, for which this Lot-et-Garonne village is renowned even more than its rugby.

Ten of the fifteen village councillors voted against Hilditch, a Belfast headmaster, and Bishop, who lives a long way from trouble in a remote part of the South Island of New Zealand. 'These people could create public disorder,' the mayor, Christian Lussagnet, intoned. 'The people of Moncrabeau, who believe in fairness, do not appreciate the performance of these two gentlemen during the two last matches.' France lost them both.

After the Lascubé–Moscato *affaire*, the French rugby federation president Bernard Lapasset invited Hilditch to take the temperature of French rugby by refereeing a few club games. It is safe to assume these will not be in Clochemerle . . . sorry, Moncrabeau.

From *The Independent*, 1992

6
GREAT NATIONS: WALES

Obsessed with Success?

Clem Thomas and Geoffrey Nicholson

The Welsh expect success at rugby as a birthright; if they do not get it, they are vocal and angry in demanding change. Alone of the Five Nations, rugby is the national sport of Wales, and as a result Welsh rugby has a flavour like no other.

W.B.B.

If you are a Welshman, once you cross the Severn Bridge and head west from Offa's Dyke you are in the Holy Land of rugby. The game was carried there by young missionaries coming home from the grand universities of England and the great teaching hospitals of London. Its arrival coincided with the time when the rural population began to congregate at the summons of the coal and iron masters, in the coastal towns and valleys that were to become ravaged by industries which would brutally scar both the landscape and the populace.

Such conditions demanded a huge release from both spiritual and physical tensions, and the panaceas came in the form of evangelical and nonconformist socialism, religion and rugby. A small, historically subjected nation (but never permanently) had suddenly found eloquent ways to express its exploding restless virility, and in rugby football had found the means to establish and prove an identity. It began building a new grand dynasty which was to become more famous than that of its ancient warrior princes and which needed no political or financial investment, only a patch of level ground, inflated leather, unusual skills and a fair amount of courage.

Strangely, the immigration into the eastern and western valleys in search of work in the new industries was cosmopolitan and, if you examine the programme when valley or seaport clubs play each other often more than half the players are of largely English origin. They have surnames which sound Saxon and Norman – Cobner, Squire, Butler, Gregory, Perkins, Leleu, Alexander, Cooksley and Swain – and these are interspersed with the inevitable Irishmen like O'Sullivan, O'Connor or Reilly. In recent Welsh teams names such as Blyth, Fenwick, Keen, Holmes, Wheel, Ringer, Martin and Squire could in no way be Welsh. This was one reason why the language almost died, but within a generation the intruders were absorbed and became Welsh by adoption and in spirit as the new communities, built on hard graft, suckled and nurtured them to become a new mongrel nation, integrated through hardship, fellowship and the new nonconformist culture.

There is, therefore, no ethnic reason why the Welsh should be better at rugby football than any of the other nations which make up the four Home Unions. The explanation is more likely to be found in the fact that, unlike the working class population of industrial England or Scotland, the Welsh working man, particularly in the smaller communities, chose to embrace rugby. Perhaps a hard life ripping out coal, or cooking steel, needed just such a hard physical game, with its strange ethics and intellectualism. Villages and towns were like separate tribes: they tended to be of different religious denominations or sects; they worked in different collieries and steelworks; and therefore the rivalry of the Eisteddfod and of industrial output was a way of life. Rugby was their means of warring with one another, and the tradition survives to this day. Welsh local derbies can still be a terrifying experience for those who do not understand the undercurrent and/or realize that there is no personal malice.

With the rise of the great industrial centres at the ports of the South Wales seaboard, Cardiff and Newport in the east, Llanelli and Swansea in the west, with Aberavon and Neath in between, soon became major clubs and they were rapidly reinforced by clubs in the new hinterland, such as Ebbw Vale, Maesteg, Pontypool and Pontypridd. Inevitably the Welsh established their major shrine in the capital city, for although St Helen's, Swansea, had its followers until the last international was played there in 1954, the great cathedral of the game became Cardiff Arms Park. I still prefer to call it that, not the National Stadium, which seems impersonal and sounds like a nationalized industry, which is almost what it is or would be if only they prevented the rich from buying all the seats.

Here in the nave the congregation produces the ultimate sound of their personal expression of nationhood, a combination of the lively fortissimo of grand opera and of the doleful hymns of Welsh Tabernacles, Ebenezers, Siloams and Gibeas. The more lachrymose hymns draw out the best descants and harmonies from what is the largest and most skilful choir of its kind in the world, so funereal at times that they have buried the expectations of many a fine foreign team before the kick-off. I remember it well, for although it is almost twenty-two years since I last appeared as a Welsh gladiator waiting to be unleashed at English, Irish, French, Scottish, Australian or New Zealand Christians, I can still recall the feeling of the hair rising at the nape of the neck, bristling like a wolf waiting to lunge at his prey, and, for the first fifteen minutes of an international, no Saxon, French or Celtic boot or bone seemed capable of penetrating a mystic armour.

From *Welsh Rugby: The Crowning Years* by Clem Thomas and Geoffrey Nicholson
(Collins, London, 1980)

The Old Enemy, England

Gareth Edwards

I have been scoring tries against England since the age of four. My first memory of rugby was that I *had* to be Wales, and my younger brother Gethin was left with England. In Wales the England–Wales rivalry has always been the traditional battle, and even as a child I can remember knowing when any game between the two countries was going to be played. There was an electric atmosphere in the valleys.

It is very difficult for outsiders to appreciate the feelings of the Welsh. If you ask any Welshman which team has to be overcome during each season it's always England – for a hundred different reasons. Everyone wants to beat England. To go to Twickenham and win is great. On the other hand, Welshmen can't believe they can lose at Cardiff, and when it happens the nation bleeds. It is not that Welsh people today feel any inferiority complex (though sometimes we think the English believe we are still painted up in blue and chucking spears). It goes back to the past, when the Welsh looked upon the English as the oppressors and possibly their superiors. Now that that is all over the only resemblances to those ancient battles are the annual rugby internationals.

From *Gareth – an Autobiography* by Gareth Edwards
(Stanley Paul, London, 1978)

The Toughest Battle Had Been the Last

Gareth Williams and David Smith

No nation likes to beat the English more than the Welsh and for the greater part of my own rugby career, no nation was more successful at doing so. If Welsh rugby is only just emerging from a painful decline, the Welsh side of the 1970s was one of the finest national sides of any era, brimming with talent in every department, from the fearless J.P.R. Williams at full-back, through magnificent half-backs Barry John, Gareth Edwards and Phil Bennett, to the granite prop Graham Price and the peerless number eight Mervyn Davies. They dominated the 1970s, but perhaps their finest achievement came in 1978–79, as this great Welsh side played together for the last time.

W.B.B.

This galaxy of Welsh stars burned brightly with its own incandescent will for one more season. It played tight, when it needed, it danced out of reach when it was required, and it had someone in its ranks with that answer to whichever question was posed. England was the first hurdle. The day was dull, the ball wet and slippery and the scores restricted to penalty goals. The satisfaction of a hard-won victory was given a special burnish by the fact that Gareth Edwards, winning his fiftieth cap, had kicked England back through the driving rain, on one occasion with a wholly incredible narrow-angled, sixty-five-yard touch-finder which thrust Wales back onto an offensive they never then relinquished, in a knowledgeable wet-weather performance that promised the receding hairline would be an optical illusion for a while yet. Against Scotland the Welsh team once again revealed their great strength: their unshakeable confidence in each other and their collective will to win, more particularly their ability to absorb punishment and then exert immense pressure of their own in a decisive ten-minute onslaught. On a bitterly cold February afternoon they moved suddenly from 8–7 to 22–7 in a scoring blizzard which was matched later that evening by a snowstorm that marooned thousands of supporters in hospitable conditions in and around Cardiff for three days. Although the Scots then exploited Welsh relaxation to pull back a further seven points, Wales had outscored them by four tries to two. The first had come from an express-train dash and dive for the line from a scrummage twelve yards out. It was predictable, and the crowd buzzed with expectation as the scrum had formed, but its power and energy were always unpredictable when it eventually came, and it was totally unstoppable. The lunging scarlet-jerseyed figure cradled the ball reverentially with his top hand before planting it over the line. It was the last of Gareth Edwards' twenty tries for his country. His appetite for the line had grown sharper over the years; that compulsive hunger would never be properly assuaged. He warmed even a sub-arctic day which suggested that the Welsh winter preferred freezing Gareth Edwards in perpetuity to losing him.

The Irish on their way to a possible Triple Crown did not really mind how Edwards was embalmed so long as it was on the March day in Dublin. Their improving side had a fly-half who delighted Welsh eyes with his bubbling play, though the bruising tactics of the Irish forwards were not quite as pleasing. J.P.R. Williams so far forgot his Hippocratic principles as to late-tackle his friend Mike Gibson when commitment out-stripped his judgement. The true mortician, however, was the deadly Fenwick. The ice-warrior from Taffs Well, unperturbed by a frenzied Irish crowd, kicked four penalties and scored the first of Wales's two tries to take sixteen out of the winning number of twenty, and thus equal Ireland's total score himself. Cobner had exhorted Wales to renewed forward power in the way he had done in New Zealand the previous summer. The team was, undeniably, wilting psychologically under the strain of encroaching age and the sheer loss of that inner energy which can be summoned up for only so long. They sat, speechless and exhausted, still in full kit, waiting for a collective return to the normal pace of rugby life before they left the dressing room together after one of the most mentally and physically draining matches ever played by any Wales team. This XV had dredged their last resources of experience and skill to pull away from a 13–13 stalemate to a final score of 20–16. What they had accomplished was not normal. This Welsh side was the first in anyone's history to win the Triple Crown in three successive years, and the toughest battle had been the last. Not the last for the Championship, though. Phil Bennett's cup would run over if France could be taken to bring a third 1970s Grand Slam to Wales. The giant French No. 8 Bastiat brought with him the nucleus of the 1977 French Grand Slammers with new scrum-half Jerome Gallion ready to dispute, with the help of the Viking Rives and the vulpine Skrela in an accomplished French back-row, Gareth Edwards's crown. The Welshman had not announced his retire-ment yet. A warm, almost Parisian, spring day saw Wales reach half-time with a 13–7 lead. French fervour never recovered thereafter as Wales, composed and dominant, sewed up a 16–7 victory. France had scored their try and drop-goal first, and early on, for a seven points lead, but then Windsor took a ball against the head and Bennett ripped his side-stepping way over. The Welsh side, ignited by Edwards, inspired by Bennett, played combined football of the highest order for ten minutes before the interval. Graham Price was ready, once, for a bullocking charge but decided instead to wait, hold and give to Edwards who dropped a goal. The second try came on the right when four players handled before the Welsh captain put a seal on a superb individual performance by streaking, low-crouched and hard, over the line, after a pass thrown miraculously by J.J. Williams from behind his right ear.

The Grand Slam captain had no intention of relinquishing club football but there were no peaks left for this modest, distinguished man to climb. He retired having scored a record 166 points during his twenty-nine international appearances. He would not go to Australia. Nor would Gareth Edwards, who left rugby as the most-capped Welsh player with fifty-three consecutive appearances. Terry Cobner went as captain but missed the last Test because of injury. On his return he joined the ranks of the ex-Internationals.

From *Fields of Praise* by Gareth Williams and David Smith
(University of Wales Press, Cardiff, 1980)

The Crown Princes

Clem Thomas and Geoffrey Nicholson

Gareth Edwards stands supreme as the finest scrum-half of his generation, but arguments still rage up and down the valleys about whether Barry John or Phil Bennett was the better stand-off. New Zealanders would have no hesitation in nominating Barry John, but my own preference is for Phil Bennett.

W.B.B.

Barry John learned his rugby at Gwendraeth Grammar School but, strangely, failed to play for the Welsh Secondary Schools. He was born and raised in the West Wales village of Cefneithin, which was also the home of Carwyn James, his mentor and coach in the 1971 Lions. Barry began playing for Llanelli when he was a student at Trinity College, Carmarthen, before he moved to work and play in Cardiff. He played in the Welsh Trials in 1965–66, and was reserve to David Watkins for the Welsh team. He got his first cap in 1966 against Australia, and went on to win twenty-five caps for Wales before he retired at his peak, a retirement due to what he believed was the excessive pressure imposed upon him by the Welsh rugby public. In his early days for Wales his play was occasionally variable, and he was the subject of continual controversy. However, his cool computer-like rugby brain blossomed to produce the greatest tactical control I have ever observed in any outside-half. On one occasion, while appearing in a charity game at Cardiff, he was wired for sound by Harlech Television, and from a particular situation he had the blithe effrontery to announce that he was about to score – and promptly did so with a scything run which left the opposition clutching at thin air.

His true talent began to blossom with the Lions in South Africa in 1968, but then tragically he was tipped up in the first Test by that great Springbok flanker, Jan Ellis, and broke his collar bone. This gave him time to observe and think; and when in 1968–69 the Welsh XV adopted squad training, he began to play rugby of ethereal quality. It was a major catalyst in opening an amazing decade for Welsh rugby, beginning with the Triple Crown in 1969 and followed by the Triple Crown and the Grand Slam in 1971.

At that time, due to his cool confidence, he became the senior partner in one of the greatest half-back firms of all time: Edwards and John. I love the story of their first practice together, when Gareth asked him how he wanted the pass, to be told, 'You just throw it, and I'll catch it!' It was Barry who dictated the tactics of the Welsh side during their partnership; it was not until Barry retired that Gareth Edwards himself took over this role. Both went to New Zealand on the ill-fated Welsh tour of 1969, which failed largely due to the lack of commitment by the Welsh forwards. When the two were chosen for the Lions tour in 1971 they had a burning desire for revenge, and Barry in particular was determined to get his own back. Subsequently, on that tour he became the first of the rugby superstars when, at twenty-six years of age, he plotted the defeat of the legendary All Blacks and scored thirty points out of forty-eight in the four Tests. On tour he scored seven tries, eight dropped goals, thirty-one conversions and twenty-eight penalties, a tally which brought a new dimension to his now rapidly increasing stature.

Barry is the first to point out that his skills and assurance flowered because of the astute captaincy of John Dawes, and the incredible performances of Mike Gibson at his elbow in the best mid-field ever produced by the Lions. No less an authority than Gibson declares that John was the greatest outside-half of our time, and we will be fortunate if we ever see his like again. At the end of 1972 he retired, prematurely in the view of most of his contemporaries, after one of the most exciting rugby careers that I have been privileged to see; and now, as well as enjoying a successful business career, he is one of our most perceptive critics and commentators on the game.

When Barry John was King, Gareth Edwards was the prince and when Barry John retired many said that Gareth would never be the same again. How wrong they were! For he promptly built a new partnership with Phil Bennett which many believe was even greater. He went on to become a legend throughout his playing days, which included an astonishing fifty-three consecutive appearances for Wales. During that eleven-year period he scored a record-breaking twenty tries, and contributed hugely to three Grand Slams and five Triple Crowns.

Nobody has appealed more to the Welsh rugby public than Gareth Edwards; not even Barry John. Not only did they enjoy his bright-eyed charm and modesty, but they had watched him develop his skills from an early age, when there were distinct gaps in his play; his distribution for instance was often erratic and there were even doubts about his temperament. However, his determination was such that he filled in the gaps to become the most complete scrum-half we have ever seen. During his career there were many others as gifted as Gareth in some aspects of scrum-half play. Ken Catchpole of Australia got the ball away quicker than any scrum-half in our time. Sid Going of New Zealand was the more aggressive and durable and, playing behind All Blacks forwards, he had the better of Gareth except in 1971. Chris Laidlaw, also of New Zealand, had as good a pass, and indeed Edwards paid Laidlaw the highest compliment of all when he decided to copy his spin pass, thus enormously increasing the length of his service. The Springbok Dawie de Villiers, nowadays the South African Ambassador in London, was as instinctive a footballer with a beautifully balanced game. But in the end I thought that Gareth had the edge on them all, for after 1974 there was never a weakness in his game; his armoury was complete and he could produce more fire-power than any scrum-half of his time.

Gareth came to maturity after the abdication of Barry John. He was still only twenty-five, and I felt at that time in his career that he was determined to prove he was at least the equal of if not a greater player than his close friend. After all they had come from a similar background, the anthracite-mining area of West Wales, and Gareth particularly had acquired the immensely competitive feeling that exists in those valleys. With the 1974

Lions in South Africa he perfected the stabbing kick to the diagonals which proved mortal to the Springboks. Then he came back to support many a suspect Welsh pack by creating a platform for them to run on to and build up impetus, a vital factor in the three successive Triple Crowns of 1976–77–78. He had become a scrum-half without a peer in Welsh rugby, a man of great charm and charisma. He will have many epitaphs, but none more fitting than two of his greatest tries, jewels in his crown. Those who were there will never forget them: that long lung-tearing burst to complete an unforgettable try for the Barbarians against New Zealand in 1973, and before that truly marvellous try against Scotland in 1972 which epitomized the deadly thrust and competitive drive of his play.

I had the privilege of playing under the captaincy of the great Haydn Tanner in 1949, and I am often asked to compare the two. While one hates to draw comparisons between different eras I would, in the final analysis, take Edwards as the better man because of his sustained power and pace, and because his dedication to winning every major game he played in never faltered, not even at the very end of his career. He was the archetypal Welshman, both in appearance and temperament – dark, quick and intensely competitive.

Gareth Edwards said that when Barry John went, he thought his right arm had gone. But he also added that when one King is dead there are always one or even two others around the corner. How right he was, for immediately he found an equally royal partner in Phil Bennett, whom many West Walians consider the best outside-half of our time. Phil shrugged off all the criticisms of his early career, when he played for Wales as a wing three-quarter and centre before his huge heart confirmed him as the true heir to Barry John. He then went on to win twenty-nine caps and lead Wales on two Triple Crowns and a Grand Slam.

His achievements are a legend. He holds the world record of 212 points in all internationals and the Welsh record of 166 points in internationals. For a time he shared – with Roger Hosen, Tony Ward and Steve Fenwick – the record of 38 international points in a season; but in 1980 that was beaten by the Irish stand-off, Ollie Campbell, with 46 points.

My own reason for preferring Barry John was that I sensed flaws in Phil's temperament which occasionally brought breakdowns in his confidence that were reflected in his play. For instance, when he captained the 1977 Lions tour to New Zealand he found the pressures imposed upon him by the management (unfairly, I thought) too great, and this had a disastrous impact on his play. His confidence eroded to such an extent that he fell back into the fault, apparent in his early career, of failing to commit the mid-field; and consequently we saw him crabbing across-field, bunching the three-quarters and destroying their opportunity for fluency or effectiveness.

However, these occasional deficiencies in a long and illustrious career are far outweighed by the enormous pleasure he gave to the millions who were enchanted by his brilliantly instinctive running and jinking. There was never a better example of this than when, during the 1973 match between the Barbarians and the All Blacks, he initiated one of the greatest tries in the history of rugby. From deep in his own twenty-five he jinked successively past four floundering All Blacks to inspire a movement which covered the length of the field and led to Gareth Edwards scoring. Then, too, after he had been told that a spinal problem would prevent him ever playing rugby again (which happily proved to be a wrong diagnosis), he went to South Africa with the 1974 Lions: he scored 103 points in eleven matches, including another unforgettable try in the second test, and developed as the cutting edge of the Lions' running and handling attack.

It was in running and try-scoring that many considered him better than Barry John, for apart from those magnificent efforts for the Barbarians and the Lions, he scored many tries for Wales which were collectors' pieces. He was, as Barry John once said, a jack-in-the-box runner, capable of conjuring tries from nowhere with that famous jink, which seems to be a Welsh copyright, and his vivid acceleration. Barry John in my view was the cooler, the more composed and therefore the more complete tactician, but Phil's supporters can point to games where he too was the master of the field. His huge armoury of skills was completed by his prodigious talent for kicking out of the hand, as well as for the place kicking which brought him so many magnificent goals. Had he decided to play soccer at a young age, then in the opinion of many experts, including John Toshack, he could have become a First Division star.

The greatest controversy regarding Phil came in the 1975–76 season when, after the final Welsh trial, he was omitted from the Welsh squad. The man in possession was that magnificently direct outside-half, John Bevan of Aberavon, who had been selected against France, England and Scotland in the preceding season and in December had played superbly when Wales, with a powerful performance, had overwhelmed Australia. The selectors' preference for John Bevan was the result of Phil's worst game for Wales against France in 1973, when he misguidedly stood so far off Gareth Edwards' pass, and so crowded the Welsh three-quarters that they found themselves operating laterally with about only twenty yards of room and no capacity for attack. All the same, most people believed that the outside-half position was a straight fight between Bevan and Bennett, and were astonished that Bennett was not included as a reserve when David Richards, the young outside-half from Cardiff College of Education, was brought into the squad.

The decision of the selectors was probably coloured by the fact that when he substituted for Bevan at Murrayfield the season before, Phil performed abysmally. In the event fate and fortune were on his side as both Bevan and Richards withdrew with injury and Phil, to the delight of his supporters, came back to control affairs against England. That encounter will be remembered as J.P.R. Williams's match, but from here on Phil, perhaps smarting from earlier indignities, came into his own. He had found a new strength of character, and a more personally committed dimension to his game. He flowered into a fine leader of both Llanelli and Wales and became devoted to his players, 'the lads' as he always called them. He was the most likeable and friendly of men, and never at any time resented the criticisms directed at him in his early career; this was the true measure of the man and his character, and is a fine example of the way to behave in misfortune. He retired from the international scene when still in his prime because of the strain and pressure imposed upon him and his family by the time-consuming demands of the modern game on the star player. Due to his abiding love for the game, however, he continued to play for Llanelli.

From *Welsh Rugby: The Crowning Years* by Clem Thomas and Geoffrey Nicholson
(Collins, London, 1980)

J.P.R., the Threes and the Sevens

Carwyn James

As the last line of defence, the Welsh side had the magnificent figure of J.P.R. Williams. He was an utterly fearless full-back, even when subjected to the most violent treatment.

W.B.B.

John Peter Rhys Williams, a doctor himself, had seven stitches inserted to patch a facial injury. He had gone on to the field with seven others, acquired in a previous match. To Welshmen along the centuries the figures three and seven are nothing if not mystical. The figure of Williams in the distance, long hair flying in the wind, may remind us of Pwyll, Prince of Dyfed, riding majestic and mysterious in the mists of the Mabinogi; but a closer look reveals the stark realism of a warrior fully committed to battle. And at Twickenham, that day, in the cold January air, rivulets of blood congealed below his high cheek-bones. What a sight he made on television immediately after the match! The gory, victoriously happy sight of a man who had scored two winning tries – both initiated from a wheeled scrummage!

And the figure seven struck again. Pinned down at the bottom of a ruck in the first few minutes of the All Blacks match at the Brewery Field, his unprotected face was trampled upon by a vicious prop. Before leaving the field to have another seven stitches inserted he paused and gave instructions to his men. A lesser mortal would never have returned to the field of play. Characteristically, he did.

From the Foreword to J.P.R. by J.P.R. Williams
(Harper Collins, London, 1983)

General Efficiency and Tireless Zeal

Bleddyn Williams

Welsh rugby was deprived of an even greater name by Hollywood. No lesser authority than Bleddyn Williams rated Richard Burton very highly . . . an opinion shared by Burton himself!

W.B.B.

My RAF training was now in full swing and there followed orders to prepare to leave for the United States. However, before I left I played for Blackpool Services while stationed at Heaton Park, a suburb of Manchester, and appeared on the Wigan and Salford League grounds in various matches organized by Rugby League players and officials for local charities. I found it an enlightening experience, the 'professionals' being splendid fellows and just as keen on Rugby as the Rugby Union 'fanatics' of Wales or the diehard enthusiasts of the Scottish Borders. While at Heaton Park I played with a wing-forward who soon caught the eye for his general efficiency and tireless zeal. His name: Richard Burton. But it was in Cinemascope that he caught the eye after the war! A pity, because I think Richard would have made as good a wing-forward as any we have produced in Wales!

From *Rugger My Life* by Bleddyn Williams
(Stanley Paul, London 1955)

Where's the Bloody Film Star?

Richard Burton

I had played the game representatively from the age of ten until those who employed me in my profession, which is that of actor, insisted that I was a bad insurance risk against certain dread teams in dead-end valleys who would have little respect, no respect, or outright disrespect for what I was pleased to call my face. What if I were unfortunate enough to be on the deck in the middle of a loose maul . . . they murmured in dollar accents? Since my face was already internationally known and since I was paid, perhaps overpaid, vast sums of money for its ravaged presentation they, the money men, expressed a desire to keep it that way. Apart from wanting to preserve my natural beauty, it would affect continuity, they said, if my nose was straight on Friday in the medium shot and was bent towards my left ear on Monday for the close-up. Millions of panting fans from Tokyo to Tonmawr would be puzzled, they said. So to this day there is a clause in my contracts that forbids me from flying my own plane, ski-ing and playing the game of rugby football, the inference being that it would be all right to wrestle with a Bengal tiger 5,000 miles away, but not to play against, shall we say, Pontypool at home. I decided that they had some valid arguments after my last game.

It was played against a village whose name is known only to its inhabitants and crippled masochists drooling quietly in kitchen corners, a mining village with all the natural beauty of the valleys of the moon, and just as welcoming, with a team composed almost entirely of colliers. I hadn't played for four or five years but was fairly fit, I thought, and the opposition was bottom of the third class and reasonably beatable. Except, of course on their home ground. I should have thought of that. I should have called to mind that this was the kind of team where, towards the end of the match, you kept your bus ticking over near the touchline in case you won and had to run for your life.

I wasn't particularly nervous before the match until, though I was disguised with a skull-cap and everyone had been sworn to secrecy, I heard a voice from the other team asking 'Le ma'r blydi film star 'ma?' (Where's the bloody film star here?) as we were running on to the field. My cover, as they say in spy stories, was already blown and trouble was to be my shadow (there was none from the sun since there was no sun – it was said in fact that the sun hadn't shone there since 1929) and the end of my career the shadow of my shadow for the next 80 minutes or so. It was a mistaken game for me to play. I survived it with nothing broken except my spirit, the attitude of the opposition being unquestionably summed up in simple words like 'Never mind the bloody ball, where's the bloody actor?' Words easily understood by all.

Among other things I was playing Hamlet at that time at the Old Vic but for the next few performances after that match I was compelled to play him as if he were Richard the Third. The punishment I took had been innocently compounded by a paragraph in a book of reminiscence by Bleddyn Williams with whom I had played on and off (mostly off) in the RAF. On page 37 of this volume Mr Williams is kind enough to suggest that I had distinct possibilities as a player were it not for the lure of tinsel and paint and money and fame and so on. Incidentally, one of the curious phenomena of my library is that when you take out Bleddyn's autobiography from the shelves it automatically opens at the very page mentioned above. Friends have often remarked on this and wondered afresh at the wizardry of the Welsh. It is in fact the only notice I have ever kept.

Anyway, this little snippet from the great Bleddyn's book was widely publicized and some years later by the time I played that last game had entered into the uncertain realms of folk legend and was deeply embedded in the subconscious of the sub-Welshmen I submitted myself to that cruel afternoon. They weren't playing with chips on their shoulders, they were simply sceptical about page 37.

I didn't realize that I was there to prove anything until too late. And I couldn't. And didn't. I mean prove anything. And I'm still a bit testy about it. Though I was working like a dog at the Vic playing Hamlet, Coriolanus, Caliban, The Bastard in *King John*, and Toby Belch, it wasn't the right kind of training for these great knotted gnarled things from the burning bowels of the earth. In my teens I had lived precariously on the lip of first class rugby by virtue of knowing every trick in the canon, evil and otherwise, by being a bad bad loser, but chiefly, and perhaps *only* because I was very nippy off the mark. I was 5 ft 10½ in in height in bare feet and weighed soaking wet, no more than 12½ stone, and since I played in the pack, usually at open side wing-forward and since I played against genuinely big men it therefore followed that I had to be galvanically quick to move from inertia. When faced with bigger and faster forwards, I was doomed. R.T. Evans of Newport, Wales and the Universe for instance – a racy 14½ stone and 6 ft 1½ in in height was a nightmare to play against and shaming to play with, both of which agonies I suffered a lot, mostly thank God, the latter lesser cauchemar. Genuine class of course doesn't need size though sometimes I forgot this. Once I played rather condescendingly against a Cambridge college and noted that my opposite number seemed to be shorter than I was and in rugby togs looked like a schoolboy compared with Ike Owen, Bob Evans or W.I.D. Elliot. However this blond stripling gave me a terrible time. He was faster and harder and wordlessly ruthless, and it was no consolation to find out his name afterwards because it meant nothing at the time. He has forgotten me but I haven't forgotten him. This anonymity was called Steele-Bodger and a more onomatopoeic name for its owner would be hard to find. He was, I promise you, steel and he did, I give you my word, bodger. Say his name through clenched teeth and you'll see what I mean. I am very glad to say that I have never seen him since except from the safety of the stands.

In this match, this last match played against troglodytes, burned to the bone by the fury of their work, bow-legged and embittered because they weren't playing for or hadn't played for and would never play for Cardiff or Swansea or Neath or Aberavon, men who smiled seldom and when they did it was like scalpels, trained to the last ounce by slashing and hacking away neurotically at the frightened coal face for seven and a half hours a day, stalactitic, tree-rooted, carved out of granite by a rough and ready sledgehammer and clinker, against these hard volumes of which I was the soft-cover paperback edition, I discovered some truths very soon. I discovered just after the first scrum for instance that it was time I ran for the bus and not for their outside-half. He had red hair, a blue-white face and no chin. Standing up straight his hands were loosely on a level with his calves and when the ball and I arrived exultantly together at his stock-still body, a perfect set-up you would say, and when I realized that I was supine and he was lazily kicking the ball into touch I realized that I had forgotten that trying to intimidate a feller like that was like trying to cow a mandrill, and that he had all the graceful willowy-give and sapling-bend of stressed concrete.

That was only the outside-half.

From then on I was elbowed, gouged, dug, planted, raked, hoed, kicked a great deal, sandwiched and once humiliatingly taken from behind with nobody in front of me when I had nothing to do but run fifteen yards to score. Once, coming down from going up for the ball in a line-out, the other wing-forward – a veteran of at least fifty with grey hair – chose to go up as I was coming down if you'll forgive this tautological syntax. Then I was down and he was up and to insult the injury he generously helped me up from being down and pushed me in a shambling run towards my own try-line with a bloodcurdling endearment in the Welsh tongue since during all these preceding ups and downs his unthinkable team had scored and my presence was necessary behind the posts as they were about to attempt the conversion.

I knew almost at once and appallingly that the speed, such as it had been, had ended and only the memory lingered on, and that tackling Olivia De Havilland and Lana Turner and Claire Bloom was not quite the same thing as tackling those Wills and Dais, those Twms and Dicks.

The thing to do I told myself with desperate cunning was to keep alive, and the way to do that was to keep out of the way. This is generally possible to do when you know you're out-classed, without everybody knowing, but in this case it wasn't possible to do because everybody was very knowing indeed. Sometimes in a lament for my lost youth (I was about twenty-eight) I roughed it up as well as I could but it is discouraging to put the violent elbow into the tempting rib when your prescience tells you that what is about to be broken is not the titillating rib but your pusillanimous pathetic elbow. After being gardened, mown and rolled a little more, I gave that up, asked the captain of our team if he didn't think it would be a better idea to hide me deeper in the pack. I had often, I reminded him, played right prop, my neck was strong and my right arm had held its own with most. He gave me a long look, a trifle pitying perhaps but orders were given and in I went to the maelstrom and now the real suffering began. Their prop with whom I was to share cheek and jowl for the next eternity, didn't believe in razor blades since he grew them on his chin and shaved me thoroughly for the rest of the game taking most of my skin in the process, delicacy not being his strong point. He used his prodigious left arm to paralyse mine and pull my head within an inch or two of the earth, then rolled my head around his, first taking my ear between his forefinger and thumb, humming 'Rock of Ages' under his breath. By the end of the game my face was as red as the setting sun and the same shape. Sometimes, to vary the thing a bit, he rolled his head on what little neck he had around, and under and around again my helpless head. I stuck it out because there was nothing else to do which is why on Monday night in the Waterloo Road I played the Dane looking like a Swede with my head permanently on one side and my right arm in an imaginary sling intermittently crooked and cramped with occasional severe shakes and involuntary shivers as of one with palsy. I suppose to the connoisseurs of Hamlets it was a departure from your traditional Prince but it wasn't strictly what the actor playing the part had in mind. A melancholy Dane he was though. Melancholy he most certainly was.

I tried once to get myself removed to the wing but by this time our Captain had become as, shall we say, 'dedicated' (he may read this) as the other team and actually wanted to win. He seemed not to hear me and the wing in this type of game I knew never got the ball and was, apart from throwing the ball in from touch, a happy spectator, and I wanted to be a happy spectator. I shuffled after the pack.

I joined in the communal bath afterwards in a large steamy hut next to the changing-rooms, feeling very hard-done-by and hurt though I didn't register the full extent of the agonies that were to crib, cabin and confine me for the next few days. I drank more than my share of beer in the home team's pub, joined in the singing and found that the enemies were curiously shy and withdrawn until the beer had hit the proper spot. Nobody mentioned my performance on the field.

There was only one moment of wild expectation on my part when a particularly grim sullen and taciturn member of the other side said suddenly with what passed shockingly for a smile splitting the slag heap of his face like an earth tremor.

'Come outside with us will 'ew?' There was another beauty with him.

'Where to?' I asked.

'Never 'ew mind,' he said, 'you'll be awright. Jest come with us.'

'OK.'

We went out into the cruel February night and made our way to the outside Gents – black-painted concrete with one black pipe for flushing, wet to the open sky. We stood side by side in silence. They began to void. So did I. There had been beer enough for all. I waited for a possible compliment on my game that afternoon – I had after all done one or two good things if only by accident. I waited. But there was nothing but the sound of wind and water. I waited and silently followed them back into the bar.

Finally I said: 'What did you want to tell me?'

'Nothing,' the talkative one said.

'Well, what did you ask me out there for then?'

'Well,' the orator said. 'Well . . . us two is brothers and we wanted to tell our mam that we'd 'ad a . . . '

He hesitated, after all I spoke posh except when I spoke Welsh which oddly enough the other team didn't speak to me though I spoke it to them. 'Well, we jest wanted to tell our mam that we had passed water with Richard Burton,' he said with triumphant care.

'Oh 'ell!' I said.

From *Touchdown*
(RFU, London, 1970)

Wales in Turmoil

Clem Thomas

Nothing has been more sad to watch than the painful decline of Wales after the break-up of their great side of the 1970s. That acute writer Clem Thomas, cast a keen, but not unsympathetic eye, over the Welsh fall from grace.

W.B.B.

No leading rugby nation has lost its way more fundamentally than the Welsh in the last decade. Their demise from being pre-eminent both on and off the field in the Seventies, is not a matter for any rejoicing by the other nations for it is a calamity when a country with such a proud rugby tradition loses belief in itself.

Tony O'Reilly once said to me: 'Whether we like it or not, and most of us don't, rugby football is simply not a game without the Welsh.' Tony was thinking about the innate ability, invention and natural competitive instincts of the Welsh, exemplified by that vicarious whiff of danger felt by their opponents.

Alas, for the time being at least, those days are gone. People are already talking about Wales being a killing field for the All Blacks and are talking in telephone numbers concerning the margins of the Welsh defeats in the seven matches New Zealand will play in Wales.

It is perhaps too easy to blame it all on the Welsh Rugby Union, nevertheless they must accept a large proportion of the blame.

They are currently being indicted for bad stewardship, parochialism, appalling press and public relations and lack of open government. They are also accused of failing to develop the game by not providing sufficient money because of their obsession with paying off the debt on the national ground, authoritarianism, lack of accountability, and just about anything else that one can think of.

They are guilty on most of these counts, but equally culpable are the clubs and the rugby public of Wales who have given insufficient consideration to the criteria required to provide an effective governing body. No thought has been given to the levels of expertise in the commercial, professional or perhaps more essentially, the rugby sense.

Many of the first class clubs, basking in past tradition, can also be accused of neglect. Unwilling to accept the possible loss of their self-perpetuating status, they have fiercely

132

resisted change and the formation of a league structure. Consequently Welsh rugby has lost its competitive edge.

In the meanwhile England, Scotland and France, not to mention the Southern Hemisphere, have been honing their combativeness to a level of organized belligerence which the Welsh at club and national level are unable to match.

Ignoring the overwhelming evidence of the last three harrowing defeats by the All Blacks, the paucity of success in the Eighties and the rising tide of defeats by English clubs, the Welsh merit table clubs have seen the focus of the media move from Wales to England. In becoming a union within the union, they have become alienated from the WRU and in some cases from the second-class clubs which feed them.

The failure of the WRU to develop the game in Wales is paralleled by the failure of the first-class clubs to develop the game in their own spheres of influence. Many of them do not run more than one team and do little to encourage youth and schools rugby.

The recent convulsions brought about by the ill-considered over-representation of the Welsh on the recent tour of South Africa were, dare one say, far out of proportion to that of the other countries involved and are only an indication of deep rooted problems. Grant Nesbitt, the New Zealand commentator, was to say on New Zealand television, totally deadpan and without a flicker of a smile: 'Over the weekend eight more Welshmen arrived in South Africa to weaken the touring party'.

Some good must surely emerge from what has become the nadir of Welsh fortunes both on and off the field. The WRU committee must now know that they are accountable to Welsh rugby at large and that reorganization, open government and better PR are essential to put the game in Wales back on its feet.

It will need time and an enormous amount of work, with the priority being the improvement of the game itself in Wales, for which there is an enormous fund of enthusiasm and goodwill. To which I am sure all rugby people in the British Isles will say God speed and good luck.

From *Rugby News*, November 1989

Push, Push, Push

Richard Llewellyn

Whatever the problems of the national side, club rugby in Wales remains unique. It is captured magnificently in Richard Llewellyn's *How Green Was My Valley* and in the writing of Gareth Williams and David Smith

W.B.B.

A healthy sound is the tamp of the leather ball on short green grass and pleasant, indeed, to watch it rise, turning itself lazily, as though it were enjoying every moment of the trip up there, against blue sky, and coming down against the green, in a low curve right into the ready hands of a back.

A whistle from Ivor, and the captain on the other side takes his run and kicks, and as you watch the ball climb you see the teams running into position to meet one another underneath it.

A forward has it, but before he can so much as feel it properly, he is flat on his back, and the two sides are packing over him. A whistle from Ivor, and the first scrum, and shouts for Davy as he lifts his arms to bind his front men. In goes the ball, and the tight, straining muscles are working, eight against eight, to hold one another and then to push each other the length of the field, but the ball comes free behind the pack, and their fly-half has it so fast that nobody knows till he is on his way toward our touch line with his three-quarters strung behind him and nothing but our full-back in his way. Shout, crowd, shout, with one voice that is long-drawn, deep, loud, and full of colour, rising now as the fly runs pell-mell and Cyfartha Lewis dances to meet him, and up on a rising note, for inches are between them, louder with the voice in an unwritten hymn to energy and bravery and strength among men.

But Cyfartha is like a fisherman's net. The fly has been too clever. He should have passed to his wing long ago, but he is greedy and wants the try himself, and on he goes, tries to sell a dummy, and how the crowd is laughing, now, for to sell a dummy to Cyfartha is to sell poison to a Borgia. The fly is down, and Cyfartha kicks the ball half-way down the field to our forwards, and has time to offer his hand to poor Mr Fly, who is bringing himself to think what happened after the mountain fell on him.

And my father is laughing so much that his glasses are having trouble to settle on his nose. Owen and Gwilym are shouting for all they are worth, for Davy has the ball and his forwards are all round him to push through the enemy. Shoulders and knees are hard at work, men are going down, men stumble on top of them, fall headlong and are pinned by treading, plunging boots. Red and green jerseys are mixed with yellow and white, and mud is plenty on both. On, on, an inch, two inches, bodies heave against bodies, hands grab, legs are twisted, fall and crawl, push and squirm, on, on, there are the white posts above you, but red and green jerseys hide the line and form a wall that never shows a gap. On, yellow and white, pack up behind and keep close, pull the ball into the belly and shield it with your arms, down with your head, more shoulder from the pack, keep closer at the sides, push now, push, push, push. A red and green down in front, another, who carries away a third. Another push now, and the ball is slipping from him. A hand has come from the press below and grasps with the strength of the drowning, but a wriggle to the side and a butt with the hip loosens it and on, on, half an inch more, with an ankle tight in the fist of red and green who lies beneath two yellow and white and only enough of sense and breath to hang on.

Down with the ball now, full flat, with eight or nine on top of you, and there is the whistle.

The ball rests an inch over the line.

Then see the hats and caps go into the air, and hear a shouting that brings all the women to the doors up and down the Hill, and some to lean from the back windows.

Again the whistle, and Maldwyn Pugh looks up at the posts, makes his lucky sign, and takes his run at the ball that rests in its heeled mark, and kept there by the hand of Willie Rees, who lies full length in the mud with his face turned away, not to be blinded by the slop that will come when the boot leaves his hand empty.

Empty it is, and the ball on its way, and the crowd quiet, with the quiet that is louder than noise, when all eyes are on the same spot and all voices are tuned for the same shout.

The ball travels high, drops in a curve, turns twice. The crowd is on its way to a groan, but now the wind takes it in his arms and gives it a gentle push over the bar, no need for it, but sometimes the wind is a friend, and there it is.

From *How Green Was My Valley* by Richard Llewellyn
(Michael Joseph © Estate of Richard Llewellyn 1939)

Play for Wales

Gareth Williams and David Smith

Welsh rugby is a rainy night at the end of the Llynfi valley watching Maesteg drive forward on their table-top ground; it is a sparkling Easter Monday in Swansea watching the Barbarians on their traditional, carefree tour; it is a cold Boxing Day on Cardiff's new ground as Pontypridd's grizzled veteran Bob Penberthy remembers over 750 first class games for his club since 1962 and leaps for more; it is the yell for the 'Scar-lets' that rebounds around Stradey; it is the rising crescendo of 'Come on the Po-art', the bass intimidation of 'Neath! Neath!', the drumming affirmation, for a beaten W.R.U. Cup semi-finalist, of 'Ebbw, Ebbw, Ebbw'; it is the youth coach, the ex-referee, the man who runs the line for the Athletic XV, the unsung, dedicated enthusiasts who turn up to offer their skills and knowledge, in all weathers, so that the game is never neglected at any level. It is men who bridge generations like Rhys E. Williams, still serving Crynant as club secretary after more than fifty years. It is seeing for the first time the boy who will 'play for Wales'; it is applauding your better opponents or, better still, your superior selves; it is the much-fingered programme, the rugby annuals, the pink 'uns, the torn tickets, the heated arguments, the warm reconciliations, the legendary trips, the cursed and blessed selectors, and above all, the game which is, first and last, for the players and those who go to watch them. John Dawes remembered for himself what can, and should, apply for all – ' . . . there is so much enjoyment you can get from that eighty minutes if you're prepared to work at it in training and . . . in organization and coaching, that there's no price you can put on it. You can't buy it. The enjoyment from that eighty minutes is, in sport, the most I've ever had and . . . the magnificences of the game were something to be envied. We played, and displayed so much enjoyment for ourselves [and] the spectators . . . that they used to come . . . to enjoy . . . it.'

After the first century, there is another.

From *Fields of Praise* by Gareth Williams and David Smith
(University of Wales Press, Cardiff, 1980)

7
GREAT NATIONS: ENGLAND

Am I Wrong?

Denis Lalanne

There has been a constant complaint over the years that English rugby has not produced the results that it should at international level. Even when England has produced winning sides, the armchair critics have been quick to complain about the style in which the results were achieved.

The Frenchman Denis Lalanne, author of one of the finest-ever accounts of a rugby tour, 'The Great Fight of the French XV', brought an outsider's eye to bear on the English way of rugby.

W.B.B.

Frenchman that I am, I always picture English rugby ideally as the game of endless youth and freedom, a rugby in which fear of losing does not stifle the delight of playing. It is true that my views on rugby are not always taken from a French standpoint, in the sense that I try above all to see the game from the standpoint of rugby itself. So to me rugby and English rugby are one and the same.

Perhaps the picture I have in my mind's eye of rugby in England is a little too idyllic; perhaps English rugby also has its collection of less desirable individuals since all sorts are needed to make a world. But I would like to tell you a secret. My own somewhat brief rugby career was as a somewhat inept centre three-quarter with a somewhat obscure club. It was in France, in other words in a country where the last thing I must do is boast about it. But I am certain that if this far from brilliant playing career of mine had been with an English club, it would have lent a much greater measure of wonder to my youth, it would have gained me a much greater number of true friends for life, and greater appreciation from them. I would have lived with that sense of humour which enlivens your outlook.

I was lucky enough to experience this much later when, thanks to the beer they had consumed, I was at last able to hold my own with authentic English internationals in matches between the veterans of the two countries. During the game, and especially afterwards, they created and maintained in me the illusion that we were not players of different class but simply people with the same aim in life. It was a delightful experience. I wish at eighteen I could have drunk my beer at Richmond to brush away exhaustion, disappointment, and all those bumps and bruises.

For me it is in England that rugby has its most natural setting – I am thinking not only of the majesty of Twickenham, of its grey skies, its marvellous crowds, but also of more modest clubhouses filled with human warmth and laughter – and has the young men most true to its tradition.

Shorts have got shorter and hair has got longer, the techniques of the game are studied more demandingly. There is even talk of a club championship. But it is still the same boyish masculinity that inspires the devotion of the English to rugby.

The English have also given me the impression of being capable of rousing themselves to the highest pitch of endeavour about victories which matter little, of being able to recreate on a rugby pitch the Bridge on the River Kwai or Montgomery in the desert. More clearly than with other nationalities – in whom I have often recognized resentment at being beaten by those dirty Frogs – I have noticed in the English a contempt for defeat so long as they are conscious of having done their best. The French, officials and players alike, could well envy the English this facility.

To tell you the truth, even if I am wrong, I like to look upon England as the country where rugby has its greatest freedom, where the game is left most willingly in the hands of those who keep it in being, that is to say, the players.

I don't say that just to please or to flatter, or out of respect for Bill Ramsay for all the treasured friendship he has given to the game in France. After all, the French also have other things than compliments to express to English rugby. I mean that we French have not always understood how an England team, better endowed in individual technique, in the combined moves and drills of the game, in sheer athleticism and, it goes without saying, in fire and determination, has so often managed to be beaten by a weaker French side.

The English account for this by referring to French genius and, frankly, this explanation has seemed very naïve to us. It is in this perhaps that the English, to our way of thinking, draw a distinction between themselves and the All Blacks, the Welsh and the Irish of vintage years. The English do not always fulfil their true potential; they do not reach the peaks we believe they could. Am I wrong?

From *Touchdown*
(RFU, London, 1970)

The Great Day

P.G. Wodehouse

One man who has proved Denis Lalanne wrong more often than most is England's record try-scorer Rory Underwood. In recent seasons Rory has had plenty of opportunities to run at defences and has repaid the investment with a string of world-class tries, but in the earlier stages of his career he often waited in vain for a pass. Alan Watkins bemoaned the shameful neglect of Underwood's talent at the time:

> Underwood, with his south-east Asian face and prop forward thighs, has the gift which all great sportsmen possess, that of communicating excitement. Whenever he gets the ball, as he does quite often for Leicester, less often for England and hardly at all for the Royal Air Force, there is a whiff of danger, of fire and brimstone in the air.

At that stage of his career, Underwood would have sympathized with another air force wingman, Group Captain Cyril Lowe, who won twenty-five caps before and after the First World War, but who rarely received a pass. P.G. Wodehouse sarcastically celebrated the great day when Lowe finally got the ball.

W.B.B.

'*Lowe has yet to receive a pass in International football*' The Press passim.

I can recollect it clearly,
Every detail pretty nearly,
    Though it happened many, many years ago.
Yes, my children, I, your grand-dad
A reserved seat in the stand had
On the afternoon when someone passed to Lowe.

There he stood, poor little chappie,
Looking lonely and unhappy,
    While the other players frolicked with the ball.

For he knew he could not mingle
In the fun with Coates and Dingle;
    He could simply go on tackling – that was all.
I had stopped to light my briar,
For the wind was getting higher,
    When a thousand voices screamed a startled 'Oh!'
I looked up. A try or something?
Then sat gaping like a dumb thing.
    My children, somebody had passed to Lowe!

I remember how he trembled
(For to him the thing resembled
    A miracle), then gave a little cry;
And spectators who were near him
Were too overcome to cheer him;
    There were sympathetic tears in every eye.
His astonishment was utter.
He was heard to gulp, and mutter,
    'What on earth has happened now, I'd like to know?'
And incredulous reporters
Shouted out to the three-quarters;
    'Do we dream? Or did you really pass to Lowe?'

There was sweat upon his forehead
And his stare was simply horrid:
    He stood and goggled feebly at the ball.
It was plain he suffered badly,
For the crowd, now cheering madly,
    Saw him shudder, start to run, then limply fall.
Then a doctor, who was handy,
Fanned his face and gave him brandy;
    And at last, though his recovery was slow,
He regained his health and reason
By the middle of next season;
    But the shock came very near to killing Lowe.

Rory Underwood

Robert Armstrong

England were soon to remedy their neglect of Underwood's talents and his career total of international tries is testament to his qualities. If he is not more widely recognized overseas as one of the world's great wingers, it is probably because Rory lacks the extrovert nature and the flamboyance of a Campese or a Kirwan.

W.B.B.

It would be easy to gain the impression that the England team are just a bunch of ordinary blokes capable of doing extraordinary things with a rugby ball. At first sight no one fits that deliberately low-key image better than England's most capped player and record try-scorer, Rory Underwood, the soul of modesty and good sense in a squad of feisty characters.

Not for Flight Lieutenant Underwood the canny pre-match propaganda of Brian Moore, the camera-caressing charm of Will Carling, or the flyaway modelling assignments of Jeremy Guscott. Unlike these high-profile bachelors, Underwood keeps his distance from the media, preferring to use spare evenings to help his wife Wendy look after their two small daughters, Rebecca and Alexandra.

Clearly the man who flies a Canberra jet to help maintain Britain's electronic air-defence system likes to keep both feet on the ground. On first acquaintance Underwood, who is stationed at RAF Whitton, may seem ordinary enough, yet his ability to shrug off the hype engendered by a remarkable thirty-five tries in fifty-four internationals sets him apart in a peer group that includes the likes of David Campese and John Kirwan.

The paradox of Underwood is that the more attention his achievements on the field attract the more he tries to fade into the background.

If Underwood does quit, some of the glory is bound to go out of the English game. Few sights are more exhilarating than the former Barnard Castle schoolboy taking a pass in his own half – as he did against Scotland in January – accelerating rapidly over the first thirty yards and outflanking the entire defence to score at the left flag.

In a match against Fiji in 1989 he set an England record by scoring twenty points, all from tries, against a back division not noted for its lack of pace.

England's stultifying game-plan in the World Cup gave him few opportunities to show a clean pair of heels – a grim reminder of the mid-Eighties when he scored only four tries in his first four international seasons. Underwood, though, has no regrets about the dog days that followed his first cap in 1984, pointing out that at least he was still fulfilling his ambition to play for his country as often as possible.

When asked to name his favourite try, Underwood usually plumps for the dazzling piece of artistry he produced against Ireland in Dublin a year ago. 'It was very wet, there were ten minutes to go and we were losing what had been a very hard game,' he recalled. 'Suddenly the ball came to me on the edge of the twenty-two and somehow I managed to squeeze through to the left of the posts.'

Characteristically, Underwood omits to mention the fact that he jinked past four Irish defenders on a skidpan surface which made staying on his feet an achievement in itself. And, in the Grand Slam decider which was distinguished by three French tries, Underwood's splendid solo score, which left his marker Lafond clutching at air, made the crucial difference between a two-point victory and a potential two-point defeat.

He used to cop a fair amount of flak for his alleged lack of concentration and neglect of defensive duties, even though overseas observers regarded him as one of the most gifted wingers in Test rugby. Men such as Alan Old, Dusty Hare and Mike Harrison, whom he has known for years, helped maintain his morale with advice and encouragement.

He traces the upsurge in his fortunes to the appointment of Geoff Cooke and Roger Uttley as the England management team in late 1987. Since Cooke, who used to coach Underwood in the Yorkshire side, took over, the England wing has scored thirty-one tries in thirty-five matches, easily the best strike ratio in the world. Since 1982 even Campese has needed sixty-four games to score forty-six tries.

Mark Bailey, a former England team-mate, believes that upper-body strength is the key to Underwood's success. 'It borders on the phenomenal and makes him extremely explosive,' said Bailey.

'That kind of strength makes him difficult to knock over, so many times he is able to ride the tackle and nick into the corner for a try.

'Rory has kept his place in the team so long because he is very fit, has managed to stay clear of injury, and, I suspect, has sustained his interest very well indeed. On top of that he has become a much cannier footballer, reading the game well and putting other people into attacking positions.'

All of that might soon be consigned to memory. But perhaps Underwood, the family man, could be persuaded that loyalty to his younger brother Tony might be best served by sticking with England. Nothing would give Rory more pleasure than to line up in the same team as the twenty-two-year-old Cambridge student and England B wing. As Rory once remarked: 'Tony is like me when I was twenty, a free spirit, willing to give it a go.' Enough said.

From *The Guardian*, March 1992

England Steer a Crooked Course

Tony Lewis

David Duckham was another richly talented English winger, who was often shockingly underused. He failed to receive a single pass during one of England's routine defeats by Wales during the 1970s. Tony Lewis's report of that match in February 1975, was described by the late Carwyn James as the best he had ever read, combining mood, fact and opinion.

W.B.B.

England went as peacefully as lambs; white, bewildered, dutifully doing the things they have always done with the same disastrous end.

Wales caught them firmly by the ears from the start – seven points in ten minutes – and though they wrestled with their conquerors fitfully, especially among the forwards, the score mounted and it was clear by the finish that the victims were well and truly skewered.

It is impossible for a Welsh correspondent not to feel the elation of all his fellow countrymen who crowded in, all 60,000 of them, to a packed Cardiff Arms Park. Just as I left the ground I overheard unrehearsed choristers, arms linked and red and white scarves waving, stumping their way along the narrow streets. They sang the sad hymn tune 'Llef' sounding like a dirge, but I was moved as ever by the fact that only the Welsh can express great joy in the minor key.

It was not a game of rugby to send people singing to their homes. Wales efficiently destroyed England by taking their chances, but there was little romance to this hard, uneven, painful pressures affair.

Wales won less ball in the line-out and were put under painful pressures in the rucks and mauls. England's forwards have never let them down in the gritty matter of ball winning.

As against Ireland and France, so now against the Welsh it was what they did with the ball that mattered. Cooper and Webster (who left the field with an injured knee after eighteen minutes) then Cooper and Steve Smith, who substituted, never produced the footballing answer. There was no direction where it should have been, at half-back.

It was rather like a super car, all the mechanism in perfect order but with a faulty steering wheel. The English engine purred silently and efficiently up front, but once again it was driven into a ditch.

The legendary Prince Obolensky, January 1936.

Above left: Colin Meads of New Zealand supported by Ken Gray in the first test against Australia at Sydney cricket ground.

Above: Lions coach in 1971, Carwyn James.

John Dawes makes the break which gives Gareth Edwards the first try in the Barbarians v New Zealand match of January 1973.

Gareth Edwards playing against England in 1974.

Above: Andy Irvine of Scotland playing against Ireland, February 1977.

Above right: Willie John McBride for the British Lions against the Northern Transvaal, July 1974.

The New Zealand v British Lions 2nd test, 1977. Sid Going of New Zealand kicks as Graham Price attempts to charge down.

Phil Bennett encourages fellow Lions team-mates in a match against the Bay of Plenty, 1977.

Above: Morne du Plessis leading the Springboks onto the pitch to play the British Lions in the 2nd test of 1980.

Above left: G. Mourie tackles J. J. Williams in the All Blacks v Wales match of November 1978.

Bill Beaumont commiserates with Jean-Pierre Rives at the end of the France v England match of 1980.

Bill Beaumont bears down on Jim Renwick, with Roger Uttley in support, during England v Scotland, March 1980.

Above : Ollie Campbell of Ireland.

Above right : New Zealand's Dave Loveridge in the 3rd test against the British Lions, July 1983.

Australia's Mark Ella makes a reverse pass to Roger Gould against England, 1984.

Rory Underwood evades Australia's Peter Grigg in the round 1 match of the 1987 World Cup.

Serge Blanco's decisive try for France in the 1987 World Cup semi-final against Australia.

David Sole of the British Lions against New South Wales, June 1989.

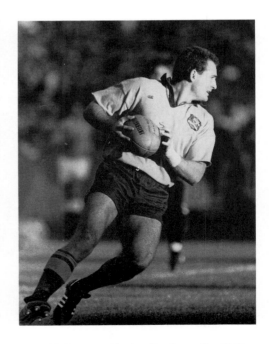

David Campese playing for Australia, 1989.

Scotland's John Jeffrey in mid-air in the Scotland v Wales match, March 1990.

Andrew Kemberey of Neath is sent off by Clive Norling as he points to the dressing room.

England's Mike Teague emerging victorious with the ball in the match with Ireland, March 1991. The final score was England 16, Ireland 7.

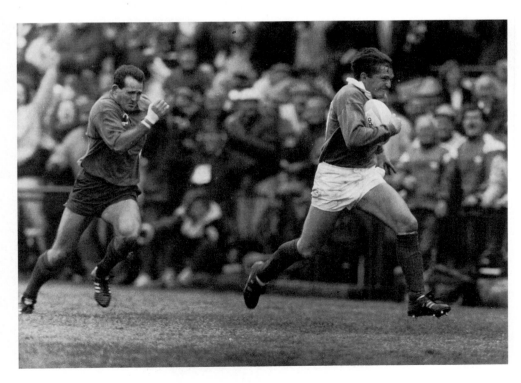

Gordon Hamilton beats David Campese to score a dramatic try for Ireland in the World Cup quarter-final in 1991.

Still, the Welsh forwards will surely know that they have been in a battle. Horton, Uttley and Ralston did exceptionally well in the line-out and their rucking was clean and organized. However, a great deal of pressure was put on both scrum-halves by aggressive wing-forward play.

With a slippery ball forcing Edwards and Steve Smith to be slightly slower and more certain of their grasp, Neary, Cobner and Evans in particular found their way into the game in the most direct and dangerous fashion.

Wales held the distinct advantage of overall control and it stemmed from the talent of Edwards, who managed to make time for himself in the face of repeated problems. He sent long rolling kicks to touch and stretched full-back Jorden to his discomfort.

Wales also killed potential English movements with speed yet calm. Quick interpassing and shielding of the ball got it back to Edwards, who bounded away up field – demoralizing to an England side which badly needed to take a lead.

As it was Martin put over two superb penalty goals, one from fifty yards and the other from forty. Oddly enough, Mervyn Davies chose to persevere with Fenwick's kicking in spite of his poor form. J.J. Williams and Gerald Davies scored tries before half-time, Martin converting the second.

The first came in one of the very rare bouts of handling. England's backs lay up so flat on Bevan, after a ruck, that he had no option but to work a scissor with his centres. Gravell obliged, ran into space which England might have hoped to be occupied by their back row, then he swerved back out to the left wing and Fenwick put J.J. Williams over with an overhead pass.

Wheeler went off with an injured shoulder after twenty minutes and Quinnell substituted. It was Quinnell who helped set up a ruck under England's posts, and the ball moved to the right with J.P.R. Williams in the line. He showed the instincts of a great ball player by swinging a pass over the head of the centre three-quarter next to him and finding Gerald Davies unmarked and unopposed on his way to the try-line. That was the try which Martin converted from a wide angle and brought England to the halfway stage 16–0 down.

Pullin replaced Wheeler shortly after the interval and in doing so deprived England of their second goal-kicker. This was important because Jorden, after three fairly straightforward misses, was clearly losing confidence.

Keith Smith ultimately had one long-distance attempt which went adrift, and this underlined how much luck was going for Wales. Their short-distance kicker, Fenwick, was failing in four attempts and two conversions as the long-range man, Martin, was succeeding.

England 'sang in their chains' especially in the second half. Play continued to be disjointed. Watkins prepared to launch himself at the try-line as Gerald Davies landed on his back, J.P.R. Williams scythed down Squires with a crunching tackle and Squires was again forced out of play near the corner flag by Edwards. As for England's other match-winning performer, Duckham, he received no pass at all during the game.

England had their consolation after a brief spell of pressure – Horton falling over for a try from a line-out on the Welsh line. However, Wales returned to the attack and, after several rucks had been set up with Cobner and Evans appearing many times in the move, Fenwick scored a try near the corner.

The result from France, which told of Scotland's defeat, now reduces the Calcutta Cup to something of a selling plate. But then again, with Welsh suspicion, justified by history, I fear the Scots may produce the unexpected at Murrayfield.

From the *Sunday Telegraph*, 16 February 1975

Nero

Alan Shuker

Rory Underwood would certainly be in my all-time great English XV. So would Tony Neary, a man I played alongside many times for Lancashire, England and the British Lions. 'Nero' had the lot, the most complete back-row forward of his era.

W.B.B.

'Nero' was lucky to be born with all the gifts required to make a world-class open-side flanker, for he had consummate ball ability, physical presence and dexterity, mental hardness and vision, and an awareness on the field which caused his decision-making to appear intuitive.

Although he was 6 ft 1 in he always jumped 6 ft 5 in in the line-out with the ability to cup the ball one-handed between palm and wrist – which in itself was an indication that you were in the presence of a player of enormous ball-playing skills. With the ball in his hand he had the almost innate ability to take one or two of the opposition out of the game, be it at a line-out, maul, or in the open, and at the same time make the ball available to a supporting player, whom he would then instinctively support in turn. An illustration of this was a try he scored at Murrayfield a number of years ago when, having received a long flat ball following a penalty from Jan Webster, he ran at a Scottish defender, dipped his right shoulder into his midriff – so committing him fully – and put Andy Ripley through the gap created. Andy then ran approximately fifty metres before being held on the line. On the instant 'Nero' was at his elbow, took the ball, and dived over for a try. A great example of his creative, supporting and finishing ability.

In addition to his ball-playing skills, his mental and physical dedication in the tackle were both resolute and absolute, as was his single-mindedness in digging the ball out of standing tackles and mauls. Summing up, he was the most complete open-side flanker of the modern era, and possibly since the time mental awareness and ball-handling ability became essential ingredients for quality back-row forwards.

From the *Centenary Brochure of the Lancashire RFU*, 1981

A Wonder and a Wild Desire

Alec Waugh

The excitement of rugby is not confined to free-scoring wingmen or world-class wing forwards, of course. Every player of the game knows the tumult of emotions experienced in a close match. Alec Waugh's splendid account of a public school house match could apply to any game, anywhere.

W.B.B.

Rain fell steadily all night, and though it cleared off about break, the ground was already under water. It was a cold, gusty day.

By lunch the whole House was unbalanced. There was much loud laughter, then sudden silences; an atmosphere of restlessness lay over everyone. Very slowly the minutes dragged by. Gordon sat silent in a far corner of the pavilion. At last the whistle blew, the magenta and black jerseys trailed out on to the field. A cheer rose from the line.

The next hour passed in a whirl of white jerseys, gradually turned black with mud, of magenta forms dashing on to the School forwards, of wild, inarticulate black insects bawling on the touch-line. The pervading impression was mud. Everything was mud; he was mud, the ball was mud. Lovelace was indistinguishable. His own voice leading the scrum seemed strangely unreal. There was a vague feeling of disquiet when, early in the first half, he found himself standing under the posts, while the Buller's half placed the ball for Whitaker to convert. Nothing tangible; then the disquiet passed, the magenta jerseys swept forward, dirty white forms came up and went down before them. Morgan rolled over the line. A kick failed. Half-time came, Hazelton came on, and said a lot of things to him, which he answered unconsciously.

A whistle blew. Once more the magenta jerseys swept everything before them. There seemed no white jerseys at all. Numberless times he watched Lovelace taking the place kick. He thought he heard Mansell shrieking: 'Heave it into them! Well done! Now you've got them!' Once he had a sensation of kicking the ball past the halves; he seemed clear, the full-back rushed up and fell in front of him, the ball stopped for a second, then rolled on. He heard someone coming up behind him; the line grew dimly white under his feet; he fell on the ball; there was a roar of cheering. The whistle went in short, sharp blasts. The game was over.

And then he realized that the House had won, that his hopes were satisfied, that the

Buller crowd had been routed, that the cup would shimmer on the mantelpiece. A wave of wild exultation came over him. The House poured over the touch-line, yelling and shouting. It was all 'a wonder and a wild desire'.

From *The Loom of Youth* by Alec Waugh
(Geoffrey Bles, London, 1917)

England Stand on the Verge of Greatness

Chris Rea

The arguments continue about whether England's double Grand Slam side of 1991 and 1992 ranks among the all-time great teams, but as far as I am concerned there is no argument; any side as successful as that England team are a great side. Some correspondents still harbour reservations, though that is perhaps a measure of how much English rugby has advanced. To beat Wales 24–0 and still be criticized is a novel experience for English sides!

Whatever the real or perceived faults of previous England sides, however, the double Grand Slam team stands comparison with any . . . and they did pass the ball to Rory Underwood!

W.B.B.

Whether the present England side is the best in the country's history is, and will continue to be, a matter of considerable if unresolvable debate.

What is not in doubt is that few England teams have been harder to beat. Since Geoff Cooke assumed control of the national side there have been any number of performances superior to those England produced against Scotland and France this season, yet, despite the fact that England were some way short of their best, both matches were won by record scores, and it is this ability comprehensively to win games that could just as easily have gone the other way which distinguishes the very good from the merely competent.

Australia won the World Cup final well short of their peak and even after the brilliance of their display against England last summer, several Englishmen left the field convinced they had not seen the Wallabies at their best and not the least of Cooke's many achievements with England has been to instil into his players the need for constructive self-criticism combined with a sense of realism. Both Cooke and his players have been quick to learn from their mistakes. This season there have been no sullen marches into battle, and no peevish silences afterwards. The joylessness of last season's Grand Slam has been replaced by a relaxed, easy-going spontaneity which has been there for all to see on the field as well as off it. The team are playing with intelligence, integrity and zest.

If there is a difference in England's style under Dick Best it is, perhaps, a greater willingness to carry play beyond the narrow confines of the forwards' domain. It is no coincidence that Will Carling, now liberated, is looking more like the thoroughbred he undoubtedly is than the willing but lamentably miscast workhorse of last season. An outstanding example of the trust that England are putting in themselves, and of the lacerating skill of their backs, came at a crucial stage of the match in Paris a fortnight ago when the French midfield collided and the ball was lost. In spite of the melancholy and undignified tangle of ill-fortune, the French still had enough players behind the ball not only to defend adequately, but also to launch an effective counter should England err. The safe option would have been for Carling to run straight, make ground, take the tackle and await the imminent arrival of his supporting forwards. Instead, he unhesitatingly chose the more dangerous but infinitely more rewarding route, to Rory Underwood's wing.

If England this season are displaying a greater sense of adventure and are proving more deadly at taking the opportunities presented to them, they have also made such significant improvement in their defence that, like the Australians, it has become one of their most potent weapons in attack.

Mick Skinner's greatest hits may receive more prominence, but it is Peter Winterbottom who has more of them in the charts. Furthermore, Carling and Jeremy Guscott are as menacingly destructive in midfield as the Australian pair Tim Horan and Jason Little.

Alan Davies, the Welsh coach, has always considered this to be one of the main hinges upon which events turn at the highest level. He knows that his young midfield trio have not yet the maturity or the stature as international class players to compare with England at Twickenham on Saturday, but must hope that ambition, motivation and footballing resourcefulness can disguise their obvious limitations elsewhere. The Welsh, like the Scots, Irish and French before them, will doubtless make frantic endeavours to exploit and to splinter England's line-out which many see as their Achilles' heel.

But as the season has progressed so has England's line-out organization improved, a fact surely not entirely unconnected with the return of Dean Richards. Martin Bayfield, who still requires and deserves better protection, is, nevertheless, beginning to settle, and there were those present at Parc des Princes a fortnight ago, pillars of sobriety all of them, who swear to the fact that Wade Dooley managed to get airborne.

Richards, who bestrode the game for twenty minutes at Murrayfield, and was the most vigilant of sentinels during the height of the French offensive in Paris, is certain to be at the heart of England's affairs again on what might be his last international appearance.

Against Ireland a breakdown in communications between Tim Rodber and the rest of the pack meant that England surrendered the early scrummage initiative, a misunderstanding which, one assumes, will not be allowed to happen on Saturday against a Welsh scrum no longer meriting the contempt that was being heaped upon them in some quarters earlier in the season. Even so, Jason Leonard, whose learning curve shot vertically upwards during his World Cup encounter with New Zealand's Richard Loe, has a rare opportunity to establish himself as the leading loose-head prop in the Championship.

Upon the depth of the resistance up front will depend how soon England's forwards release the ball to Dewi Morris, who surely received the ultimate accolade recently when his coach at Orrell, Des Seabrook, the least impressionable and effusive of judges, compared him to Gareth Edwards. Good as Robert Jones is, there are not many Welshmen who would place him above Edwards in their roll of honour, but then Jones has seldom enjoyed the same protection that was so often afforded to his illustrious predecessor. And, once again, too much may be asked at Twickenham of Wales' most gifted player.

The improvement in the shuttle service between England's forwards and backs has, of course, increased the risk factor and England are still making mistakes. They are mistakes which have so far escaped harsh punishment for the very good reason that the opposition England have encountered in the Five Nations' Championship has been outclassed.

There is the inescapable feeling that, even if an Englishman were to commit as profound a misjudgement as it is possible to make, there would be a colleague on hand to save the situation. In other words, while England can afford the luxury of human error their opponents cannot. It is this which has helped bring England to the brink of history and is surely one of the hallmarks of a side on the verge of greatness.

From *The Independent on Sunday*, March 1992

Winter Tale of Power and Glory

Steve Bale

In one respect at least, this England are the equal of that Wales with whom comparison was relentlessly made as we awaited the triple coronation and grand slamming. The England of the Nineties, like the Wales of the Seventies, have set themselves standards that are impossible to maintain.

Not all the time, anyway. One indifferent performance in four Five Nations' matches is more than excusable, and when it still gives you as overwhelming a victory as this it seems churlish to complain. Imagine how Wales – or Scotland, Ireland and France for that matter – would have felt if the boot had been on the other foot.

In fairness to England, and in deference to their colossal achievement in completing the first back-to-back Grand Slams in sixty-eight years, we should not allow the squib that concluded the firework display to blow away the memory of the technicolor explosion that went before. For the most part, they have distilled an alchemist's blend of efficiency and adventure which has meant rugby of breathtaking quality. For the most part, it has been pure gold.

So England should be ringingly saluted, though the question is left hanging for ever, tantalizingly unanswered: how good are they? So what. Historical comparisons being odious, the one that matters is with the other four nations as they are now and it is as unflattering to them as flattering to England that in winning the Championship Will Carling's team accumulated points in unprecedented numbers and more tries (fifteen) – a truer comparison since scoring values have changed – than anyone since the Thirties.

Perhaps the problem against Wales was that it was too easy, not in a physical sense because the Welsh niggled and scrapped and made life frustratingly difficult, but in the sense that England knew all along they were going to win. Mistakes proliferated, more of them than in their other three matches put together, but somehow they did not matter.

In fact once Carling had scored his first-minute try, nudging the badly positioned Anthony Clement out of the way in pursuit of Rob Andrew's garryowen, the knowledge was confirmed that they did not really have to bother too much. Tight discipline and careful tactical appreciation were no longer imperatives; the mixture of pressure and tension on which England had thrived simply did not exist.

This was reflected in post-match comment which fell short of elation even after the high emotion of an unprecedented balcony appearance by Carling and company. 'Everyone is a little disappointed with the quality of the performance but we just couldn't control it for long enough,' Geoff Cooke, the manager, said. It comes to something when 24–0 is disappointing – and it comes to something when a Welsh side derive comfort from such a defeat.

At least Alan Davies, the Wales coach, injected a note of realism when he said: 'We defended well. That's really all the players can latch on to.' But Ieuan Evans, the captain, pleaded for patience for the umpteenth time and for his players to be granted the same courtesy – time – that Cooke's England were four years ago.

'I don't feel that was a nightmare,' Evans said. Fair enough, it wasn't by comparison with some that have befallen Wales in the recent past, but put it in historical perspective and after all it is pretty nightmarish. Since scoring was first quantified in points in 1891, Welsh defeat by England has only twice been more severe.

As one of the two occurred here at Twickenham as recently as two years ago, I suppose we must conclude that progress is being made. 'We are a very young side, average age twenty-four, and people have to bear with us,' he said. 'England were allowed leeway and we should be given the same.'

Evans had a fine game policing Rory Underwood and his side were stubborn in their tackling, remorseless in their determination to disrupt England at the cost of conceding penalties and constantly interrupting the flow of the game. Having worked out the referee, they freely killed the loose ball and so denied England the continuity that had been central to their previous successes.

This was the negative and there was very little positive to accentuate. Welsh handling attempts were doomed by the inability of their forwards to build any momentum and there was a characteristic lack of judgement which consistently played into the voracious hands of the England back row. For a midfield back to run straight at Pete Winterbottom, for instance, makes no sense at all.

Especially when Winterbottom is playing like this. His back-row mate Mick Skinner was a try-scorer and another old stager Wade Dooley, fifty caps to his name, raised Twickenham's roofs with his try, but in the autumn of a superb career Winters more than any England forward took Wales with the seriousness the occasion warranted.

Nor did he permit himself to be deflected by the underdog yapping which infuriated some of his colleagues. To take the most obvious example, Garin Jenkins was hell-bent on upsetting Brian Moore and succeeded, at the same time creating an unpleasant atmosphere which even had Evans and Carling ill-naturedly jostling each other at one point.

Only once did Wales threaten the England line whereas their own was under regular threat. That they restricted England to three tries was an achievement, but Jon Webb's twelve points – creating a season's Championship record of sixty-nine and England career record of two hundred and forty-six – taught a paradoxical lesson in showing how an expansive strategy, as much as a more limited one like Wales's, demands accurate place-kicking.

Instead, Neil Jenkins missed a couple of fleeting chances and Wales drew a blank for the first time in twenty-two years. The Welsh Rugby Union is pleased to call its team the Dragons, a sobriquet that has yet to catch on, and it is an infelicitous choice. The dragon, after all, was a mythical beast – and even in mythology it was slain by St George.

From *The Independent*, March 1992

Cooke's Victors in Need of a Vice

Ken Jones

It is never possible to attend a match between England and one of the Celtic nations without being touched by issues that run deeper than sport.

'And stuff you too Mrs Thatcher,' cried an Irish supporter in 1985, throwing his hat into the air when Michael Kiernan's dropped goal saw off England in Dublin to win a Triple Crown.

'Look at them with those white shorts pulled up around their backsides, they've only come down here to take the piss out of us,' growled Jimmy Murphy, their manager, before Wales played a football international against England at Ninian Park, Cardiff.

Injustice, real and imagined, is evoked on these occasions, often depressingly so, but history rises up with the steam of commitment; it cannot, will not, be denied.

Thus, perhaps a metaphor in England's slow, rolling mauls, their apparent obsession with grinding down frantic defence when with a cushion of fifteen points they could have fed the ball from scrummages on the Welsh line and completed another hugely impressive Grand Slam with a glorious flourish; physical rather than cerebral supremacy; drive them back into their holes. 'Land of Hope and Glory', a lyric disowned by Elgar, provocatively resonant with imperialism ('wider still and wider'). 'We sing about people stealing *our* land,' a Celt muttered.

Fanciful you may think, but in the scolding manner of England's victory, and the disruptive spite that Wales brought to Twickenham there was plenty of the past.

By the standard of their achievements England were disappointing, and it is nonsense for anyone to suggest that Wales were entirely responsible for it being an untidy and at times snarling match, the most boring of this season's championship. There is no question that the principal Welsh objective was damage limitation, but a wider question relates to where this England team stand in the annals of the game.

Supreme in the northern hemisphere, success has come steadily, convincingly since Geoff Cooke was given the responsibility of marshalling England's resources, and yet doubts remain about the true quality of Will Carling's team.

Afterwards, on television, Gareth Edwards, one of the great players Wales sent out in the 1970s, their golden era, said, 'Of course I'm biased, but if England search their souls they cannot be satisfied.'

England at play have never been comfortable with the notion of spontaneous brilliance. There is little room for romance on the cross of St George. Efficiency, high morale, is a common thread. It is easy to sympathize with this, for they are doing no more than being true to their nature.

No one auditing the bright post-game chatter at Twickenham, the raucous choruses that rose up in the stands, could fail to appreciate the satisfaction brought by another national triumph.

Victory was enough as in 1966 when Sir Alf Ramsey won the football World Cup after rejecting Jimmy Greaves, the most naturally gifted English goalscorer of his generation. The real virtuoso must exist between the dissolves of expediency; thus David Gower can only look on at the cricket World Cup. The trick is to go beyond the critics and reach toward the soul. But that in itself leads to the prospect of collapse under pressure. It is too much for anyone to handle by himself; better to be sure.

The parallel threat is a fear of waning powers. 'It would be wrong for England to put pressure on players who are seriously thinking about retirement from international rugby,' Cooke said when coming to appraise England's performance. 'But we shall have to wait and see how some of them feel after taking a rest.' Tireless time assaults even the most resilient of players, and Cooke will have to replace important forces in his team.

England have been borne aloft by audiences at Twickenham, and gained undying respect in other centres of the game. But being at one with great artists is not a quality acquired without scrutiny. Once you accept a popular premise you are, for good or ill, quite lost.

At the beginning of it all Cooke spoke eloquently and with great passion about the responsibility England's players would have to accept. He appeared to be thinking less about Grand Slams than leaving a monument in the game. In an era when success is paramount he cannot be condemned for compromise. And yet in sport there is always room for a small vice, the urge to gamble slightly beyond means.

From *The Independent*, March 1992

Eluded by Mantle of Greatness

John Hopkins

So farewell Rory, Simon, Wade, Peter, Jonathan and Mickey. Or is it *au revoir*? We will not see you again. Or will we?

On a day when the sun touched the turf at Twickenham and Will Carling ran like the wind, we had hoped for a spectacle to mark England's second Grand Slam in as many years. We wanted you to quit the scene with a flourish worthy of the achievement – matching a record last set in the Twenties.

And so, no doubt, did you. You wanted to show us you were the greatest England side ever. Thousands came to Twickenham to acclaim you, to cheer you on to Carling's twenty-second victory in twenty-nine matches. They left bedraggled, muted and disappointed, far less satisfied than two years ago, when England won 34–6, their biggest win in the modern era.

Where stand England now, four years, one month and one day after they lost a championship match at HQ? I think England would have beaten any other England team, any French team and, deep breath, even the great Welsh teams of the Seventies.

This is not to say that man-for-man England's white tornadoes are better because, patently, they are not. John Webb v J.P.R. Williams? J.P.R. naturally. Gareth Edwards v Dewi Morris? Gareth Edwards. Barry John or Phil Bennett v Rob Andrew? John and Bennett.

But the total of this England team is greater than those individuals, even individuals as luminous as those mentioned above. Playing in leagues and cup matches most weekends has given them a resolve that is irresistible. They have learnt how to soak up everything that is thrown at them – and then break out in dangerous, dizzying attack.

They squeezed and squeezed and squeezed. Then, in the blinking of an eye, Underwood is clear, Webb is striding upfield, Carling is bursting and darting through as he did so dazzlingly before he went off yesterday.

The shame is that England could not cap this wonderful season with a crowning performance against Wales. It looked as though they might when Carling scored that try barely one minute into the game. It could have been a scene-setter. Instead it was a false promise. England dropped more passes, botched more moves, conceded more penalties than in any other two matches this season. It was their worst performance in the championship. Yet what happened, England won by three tries, twenty-four points to zero.

Perhaps the greatest achievement of this England side is in raising the level of fitness to a standard never before approached. 'England are twenty per cent fitter than our players,' says Alan Davies, Wales's coach. Many of England's players have an oxygen uptake level approaching trained athletes', professionals that is. Wales's equivalent figures are those of trained amateurs.

England have brought on players in a way that few countries have been able to before. A good example is Wade Dooley whose try yesterday deserved and received a standing ovation. The difference between the lumbering Preston Grasshopper who first turned out for England seven years ago and the sleek, strong and fast forward who won his fiftieth cap yesterday, is as that between chalk and cheese.

Moreover, England's forwards last longer, like Duracell batteries. In this season's championship England's opponents won only one scrum in England's twenty-two in the second half. Scotland couldn't do it, nor could France and certainly not Ireland. Only Wales managed it – in the sixth minute yesterday. And a fat lot of good it did them. Thereafter they were held, vice-like, deep in their own half.

In the Seventies, Wales won the Grand Slam three times and won or shared the championship on four other occasions. They assimilated new players into the winning team seemingly without a hiccup. This is the greatest challenge facing England.

Geoff Cooke, their outstanding manager, has spoken lately of only having done half a job. He is right. Dominance in Europe is only a start. New Zealand and Australia await. So does the mantle of true greatness.

From *The Independent*, March 1992

8
GREAT NATIONS: SCOTLAND

Greenyard Memories

Bill McLaren

Think of Scottish rugby and one name comes instantly to mind – my fellow BBC commentator Bill McLaren. His love and knowledge of rugby shine through in every word he speaks and in every word he writes. As a devout Borderer, 'Sevens' is dear to Bill's heart, a form of the game invented at Melrose. Though a Hawick man himself, for Bill, the Melrose Sevens will always be his favourite rugby event.

W.B.B.

It continues to be a matter of some puzzlement to Rugby men in other parts of the United Kingdom that we Scots devote so much of the season to the seven-a-side game. Perhaps they would begin to see the light if they could be present at the Greenyards today to sample the flavour of the short game in its birthplace – a rich flavour indeed with its amalgam of family picnic atmosphere laced by the keen rivalries, intense commitment, high drama, vociferous audience participation and flowing action, all of that set against one of the most picturesque backdrops to any sporting arena in the great wide world.

It is no secret that Melrose sevens always has been the Rugby event of the season for me even allowing for the very special attractions of the National Leagues programme, the inter-district championship and those great international occasions that now raise the passions so high. But a Melrose sevens enclosure seat alongside my wife, Bette, on a crisp, sunny day, a pot of hot, sweet and milky coffee to hand and in the other hand, a Hawick meat pie dripping warm gravy – that has to be as near to the promised land as one might ever hope to reach – especially if Hawick are leading Gala by 38–0 with time almost up!

That renowned sevens exponent, the late Andrew Bowie, wouldn't have found it difficult to convert any sceptics to the abbreviated version. He simply loved 'sevens' and had a special fondness for the Melrose tournament. He often told of how, as a boy of eight, he was livid at not being allowed to stay up late to see his uncle, Sandy Burns, who was coming to the house to show his folks the Melrose sevens trophy. Sandy had been captain of the winning Hawick seven on that afternoon in 1908 and when he turned up, young Bowie was asleep. But the lad was up with the lark next morning and off to his grandmother's house like a shot – just to see and touch the Melrose cup. It was at the 1927 Melrose tournament that Hawick met Stewart's F.P. in the final and when Stewart's scored first a thunderous roar went round the ground. As the Hawick players, who eventually won, stood behind the posts waiting for the goal-kick, they heard Doug Davies grunting: 'By hell, there's shairly a bluidy lot o' Edinburgh folk here the day'!

Recollections of Melrose sevens simply flood into the mind. I remember seeing the 1935 London Scottish seven on their first visit and how, to my youthful eyes, their international lock, George Horsburgh, seemed positively massive. My father used to stress to me the virtues of the clever Heriot's F.P. forward trio of the late thirties, Charlie Brow, Ernie Oxley and Wallace Deas. When John Smith, the current president of the Rugby Union, and Brian Boobyer were sizzling over the Greenyards turf in the winning Rosslyn Park Seven of 1951, one was taken aback by such speed. There were the Scotland brothers, Ken and Ronnie, as opposing stand-offs in the Cambridge University v. Heriot's F.P. final of 1960. Who could forget the Melrose 'weans', Keith Robertson and all, who swept all before them in 1975? And how would they have fared a decade before against that magnificent London Scottish seven with Iain Laughland as their orchestra leader?

It pains me to have to admit membership of Hawick sevens who lost in the first round of successive Melrose events – once to an alleged drop goal by Archie Lockie for Kelso that was miles wide and once in a tie with Watsonians (George Thomson has chortled about this ever since!) when, in the dressing room afterwards, none of us could remember having the ball in our hands – and that included Jackie Wright for whom such an event merited a mention in the Guinness Book of Records! Once, I was in a winning seven at the Greenyards but that was when the Earlston tournament was played there just after the war. It just wasn't the same. A Melrose winner's medal, after all, is in a class of its own.

From the *Melrose Sevens Centenary Brochure* (1983)

The Jubilee Year

'Fly-half' (Walter Thomson)

The mist of memory broods and floats
The Border waters flow
The air is full of ballad notes
Borne out of long ago . . .

Will Ogilvie cetainly hadn't Melrose Sports in mind when he wrote these lines, but they seem apt. For all but the very youngest spectator, memories do brood and float on Sevens day at Melrose. Everybody remembers some special passage of play, some dramatic upset, some of the great characters who seem etched in time; even the appetizing whiff of the Gala 'chipper' belching smoke, evokes Melrose memories.

In the centenary year I am maybe luckier than most because not only was I at the Jubilee Sevens but I had the privilege of reporting them . . . not, one must hurriedly add, from the sybaritic comfort of the present press-box, which was in a sense spawned at the Jubilee Sevens, but from a table and chair set out on the touch-line near the turnstiles with the rain unceasing for five sodden hours and a notebook resembling nothing so much as a trainer's sponge. The year was 1932. The weather, perhaps, was a judgement on Melrose for daring to celebrate their jubilee a year too soon!

It is difficult now to recall the intensity with which Rugby was followed on the Borders. There were no distractions. One spoke of nothing but the Sevens for weeks before – and of little else for weeks after. Especially that Jubilee year. For hadn't Melrose, always the most enterprising of entrepreneurs, chosen to lift their tournament to a higher rung by inviting the mighty Barbarians to be their first major guest side? It was a great coup and the names of these wondermen were awaited with anticipation – and trepidation.

Drawn from the cream of England, Ireland and Wales, with six caps in their midst, it seemed that the day would be dedicated to the pursuit of runners-up. Everyone knew where the cup would go. But it didn't work out like this at all. The weather took a hand, leaving the pitch like a bog and pouring heaven's hard on the eight thousand spectators without a hint of remission.

My abiding memory of the conditions was provided at the finish of the Gala–Hawick semi-final. Victory went to Gala by 3–nil and, perhaps secretly relieved that release was at hand, that rotund citizen of Hawick, Jerry Foster, keeled over and sank, as someone unkindly said, in the swamp 'like a ruddy hippopotamus'. The record skid of the day was credited to F.M. Matheson, the Gala wing, who slid fifteen yards, taking his tackler with him.

In such conditions the form book could be thrown away. The greatest upset came in the other semi-final where Kelso, with that flamboyant farmer from Kaimflat, Jimmy Graham, whipped his side to such a frenzy that they beat the Barbarians. No wonder the Eildons trembled. The effort left Kelso drained and they were beaten by Gala in the final by two typical opportunist tries by that laconic half-back, W.W. Barbour.

When it was all over, and we had begun to dry out, the prime talking point was that astonishing performance by Kelso. How odd that when Barbarians next appeared at the Greenyards they should lose again, short of the final, to Kelso with Jimmy Graham's son in the side. But, then, Melrose Sports are full of odd bits of family history. When Gala won that Jubilee tournament Henry Polson, the first Braw Lad, stood shoulder to shoulder with the redoubtable Jimmy Ferguson. Polson's dad had been in the Gala seven when they last won at Melrose – as far back as 1903.

From the *Melrose Sevens Centenary Brochure* (1983)

Scotland's Long Dark Tunnel

Bill McLaren

Bill McLaren's reign as king of the commentators has been a long one, covering almost forty years. In that time he has seen the best and the worst of Scottish rugby, beginning in the depths of a sequence of seventeen consecutive defeats, and culminating in the 1990 Grand Slam victory against England – a result that came as an equal surprise to both of us!

W.B.B.

My entry into commentary work coincided with the darkest period in Scottish rugby history. Happily the two were not connected. Between February 1951 and February 1955, Scotland lost seventeen major international matches in a row. My first nine radio commentaries of Scottish games were all of defeats.

The defeat that sticks in the memory is that 0–44 thrashing from the South Africans at Murrayfield on 24 November 1951. They were just awesome. It was like sevens played by fifteen men. I had never seen anything quite like them. I had never seen a prop forward run as fast as Chris Koch, had never seen such a huge a man as 'Okey' Geffin kick goals, had never seen very big forwards, such as Ernst Dinkelman, Jan Pickard, Gert Dannhauser, Basie van Wyk, 'Saltie' du Rand and Hennie Muller, running and handling with such dexterity. When they were launched it was like watching a cattle stampede; with remarkable skill and ball transference they brought a new dimension to forward play. How their backs prospered – Rik van Schoor, of the crew-cut dome, Tjol Lategan, elegance at speed, 'Chum' Osche and Paul Johnstone on the wings; and then there was that combination of shrewdness and physical strength from P.A. du Toit at scrum-half and quickness of thought and action from J.D. Brewis at stand-off. Behind them was the twenty-one-year-old Johnny Buchler, safe as houses in catch, clearance and tackle. They won thirty of their thirty-one matches.

At Murrayfield the massive Geffin thumped over seven goals in nine attempts from all over the pitch, with the old-fashioned style of having the ball sloping towards the goal and with a dead straight run-up. Perhaps the Scots had London Counties to thank for being at the receiving end of a South African backlash, because, just nine days before, the representative side had administered the only defeat of that South African tour by 11–9, when their hero was the Harlequins lock, Alan Grimsdell, whose second half penalty-goal was the match-winner. That 0–44 defeat stood as the biggest in an international until Ireland beat Romania 60–0 in 1986. On that sad day at Murrayfield, as the South Africans cantered away to a 17–0 margin, I whispered to Bette: 'We're going to see history made today.' We sure did! That prediction wasn't all that clever because, just a month previously, I'd been lucky enough to see those Springboks beat a combined Glasgow–Edinburgh fifteen 43–11 in Glasgow. It was a remarkable game in that their magnificent loose forward, Hennie Muller, showed another side to Springbok all-round skill by slotting home four superb goals as well as romping in for his try. In that game their prop-forward Chris Koch scored two tries and, as he had done the same against Scotland, I had the privilege of seeing a prop-forward register four tries in two games. That was very unusual in those days when forwards still were regarded as the ball providers, the piano shifters who were expected to leave the piano playing to the aristocrats behind them. Koch not only could run about the paddock at a rate of knots, but he was a fearsome scrummager as well. My Hawick friend, Hugh McLeod, was only nineteen when he played for South of Scotland against those Springboks, whose props that day were Koch and 'Okey' Geffin. The match was memorable for me, too, in that it was the scene of the audition commentary that launched me on my career in radio and television. What is more the South lost by only 3–13, in retrospect, some effort against that side.

From *Talking of Rugby* by Bill McLaren
(Stanley Paul, London, 1991)

Scotland Rejoices

Bill McLaren

The atmosphere was almost overpowering as England's warriors took the field. When the Scots followed the noise was deafening and such was the sense of occasion that I have to admit I did not notice that David Sole had marched his team on to the field, instead of running, in the grimly determined gesture that became front-page news the following day. I have never known such a lengthy greeting for a Scottish side in all my experience of international attendance. I remember feeling a sense of satisfaction that 'God Save the Queen' was given a comparatively unhindered and vociferous rendering and then came the moment that Scots will never forget – the sight of Scotland's fifteen joining with the fifty-three-thousand-strong crowd in the most inspiring rendering of 'Flower of Scotland' that one ever could imagine. It was quite overwhelming. As a commentator I always have sought to be objective and fair but as a Scot, and proud to be a Scot, I have to admit to a feeling of high emotion and intense national pride at that wonderful rendering. It seemed as if the whole of Scotland was united in anthem behind the national side. I don't know what it did for the English players but it certainly stirred the blood of every Scot.

Rob Andrew said that even on four visits to Cardiff Arms Park he had never felt quite the same challenging atmosphere as that at Murrayfield on that 'Grand Slam' occasion. In all my experience of rugby grounds I have never come across anything in terms of atmosphere and national passion to match the singing of 'Land of My Fathers' at Cardiff Arms Park. Even as a Scot I always felt the goose pimples and the hair bristling on the back of my neck whenever the Welsh sang their hearts out at that anthem. But on 17 March 1990 my countrymen and women reached the same heights of inspiration and challenge. And, believe it or not, whenever I play the record of the Scottish team singing 'Flower of Scotland' or watch the start of the video of that historic match, I feel quite emotional with a lump in my throat.

It certainly was a great day to be a Scot. The match, supported by the Royal Bank of Scotland, lived up to the occasion, if not in continuity of spectacle, certainly in total commitment and in the ebb and flow of rival fortunes. When Jeremy Guscott dummied through for a try created by a scrummage pick-up by Mike Teague, a beautifully weighted pass from Richard Hill that rendered Scott Hastings fractionally off-line in his tackle engagement, so that Will Carling was able to demonstrate his flaring acceleration, there were many Scots who feared the worst. But one of the key factors was the inability of England's line-out giants to dominate that phase as they had done against their other rivals, because Ian McGeechan, Jim Telfer, Derrick Grant and Douglas Morgan had evolved the masterly strategy at the line-outs that upset England's well-laid plans.

The Scots opted out of conventional line-out positioning and, instead, moved their jumpers around so that virtually no line was the same as the one before it. This set the English forwards an examination they hadn't faced before, and when coupled with unceremonious Scottish engagement on England's throw, it proved vital in the battle for possession. There was, too, a repeat of Scotland's dedication to making tackles count that had marked their entire championship approach. From Gavin Hastings to David Sole, number fifteen to number one, every man tackled as if his life depended on it. And it was copy-book tackling by the legs so that the ball-carrier virtually every time was grounded and so momentarily put out of the game. The tackle contribution from Scotland's tight five forwards was a crucial element. One recalls Craig Chalmer's tap tackle at full stretch on Pierre Hontas. If the Frenchman had escaped, a try was certain and the entire trend of that match could have changed. Then, against England, there was the perfect example to youngsters watching of how to cut down a player from the side and behind. Rory Underwood was virtually certain to score when Scott Hastings launched himself and brought him down. It is true that Gavin Hastings was covering behind his brother but Underwood is such an elusive runner with instant take-off and change of pace that I believe he would have scored. Finally, there was that moment when Will Carling was in full cry with ten metres to go, when he must have got the impression of having hit a tidal wave of blue as the entire Scottish pack supported Craig Chalmers's tackle and simply swept England's captain backwards at a rate of knots.

Of course, there was the point that if England had taken penalty-goal chances in the first half they could have created a handy cushion, but the fact is that they didn't. As for Tony Stanger's try it was a special thrill to me to be providing the TV commentary because he is from my home town and is a former pupil who started his rugby as a ten-year-old at Wilton Primary School in Hawick where one of the women teachers, Mrs May Sinclair, had a lot to do with his initial development and enthusiasm in the game. That move will be engraved on the minds of all Scottish rugby folk for a long time – John Jeffrey's pick-up and feed, Gary Armstrong's cleverly judged pass, the Gavin Hastings punt that was placed on a sixpence and Tony's reach and dive. I wonder if that try would have been scored if Tony had been only five feet nine instead of six feet two? His height and reach made all the difference. It was an Englishman who expressed the opinion that Tony hadn't touched down properly. Tell that to the fifty-three thousand Scots who were there! A wee country like Scotland has long periods of hunger and of failure and short bursts of wonderful success. This had to be the greatest day in Scottish rugby history. It was a day Scots never will forget. And whilst I hope that my commentary was unbiased it was some day for me as well.

From *Talking of Rugby* by Bill McLaren
(Stanley Paul, London, 1991)

Wear and Tear

Gordon Brown

Gordon Brown – 'Broon from Troon' – was always an enjoyable after-match companion, but he was also an opponent to be respected on the rugby field. He gave his all for Scotland, often carrying injuries that would have ruled out a less patriotic or dedicated team-player.

W.B.B.

Every rugby player enjoys playing as often as possible, and as rugby is a physical-contact game, most players have a running series of bumps and bruises which tend to be ignored. It is also not normally in the make-up of players to complain too much about such ailments. However, there must come a time in every rugby player's life when the ailment requires rest and attention. Sadly, the macho side of us does not allow us to admit that we have an injury that hurts. Of course, there are other angles. We do not want to call off in case the replacement plays too well and is retained once we recover. Nor do we ever wish anyone to hang the label 'injury-prone' on our peg in the dressing-room. Generally, though, I think the burning desire to keep playing without a break weighs on us most heavily, and although no one will ever thank a player for playing with an injury, and playing badly, it is always an excuse to fall back on.

I have often felt too that the feeling of letting my team-mates down by not playing weighed on my shoulders. 'They'll never manage without me' is something I've told myself often – too often. 'They'll never manage to find someone to take my place' is an honest statement of concern, rather than a big-headed attitude.

When players have a dilemma over whether to play because of injury, the decision should be taken out of their hands as quickly as possible. Most of the time the major problem is getting the players to talk about injuries they are carrying. Despite the fact that rugby is such a bastion of amateurism, too often this is allowed to cloud the issue, thus putting all the onus for decision-making on the player. Few players are capable of making a completely fair and unbiased decision when it comes to weighing up whether they should play or not. The long-term dangers of playing while injured rarely come into the mind of most players. The real problem is always dominated by the next fixture – depending upon which team it is against.

Starting to play again before a broken bone has had the chance to reset properly or a torn ligament or pulled muscle has had the chance to become strong again is all too common in rugby. But the major danger is starting again too soon following a bump on the head – especially when concussion has occurred. Rugby captains and committees should take a far greater responsibility when it comes to deciding whether to select players who have received head knocks in the immediate past. The masochism should be ignored and players be firmly told, 'You are not playing.' Most of the time this will not be appreciated at all, but much can now be made of Bill Beaumont's premature retirement from the pinnacle of British rugby. Bill was a man's man, a player's player, and no softy. If he in his position can turn his back on rugby in the name of self-preservation, his decision must be seen as a pointer to others, especially at lower levels, to follow suit. Bill Beaumont will probably never be able to appreciate fully the far-reaching effect his sensible decision will have, and should have, on the rugby players in this country or anywhere else in the world, for that matter, where the game is played.

The normal wear and tear of rugby is demanding enough on anyone's body, but because I have played too often with injuries yet unhealed, I dread to think what state I am going to be in by the time I reach the age of sixty. I know how many joints are currently bothering me at the 'tender' age of thirty-five, so my only hope is that some time during the next decade or so a remedy is found for arthritis.

Because of what I have inflicted on myself through stupidity and pigheadedness, I am a firm believer that rugby players generally – because I am not alone – can cause more long-term damage to themselves by continually playing with injuries than any thug whom they will encounter on the field of play will ever do to them. I may still carry mental scars from my attack by Allan Hardie but, thankfully, the physical scarring is now almost invisible. The scars which I have inflicted on myself throughout my career will be with me till I die!

From *Broon from Troon* by Gordon Brown
(Stanley Paul, London, 1983)

9
GREAT NATIONS: IRELAND

The Middle Thirties

Patrick Campbell

The Irish have not always enjoyed the greatest success in Five Nations rugby, but whether winning or losing, they have given spectators and themselves some of their happiest moments. The play on the field may sometimes have erred on the primitive side, but those watching and writing about it have always had an abundance of wit and style.

W.B.B.

After a really punishing loose maul in the mud-stained remnants of my mind I still find it curiously difficult to get the ball – as it were – out and as far back as Lansdowne Road in the middle thirties.

I can see in my mind's eye, blurred as it is by many a belt from life, shivering figures in green jerseys and almost white shorts down to the knee standing roughly to attention as the Garda Si'ocha'na Band blasts out 'God Save the King', their blowing and banging affected in no way by lashing rain, whilst fifteen Englishmen, all in immaculate white, stand ramrod straight in front of them, their eyes closed in homage – not too easy to spot from the Grandstand – to their very own George V.

Or could the musical excerpts have been provided by Mary Comerford and her Girl Pipers, even if they came on for 'The Soldier's Song'?

One thing is certain, in my memory. Every man-jack of us wanted to get the music out of the way so that our lads could get at the other fellas, and especially on the occasion of the England–Ireland match.

In those days, of course, we weren't searched for bombs as we came in through the turnstiles, nor were there Gardai' with machine guns patrolling the pitch. The only weapons required for the coming war in the middle were hands, feet and a judicious elbow, and a guaranteed peace after the final whistle.

I must have attended quite a lot of Internationals at Lansdowne Road with my father, as expert and as silent an observer of Rugby as he was of racing. His first plan to stand treat to his whole family was kicked miles into touch by my mother and sister, on the grounds that even watching Ireland winning was no compensation for spending a whole perishing afternoon sitting on hard wooden benches, so that the Lord and I would go alone.

He was always well equipped for the event. A muffler, a good thick woollen rug, a silver flask of modest size and an encyclopaedic knowledge of the names, plus past and present form, of every single player on the field, including data on personnel as remote from my adolescent world as Welsh scrum-halves. As I have said, he was a remarkably quiet watcher of sporting events. As, infrequently, he saw his selection first past the post at Leopardstown, Baldoyle or Phoenix Park, his demeanour would be as gloomy as though it had come in – as it very often did – an exhausted fourth.

He was the same at Lansdowne Road. With everyone around him bawling abuse or exhortation the Lord, fanatically devoted to the game and a sage on its finer points, would greet a faulty pass with the severe comment, 'Somewhat erroneous tactics,' and follow it up with a discreet sip from his flask.

It might have been this, or just plain curiosity, that led me into the social activities in Dublin that surrounded an International match, both for several days before and often a week after the event. The result of this was that I actually got to Lansdowne Road for round about one event in every three.

Our mornings would begin outside the door of the Buttery in the basement of the Royal Hibernian Hotel, almost always as early as 10.25 a.m., to be there in good time for the throwing open of the portals at 10.30. Once inside service would be held up by George and Jack behind the bar in discussion with the older members about 'What would be good for it?' 'It', of course, was the accumulated result of the two days and nights of conjecture about the possible result of the coming match – not a matter to be lightly dismissed.

It would have been round about 11 a.m. that a number of us would decide it was high time to see what was going on in Davy Byrne's just around the corner, followed about 11.45 by an investigation into Bailey's Hotel, almost opposite, a smooth flow that led us into Jammet's back bar as early as 12.30. Seeing that at this chilly hour it was much too soon for lunch the more socially minded of us nipped around the corner of Nassau Street and back into the Buttery, where to many of us it seemed we had been only a minute or two before.

From there, some time later, we were propelled by the surge of events back around the corner of Duke Street and into a re-visiting of Davy Byrne's, followed by Bailey's Hotel, for the purpose of finding out whether Oliver St John Gogarty was still telling the story he'd been embarked upon during our first lap or, more probably, had begun again at the beginning.

All this wasn't simply a vulgar, drunken route. It was much more the vulgar excitement of feeling that the whole city was *en fête* – that hundreds of thousands of people had abandoned care, work, wives and other encumbrances and were making devotedly, if circuitously, for the ultimate Mecca of Lansdowne Road.

Rather too often lunch got in the way, in establishments as remote from the beaten track as the Red Bank or the Dolphin, where we would realize, as we took our first Irish coffee, that the whistle must have gone, miles away, for half-time, so there would be no point in breaking our necks to get there for the final touch-down. That looked after the rest of the night.

But I did get there, at least twice, to witness two of the greatest athletic feats that the Rugby world has ever seen. I must admit it's quite possible I was never there at all and heard about them from my father, a bit warmed up, thereby making them my own stories for ever. Like the one about Jammy Clinch, that heroic Irish forward, the only man made of solid concrete from head to toe who could still run quite fast despite such unusual anatomy.

Was it not Jammy, looking, as usual, for trouble in midfield, who suddenly found the ball in his hands, emerging from some unknown source, and started to gallop, instantly, for the Welsh line? Did not two Welshmen climb aboard him in their own twenty-five, slowing Jammy a little but not significantly? And did not their full-back add himself to Jammy's load so that all four of them fell like a double-decker bus over the Welsh line, between the goal-posts, leaving a crater the outlines of which can be seen to this very day? It's a well-known fact that all this happened, no word of a lie.

Nor is it a word of a lie about Ernie Crawford, our own little hunchy full-back. Remember the day when Ernie was there with the sun in his eyes and the wind in his teeth and a big lolloping punt coming his way with three bullocks of English forwards thundering down on him and Ernie palmed the ball as if it was a marble, side-stepped and kicked for touch, while all three Englishmen ran into one another and fell down. And what happened to Ernie's kick? Bounced off the head of a bewildered three-quarter, got snapped up by the English scrum-half and shovelled out to Serge Obolensky right out on the other wing, who set out like a Maserati for the Irish line. What did Ernie do? With his crab-like lightning run he covered the whole width of the field in a single second, caught hold of good old Obo, tied him up into a neat little parcel and threw him right into the orchestra stalls, two feet short of our line.

If anyone wants to question the veracity of these epic tales, with niggling demands for dates, times, teams, weather conditions and so on, let him not come to me.

I've been in exile so long that were I to find myself in Dublin again I'd be hard put to it to find Lansdowne Road itself.

From the *Ireland v. Wales programme*
(Irish RFU, 1978)

It's a Long Way from Mutton-chop Moustaches and Dundrearies

G.A. Redmond

As Patrick Kavanagh often said about placed horses, or pigs or porter, the price of things is a holy dread. The agenbite of inwit had gnawed deeply into the bone of this most realistic, rooted poet: his generally thrown-away obiters had a very particular ring of truth (if not always that other ring of confidence). He knew the value of things as well as their price. He'd understand today's difficulty very nicely: a holy dread that it's costing the stand sitter at Lansdowne Road more to park his backside (to say nothing of herself's) for this eighty-seventh match against England than it did to go boat-and-rail excursion to Twickenham, when this year's centenary was still a long way off. All the same, aren't we the great ould warriors to be sticking it out so long and so well? I suppose *The Times* and *The Guardian*, even a certain party in the *D.T.* (the singular means a newspaper, *not* the other thing – shh! Be quiet when I'm talking to me friends . . .) will have something to say about that.

It's probably proof of the existence of God, that after a hundred years of existence Irish rugby is still talking to itself and another, that after eighty-six matches (it might have been the hundred but for twelve years lost in the two wars and no games in 1888 and 1889, for which see Ned van Esbeck's definitive IRFU history) we're still talking to England. On the statistics of the eighty-six games so far, though, it's been rather a case of England's doing the talking: they've won forty-nine, we've won only twenty-nine with eight drawn. But we've been answering back pretty well since the resumption in 1947. It's a holy dread, too, the way one has to explain to cash customers – I beg your pardons: respected patrons – every little detail we used to make out for ourselves in the old days. Like, that the Ladies' Department was situated under the East Stand. Still is, I suppose, though with many more branches now, or that Willie James Noel Thomas Eugene John Wilson Ernie MacStrap, aged 123, the legendary hero of Muicineachidirdhásháile, an advanced student of business at the Massachusetts Institute of Technology, is gaining his five hundred and fourth cap for Ireland today: You will note from the small type under the picture that the chairman of the selectors is keeping his eye on WJNTEJWEMacS's grand-daughter, who has been showing good form, even if it is a trifle square, in the recently established Maynooth College Unisex XV, Newman's idea of a university education having belatedly been noted among the glosses by an improving Minister for Education and some broad

Churchmen. But, as Mr Peter Sellers, who has not yet been capped for England, says, I digress.

It is significant that, after so long an imbalance we are at last having more equality: of the twenty-eight matches since 1947, Ireland has won eleven, to England's twelve, with five drawn. And there's a chance we could today make it four-in-a-row, something we last did in 1896–99, for 1939–49 was interrupted by the last war. Eighteen Ninety-Six . . . that's another holy dread: to think we've been at it all that time, plus a further twenty-one years. How does one grasp the enormity of such a span? Disraeli was British Prime Minister, when Ireland first played England. I suppose he hardly noticed that his Twenty had reported the victory at Kennington Oval. Shh again! I *told* you about Disraeli and what he said to the Queen: that the difficult takes time, the impossible a little longer. Ireland proved his point for him: our first win against England took until 1887 (Lord Salisbury was P.M.) and our first away win until 1894. The Nineties, of course, were a time of great things toward: The Gaelic Athletic Association just growing, the Gaelic League beginning, the smell of Home Rule and Horse Trams in the air. Irish rugby was perhaps more Viceregal then, but scarcely any less visceral than it is now: the Ryans of Rockwell, Clinch Senior (Jammie's Da), Louis Magee stating some basic playing principles that became part of a tradition.

It's a long way from mutton-chop moustaches and Dundrearies, hob-nailed boots and first-up-first-down: some modern hair-styles, to be sure, would not have been out of place on these early Irish and English teams, though what those antique Corinthians would have had to say about modern coaching and planning we may only speculate – and those short trousers . . . What they would undoubtedly recognize is that it's still Us against Them. That rugby is still played between such disputatious neighbours is a measure of the game's merits; but give both parties credit for sticking at it. Of course it's important to win, if we can; but *if* we can let's not blow about it. This is a very complicated proposition in these highly motivated times; and it was an engaging phrase, that old languid Anglo-Saxon thing about 'Gentlemen, The Game's The Thing'. Des Merrey, a famous Palmerston and Irish Defence Forces' hooker, saw that one off. As a guest for Bective Rangers against Northampton he so distinguished himself that some local Alickadoos thought he was from Coventry. Des, sucking the orange at half-time, overheard from the touch-line. 'Rather rough, what, these Irish? One thought this was a game for gentlemen.' To which Des replied: 'Begod, then if ye did, I had no such——misapprehension when I came out on this——field!' The point was resolved later over copious jars. As Sydney Smith said, beer and Britannia are inseparable . . . It's not just by courtesy of the beer – or of the box – that McBride, Gibson, Slattery – indeed, any Irish players ancient or modern – are welcomed wherever rugby is played in England, from the Coarsest Extra Bs of Michael Green-land to the deb and debenture-studded elegance of Harlequins.

It's simply that other jems were wise in their generations, elastic-sided boots and all; which helps to explain why Duckham may be measured by some against Sever, or Obolensky (though he was more a Peter Jackson man); and Jan Webster against Dickie Jeeps; Warfield and Preece against Butterfield and Davies . . . and Ensor against Kiernan, Norton, Crawford – until some practical man asks, 'Yes: but do you remember when the ground ran the other way?'

It's a gas old game: this private ritual committed in public, invented by accident at an

English public school, part of an elitist pastime that has been embraced by miners, Boers, Maoris, Frenchmen, kilt and caber men, Irishmen – Catholic, Protestant, Dissenter, Jew – and refined, not into the homogeneous anonymity of internationalism, but into nationally idiosyncratic expressions of widely shared delight in thirty bods' colliding, mind and matter, on a football field. That the game is now committed within the motions of a more calculatedly cerebral approach is no great harm: the use of force didn't begin with Plato's *Republic*, though since Greek met Greek isn't it a wonder they didn't think of rugby? Politics crept in, of course – the art of the possible: and there'll be a lot more of it before tonight's few jars are finished. Remember, though, that if Britain – someone has said – like the Bourbons, has remembered nothing, forgotten nothing, there's a decent farmer out there today, who two years ago captained England when *they* kept their word. Welcome again, John Pullin – and good luck to you that you got back after omission and injury. You said at the dinner: 'We may not be much good, but at least we turn up.' King Cotton's men will get as big a cheer today.

From the *Ireland v. England programme*
(Irish RFU, 18 January 1955)

For Ireland, Boys!

Frank Keating

It was good to be back in Dublin after long winters of cricketing, though the soft weather of centuries was more chill than I can remember as the biting north-easterly yapped in from an ice-cold Irish Sea.

But the grass was a bright green and the sky a crisp, glistening blue. 'Ah,' enquired my purple-faced, jug-eared taximan, 'for the match, I suppose?' For the match, I said. 'Ah,' mused he, 'I don't know about the rugger, sor, but it's sure a lovely day for ploughin'. There'll be a lot out ploughing tomorrow.' But he agreed that no one would be out ploughin' come tomorrow afternoon. 'Every man, woman and child is keyed up. It does the old country good, does the rugger. Livens it up. They should play these games more often.'

The city has changed radically since I was last here. They have closed off Grafton Street to cars and everything else 'up there' is one-way. The Royal Hibernian Hotel has gone for good. Nobody could park nearby it, you see – 'you never used to be able to park up there at all, but now you can't park at all, at all,' my man said. I went to make sure one of my favourite shopsigns was still there – 'Haircutting While-U-Wait'. The office-workers were taking brisk and animated constitutionals around Stephen's Green. The sacred smudge of ash from Wednesday was still on some foreheads, on the brow of solicitors and senators, and shining-faced secretaries with smiling Irish eyes and terrible Irish hang-ups. On their knees that morning, I fancy, more than a few candles were lit and prayers wafted up to Blessed Oliver Plunkett, the martyred seventeenth-century Bishop of Armagh, and patron saint of the Blessed Seamus Oliver Campbell, to whom many with their eyes on Lansdowne Road will be making their own individual prayers. Last winter Campbell's forty-six points ensured the Triple Crown for Ireland for the first time in twenty-five years. This season they are the only side who can win it again – indeed, a Grand Slam is within their grasp.

Last year in Paris the French stopped the Irish with – in the words of an editorial in a Dublin newspaper – 'head-bucking, gouging, boring, punching and similar skullduggery with the intent fully to send home the Irish forwards back across the sea in plastic bags.' So Saturday's match will be an occasion of terrible fury. But it's invariably tit-for-tat. As long ago as 1892 a J.J. McCarthy contributed thus an Irish chapter to the then definitive volume *The Rugby Game*:

Football in Ireland may be said to consist of three parts – Rugbeian, Associationist and Gaelic. The rule of play in these organisations had been defined as follows: in rugby, you kick the ball; in Association, you kick the man if you cannot kick the ball; and in Gaelic, you kick the ball if you cannot kick the man.

The rugger headquarters at Clonturk Park, McCarthy went on, was,

> conveniently situated between Glasnevin graveyard and the Mater Misericord-iae Hospital. A man has been known to pass from the football direct to the hospital, and from the hospital to the cemetery; another match being then got up to raise funds for the benefit of the next-of-kin, thus running the risk of killing a few more for the benefit of the deceased.

In spirit at least, I reckon, things won't have changed much by tomorrow. The very thought of those first two or three scrums makes me wince. For the Irish are no angels, and their battle-scarred pack has been getting in first with the retaliation for a long time now. And when admonished – oh! the innocence of those open, guileless faces.

The stokers in the engine room this week have been working at more than just looking fierce, I can tell you. A stream of curses has been pouring forth as the eight-man juggernaut has clanked and clamped and charged itself up on the practice ground at Old Belvedere.

Campbell is much more than a kicker, of course. He has a beautiful pair of hands and feet with a delicate, deceptive pit-a-pat stride. The scrum-half Robbie McGrath is by no means the quickest nor the most accurate passer with whom to be paired, yet he explained this week how last year they agreed on signals for an attempted drop goal. In the event, McGrath's pass squirted out at Campbell's bootlace – 'he was completely off balance and unready, yet he picked the thing off his toe, changed direction and intent in one stride, and took off on a mazy, bewildering run that presented a try to Moss Finn.'

Campbell is as shy as he is unaffected and friendly. He could pass, at a glance, for twenty: in fact he is thirty next year. To anyone else's knowledge he has no regular girlfriend. He works as salesman for the family's clothing firm. He still lives with Dad and Mam in the attractive Dublin suburb of Malahide. 'I'm spoiled, pampered, no doubt about it. I'm probably still tied to my mother's apron strings. If I come in late at night she'll always be up for me, just as if I was nine, not almost twenty-nine. No, she's never watched me play, since I was around fourteen. She won't even watch a recording of a match on television in case I'm murdered before her eyes!'

At Belvedere College old boys' ground on the Anglesea Road one can often find him alone at practice. Solitary. All weathers. Till the lights wink warm in the city yonder. Kick, kick, kick. Fetch and carry, fetch and carry. Kick, kick, kick. Short ones, long ones, wide ones, narrow ones. Fetch and carry, fetch and carry. Kick, kick, kick. Punting ones, torpedo ones, considered ones and hasty ones. He ends up with one from the halfway line, soccer's centre circle. He claws the mud from studs. With care he lines up his right instep against the ball, his left foot forward and alongside. He looks down at the ball, then up to gauge the distance. The goalposts are far away in the murk. Then, neither hurried nor too cautious, one-two-three-four-five steps back; a little one-and-a-half chassé sideways and left. A glance at the ball, the posts, then back to the ball. Up on his tiptoes just once, then a rhythmic, slightly curving run, eyes down, and . . . woompf! The 'H' is perfectly bisected.

Campbell's kicking is so prodigious that people in high places are talking about changing the rules and the points system. It's not a fair game when Ollie's around. Although he had been a schoolboy fly-half since he was nine he never kicked at goal – 'not even a twenty-five drop-out' – till he was seventeen. 'After that I got the taste – so started practising.' He does bridle shyly at being thought of only as a kicker – 'I actually think I do passing best,' he says. 'Though you lot would never write that, would you?'

Ned van Esbeck, doyen of the *Irish Times*, once explained how the boy had never sought to bargain with his talent: 'Ollie's a humble man. If he were locked up in a room or stuck in a lift with four other men for twenty-four hours they'd all come out of that room none the wiser as to who he was. They wouldn't even know he *liked* rugby football. His modesty is such that he wouldn't have even mentioned it.'

Last year, not long after Ireland had won the Triple Crown, there was celebrated in St Patrick's Cathedral, Dublin, an annual ecumenical service for sportsmen. One of those chosen to read a lesson was Campbell, with a passage from the first epistle of St Paul to the Corinthians. Softly, reverently, he read: 'You know, do ye not, that at the sports all the runners run the race, though only one wins the prize. Like them, run to win. But every athlete goes into strict training. They do it to win a fading wreath; we, a wreath that never fades. For my part, I run with a clear goal before me; I am like a boxer who does not merely beat the air; I discipline my own body, and make it know its master, lest that by any means, having preached to others, I myself should be a failure.'

At Belvedere, he was taught by the Jesuit priest, Fr Jim Moran, who now works in Chicago. They are still in regular touch on the telephone. 'Don't let others define your pinnacles for you: set them yourself,' says Fr Moran. He would, however, always tell Ollie throughout his schooldays, 'Just because you are a good sportsman, don't think that makes you a better *person*,' and Campbell reflects on that to this day. 'Sure, I'm enjoying the rugby, though I admit the practising did once make me very blinkered. And it's nice to do well at it sometimes. But I know it's all a very temporary, transitory thing: soon, I know, I'll just fade into the distance and be an ordinary Joe Soap again.'

On the eve of the very confrontation itself I found myself sinking the black in the snug atmosphere of Sean Lynch's bar opposite Dublin's Carmelite Convent. Sean was a Lion of a prop who helped to bring the spoils home from New Zealand for Carwyn in 1971. But it was not to Sean that I was listening: in a wet-elbowed huddle, hammering out the ifs and buts and coulds and shoulds of the morrow, I was with none other than the Irish national coach himself, the old grey fox with the button snout, Tommy Kiernan.

Perhaps it was my Benedictine boyhood. Or an Irish father. But from the winter's day in 1960 that my uncle, who was from Cork, took me to Twickenham and introduced me to the boys from home I have ever worn the green weed on my sleeve on international days. We stayed at the Knights of St Columba Club in Kensington on the eve of the game and I remember that after midnight everyone stopped bibbing the black and started ordering Green Chartreuse. Next day everyone managed to be up for Mass. They were particularly looking to luck on account of it being a young Cork lad's first international. The Chartreuse and the heartfelt *Credo* worked wonders, for Tom Kiernan, from the Presentation College, had a wonderful game.

He had the kick of a Kinsale mule, the whooshing, deadly tackle of a midsummer Sligo scythe, and still a gentle open face as serene and warm as a turf fire in a cosy cottage. He went on to become the most capped full-back in international history. I worshipped him. Indeed, from that first day I was entranced by the way the Irish played the game. And they do it to this day: a hotchpotch of jigs and jinks and darts and delicate invention and wild make-do-and-mend and all the time maintaining the most furious gusto imaginable.

The Irish scrum-half for that first team I saw at Twickenham was a smart little sprite called Andy Mulligan, who combined a mischievous break with a deal of courage and a grand pass to his out-half. He later became a friend of mine (though I haven't seen him for ages: come back Mulligan, the fiver's forgotten) and once explained the philosophy behind the fizz of those Shamrock sides. Andy's first international was long before the days of squad systems, let alone men-of-the-match. He was understandably nervous before they left the dressing-room. Two minutes to go and the captain finished doing up his laces and addressed them:

> 'Right, lads, let's decide how we're going to play this game. What do you think, Jack (Kyle)?'
> 'I think that a few wee punts at the line would be dandy, and maybe Mulligan here can try a few wee darts on his own.'
> 'What do you think, Tony (O'Reilly)?'
> 'Jasus, the programme here says I'm playing against a midget. Just let me have a run with the ball.'
> 'What about youse, Cecil (Pedlow)?'
> 'I think a subtle little mix of runnin' and kickin' and breakin' would be dandy.'
> The captain summed up: 'So it's decided, lads – Jack's puntin', Andy's dartin', Tony's runnin' and Cecil's doing all three.'

The whole philosophy was precisely presented back in the 1950s by the North of Ireland centre-three-quarter, Noel Henderson, who was doubtless lacing up his boots during that very exchange that afternoon. Said Noel: 'The state of English and Welsh rugger is sometimes serious but never hopeless; the state of Irish rugby is usually hopeless but never serious.'

The enchanting amateur feel of Irish rugby was further summed up for me when Tony Ward showed me a long-ago letter written by the late Mai Purcell to an Irish fly-half of the fifties, Mick English, on the occasion of Mick's first international match. They worked together on the *Limerick Leader*. The memo went:

> Mickie – I should like to impress on you that I'm spending me whole week's wages, *viz* £3.00, on the trip to Dublin just to see you play, and I beseech you not to make an eejit of yourself on this occasion. I furthermore request that on this auspicious afternoon, mindful of your duties and responsibilities, not only to your club and the people of Limerick, but to our country as a whole, that you keep y'bloody eye on the ball. Good luck, sir, and God Bless – Mai.

The uncommitted will feel much the same as Mai these next two March Saturdays. Bejasus, what a hooley there'd be if they made it! It's high time they did. The Triple Crown is one glorious thing, the Grand Slam quite another – and how a Grand Slam for them would do the others good. They've won one this century – at Ravenhill, Belfast, on 13 March 1948. Their winning try against Wales that day – a fly hack, an exuberant charge and a thudding bellyflop to a din that bounced all round the Mountains of Mourne – was scored by a cumbersome prop-forward called Jack Daly. At the final whistle the green shirt was torn from his back and, as he was shouldered off in triumph, the socks peeled from his feet. And still, they will tell you, little square relics of fading green cloth are in existence, to be sure, framed in passepartout on mantelpiece shelves all over the little land, right next to the nightlight in front of the Sacred Heart and alongside the fluorescent statues of Our Lady brought back with the duty free from Lourdes or Lisieux. Y'man Daly, mind you, didn't need the shirt again – his name made, he at once caught a boat to Liverpool and cashed in with the rugby league.

From *Up and Under* by Frank Keating
(Hodder & Stoughton, Sevenoaks, 1983)

Horizons Broaden

Sean Diffley

The Irish team first took the field in an international in 1875. The game was twenty-a-side and the preparations for the great day were equally idiosyncratic.

W.B.B.

When Scotland and England played the first-ever international rugby match at Edinburgh in March 1871 the event passed virtually unsung in Ireland except among the obvious devotees – the comparatively small band of rugby players. There were other matters of international importance to agitate the minds of the populace. There was, for example, the matter of the Franco-Prussian war, which took an especially unpalatable turn for the French that particular March.

Mr Gladstone was prime minister. The Lamb became the first grey to win the Grand National at Aintree and according to the *Irish Times* the other imperishable items of sporting 'intelligence' included . . . London betting . . . Doncaster races . . . Trim races . . . Mallow archery and croquet club . . . A run with the Duhallows . . . A clipping run with the Allanstown Harriers . . .

And there was a certain amount of euphoria in Ireland that particular March when the famous greyhound, Master McGrath, won the Waterloo Cup, the blue riband of coursing, for the third time in his career. Even Queen Victoria was impressed and asked to see the dog. That Royal Command brought forth the following from the *Sporting Gazette*: 'With what different emotions March will hereafter be remembered by the French and the Irish. By the Parisians it will be remembered with deep humiliation because of the occupation of their city by the Prussians – by the Irish with feelings of unmixed gratification at the distinguished and unprecedented honour paid by the Queen of England to their champion of the leash – Master McGrath.'

That, plus wars and clipping runs with the Allanstown Harriers, obviously made for a full enough life and the historic event at Raeburn Place, Edinburgh, seems to have left that part of the realm to the west of the Bailey Lighthouse singularly unmoved.

Irish rugby men were certainly keen on the idea of international matches but there were doubts, that year of 1871, that the game was yet strong enough in Ireland. After all, it was a mere three years since Barrington and Wall had given the first set of rules to the game in Ireland. There was very great interest in the deliberations and progress of the new Rugby Football Union in England and in 1872 Trinity joined the Rugby Union as a full member. (It wasn't all that strange a decision. Six Scottish clubs were already in membership.)

England and Scotland had played four international matches before the Irish really got down to the serious task of starting up some sort of central controlling body. Throughout 1872 and 1873 there were many earnest discussions particularly in the College rooms inhabited by Trinity players. As the premier club they felt they should take the lead in any moves to negotiate for international matches and the founding of controlling organizations.

The question was also exercising the minds of the North of Ireland Football Club in Belfast. North had paid a visit to Scotland in February 1874 and in a report at the end of the season (1873–74) it was mentioned that 'as a result of the trip to Scotland it was hoped that an international match might follow. It is hoped that an inter-city match between Dublin and Belfast (similar to that played between Glasgow and Edinburgh) could be played.' North played two matches on that Scottish tour – they beat Merchiston Castle School but were beaten by Glasgow Academicals.

The moves went on and in October 1874 the *Sporting Gazette* was able to announce: 'We hear on good authority that Ireland proposes challenging England to play a match according to the Rugby Union rules. It is hoped that the match will take place this year. While not undervaluing the strength of the English twenty we are of the opinion that Ireland can produce a team which will give England plenty to do.'

The match took place at Kennington Oval on 19 February, 1875 and was attended by 3,000 spectators. The pitch was 130 yards by 75 yards.

The most interesting description of that first international was given by our trenchant critic, Jacques McCarthy, who viewed the affair in his own highly idiosyncratic fashion.

'Such an enterprise, and such a twenty!' wrote Jacques. 'They had never previously seen each other; the twenty-a-side game was absolutely unknown in Ireland and some of the team did not turn up at all!

'H.L. Robinson and the celebrated "Darky" Smith, the two best backs in Dublin University, were absentees, although their names were on the cards sold about the Oval. Backs were put to play forward and vice versa, and the whole lot were immaculately innocent of training.

'Almost every one of the North men wore beards, and Ash was like Falstaff – "a mountain of mummy". On the other hand, England had been playing Scotland since 1871 and her team was thoroughly disciplined and trained.'

George Stack was the Irish captain that afternoon, but like most of the team he was to gain one cap only. Stack was a clever man, being elected a Scholar of the House in classics in Trinity in 1870; gaining his B.A. in 1873 and an M.A. in 1875. His name is quite unknown in Irish rugby, but though few have ever heard of him the rôle he played in the foundation of the Irish Football Union and his part in organizing Ireland's first international were of major importance. In a cryptic remark some years later, Jacques McCarthy revealed: 'Poor Stack, who did so much for us, afterwards accidentally poisoned himself with an overdose of chloral.'

England won that Kennington Oval encounter by two goals and a try to nil. Only A.P. Cronyn, the nippy and strong Trinity half-back, showed up well for the Irish. He seems to have been the only Irish player to merit a mention among the 'played wells' even though the critics (with the vociferous exception of Jacques) were anxious to be as benign as possible on such an auspicious occasion.

The next exciting event in the story of Irish rugby was the staging of the first international match on Irish soil. The match, between England and Ireland, took place ten months after the Kennington Oval match and it was played on 13 December, 1875, at the Leinster Cricket ground at Rathmines, Dublin.

'The international match,' enthused a Dublin newspaper, 'was brought off on Monday under circumstances of so happy a character that nothing was wanting but victory for the home team to make the success of the Football Union complete.'

The happiness accruing to the Irish Football Union (and the Northern Football Union) was diminished to the extent that England scored a goal and a try and Ireland scored nothing at all.

For the occasion the Irish team was resplendent in blue knickerbockers and white jerseys with green velvet caps and gold badges and lace. The traditional shamrock emblem was still the preserve of the Trinity club who retained it until 1880–81 when it was replaced by the College Arms, and the shamrock transferred to the Irish team at the request of the Irish Rugby Football Union.

The Englsh team was in white jerseys with rose badges, white knickerbockers and brown stockings, rose-coloured velvet caps trimmed with silver lace. But all that *haute couture* might have remained to blush unseen but for a lucky thaw. Heavy frost put the fixture in jeopardy but England travelled anyway and refused to be put off by a series of urgent telegrams from Dublin. At the last minute the weather relented and the thaw allowed the match to go ahead.

England won by a goal and a try to nil. C.W.H. Clark (Liverpool) had the distinction of scoring the first try in an international match in Ireland, but the place kick was missed. In the second half E. Kewley, also of Liverpool, went in for a try which A.W. Pearson (Blackheath) converted.

Jacques McCarthy's description was interesting: 'The Irishmen,' he wrote, 'had discarded their stout woollen green and white jerseys of the previous season for wretched thin cotton vests, but even these possessed an advantage.

'Cronyn, in being tackled,' he went on, 'was denuded to the waist and before he could get another jersey the ball came to him again. Away he went from his own "twenty-five" through almost the whole English team for no one could get a grip on his slippery skin. He dodged Clark and Collins, handed off Mitchell and Gunner, Login dropped at his knees, but he jumped over him amidst terrible excitement but, slipping on landing, Pearson pounced on him at the very verge of the goal line.

'This was probably the finest run ever made in an international match, and in that connection it should be recollected that there were twenty men to be passed.'

Another Dublin account of the match contained the following philosophical gem: 'Again the English vindicated an old theory of ours, that tackling round the legs is the best, for it drops at the root of the evil. . . . '

From *The Men in Green – The Story of Irish Rugby* by Sean Diffley
(Pelham Books, London, 1973)

Ireland Too Anxious

Louis MacNeice

Among the irregular correspondents on Irish rugby is one very distinguished name, the poet Louis MacNeice, who cast his eye over the on- and off-field events at the Ireland–France game at Lansdowne Road in 1955.

W.B.B.

At 11 a.m. sharp in the cocktail bar a North of Ireland gentleman ordered himself a half-bottle of champagne, explaining that otherwise he would not be capable of breakfast.

This is the usual sort of prelude to a Lansdowne Road international. And yesterday for the match between Ireland and France Lansdowne Road was really being itself, full to the brim with such solid and glorious veterans as W.E. Crawford and Sammy Walker and 42,000 others. And there were the pipers, of course, and a police band and the two competing tricolours and a lot of young priests and one Franciscan Friar.

The afternoon, as it should be, was grey and soft, and the turf looked softish but decent. The French team, all blue and white, looked decent, too, but too large (from an Irish point of view). Still, the Irish team, all green and white (including for the first time green stockings, which some of the old hands objected to) did not really look so small. Anyhow, there both lots were all limbering up as if they were treading water. And Henderson kicked off bang into the hands of the French full-back Vannier, and Vannier did a long kick to touch.

This was a significant opening. Right through the game Vannier, a most cool and competent player, seemed to mesmerize all the Irishmen so that they spent and wasted their time kicking the ball directly towards him with a most improbable accuracy. The other suprising thing about this match was that Ireland kept getting the ball – and failing to do anything with it. The Dublin papers had foretold that if the Irish pack could only hold the French the Irish backs would prove superior. Well, the Irish pack did hold if not master the French, but when the ball moved out – Oh, Erin, the tear and the Kyle in mine eye! Movement after movement bogged down or as often as not turned into a French counter-attack.

To begin with, Ireland appeared too anxious, kicking too often and too loosely, but they had, as it is pompously put, the territorial advantage, and the French try, when it came after about a quarter of an hour, was opportunist and surprising, beginning with a cut through by Maurice Prat around his own 'twenty-five'. Lots of Frenchmen seemed to handle (and there were lots more over) but it was Domenech, huge and fast, who scored. Vannier converted.

This was also significant. The French hardly ever heeled, but when sometimes by sheer luck but more often through Irish ineptitude or their own opportunism, they did get the ball, unlike their opposite numbers, they handled it deftly and ran with it and even showed some ideas. The Irish outsides seemed sadly lacking in ideas; towards the end of the first half Pedlow, the Irish left-wing, gathered a kick near his own line, and an Irish counter-attack went to the French 'twenty-five', where, with a man over, Henderson chose to cross-kick. This kick, needless to say, went astray, and a great opportunity was lost.

So at half-time France were leading five points to nil, but Ireland most obviously still had a chance since their pack, including three new men, were showing not only fire and stamina, but remarkable efficiency. The second half was not old before each side was reduced to fourteen, but the same pattern was repeated: Irish attacks dissolving into French counter-attacks. Then in the middle of this half, with the crowd traditionally chanting 'We want a score', Henderson landed a beautiful low trajectory penalty from near the touch-line. Five points to three – Ireland at once came beautifully to life.

The crowd came to life, too, and chanted louder and louder, but the Irish three-quarters remained indecisive (though both Pedlow and O'Reilly had at least one strong run each) and the ball continued to land in the hands of Vannier. Vannier kept sending Ireland back and Ireland kept returning (but what a strain on her forwards!).

Once the French made one of their sudden counter-attacks, and Kyle for the second time in this game accelerated out of nowhere and touched down. He is still a wonderful defender, but alas, in attack he hardly showed up today. So France won, but in spite of earlier prophecies it would be rash to bet on her winning the championship. On the other hand, one may doubt if any of the other home countries will find a pack to beat Ireland's.

It was the memory of this pack that sent us away not too unhappy as we formed the usual bottleneck to treacle at the Lansdowne Road level crossing. It had not been an elegant game, but it had been a hard-fought one – and at moments very exciting.

From the *Observer*, 23 January 1955

Heart-warming Tries Overwhelm Wales

Sean Diffley

Ireland has never been able to equal the success rate of the other members of the Five Nations; perhaps there are too many other calls on the time of sporting Irishmen, from hurling and Gaelic football to horses, and even a drop of the black stuff!

Championship successes and Triple Crowns have been rare for Ireland and there seemed little ground for optimism in 1982. Ireland were on a losing run of seven games and the selectors had gambled with a new captain, Ciaran Fitzgerald, and a stand-off, Ollie Campbell, who was only just back in the game after a long lay-off. All the gambles paid off, however, and Ireland defeated Wales to clear the first hurdle on the way to their first Triple Crown in thirty-three years.

W.B.B.

It was a green torrent again at Lansdowne Road yesterday. After the sedate trickling streams of recent times, the torrent roared with abandon. This inspired Irish performance, a marvellous marrying of the fire of the forwards and the superb skills of the out-half Ollie Campbell, gave the Irish a thoroughly deserved win in this celebration of 100 years of battle between the two countries.

The Irish won by three heart-warming tries, one converted, and two penalty goals to a single try for Wales which was converted, plus a penalty goal and a drop goal.

But seldom can a Welsh side have been so discomfited and in the history of the confrontations between the two it is not often that the Irish win consecutively in Dublin. Two years ago it was 21–7 for Ireland and the same kind of spirit was splendidly in evidence in yesterday's match.

The Welsh forwards were clearly done with long before the end, and after suffering for most of the century from superior Welsh packs it was certainly a landmark yesterday. At the finish the Irish forwards, so well motivated by the irrepressible Ciaran Fitzgerald, were simply toying with the representatives of one of the most illustrious rugby nations.

And Campbell's performance was pure, unalloyed, gold. I would label it as his best display for Ireland or the Lions. Not alone was his handling and tactical kicking of the highest quality, but this time Campbell took on the defence with some spectacular breaks. It was from two of those defence-splitting breaks by Campbell that two of the tries came.

And he paved the way for another, but for a bad pass from Michael Kiernan to Moss Finn.

It was further to Campbell's credit that he could still mastermind a talented back division that was sorely tried by injuries. Ireland lost both centres David Irwin and Paul Dean. Michael Kiernan came on to replace Irwin after half an hour and John Murphy replaced Dean at half-time. Regrettably Irwin broke his right leg and Dean has a severe calf muscle injury.

In addition, Moss Finn on the left wing played the second half with concussion and had no subsequent memory of his second-half try. Moss Keane and Willie Duggan were also in the wars, Keane with a bruised back and Duggan with arm and shoulder problems. But they all soldiered on in adversity.

The one danger to Ireland was the Welsh scrum-half, Terry Holmes, and he did pose a lot of problems with his strength and skill early on. But as his forwards disintegrated and as the Irish poured on to him in a green horde, even Holmes could not do any rescue act.

In what was the only class movement from Wales all afternoon, full-back Gary Evans created an overlap on the right – following a fine break by Holmes – but Evans chose to ignore his wing and turned inside. David Irwin caught him a couple of feet from the Irish line in a tackle that resulted in the Irish centre's broken leg.

That could have been a disastrous period for the Irish with the scrum awarded to the Welsh on the Irish line. Ciaran Fitzgerald said afterwards that the official doctor Mick Molloy had indicated to the referee that Irwin had a broken leg. But as Fitzgerald appealed to the referee (Mr Short of Scotland) for the substitute to be allowed on, the referee said that Irwin must first be off the field and then must be formally adjudged to be unfit to resume in the dressing room.

So while Michael Kiernan fretted on the sideline and while the crowd roared their disapproval of a silly, hidebound decision, the Welsh quickly made the most of their chances against the depleted side. They were awarded a free from the scrum on the Irish line, because of over-eager striking by the seven Irish forwards. They chose to bulldoze their way forward and Holmes grabbed possession to score his try which Evans converted.

That put the score after half an hour at 9–4 for Wales. Many a team would have buckled under but the Irish team were not to be denied yesterday. After half-time when Gary Pearce came on for the injured Welsh captain and out-half, Gareth Davies, the referee did not hesitate that time in calling on the Welsh substitute.

Ireland started badly and were three points down after a mere three minutes when Evans kicked a penalty goal from forty-seven yards range. But after twenty-three minutes the Irish struck form at last and took the lead. Philip Orr and Fergus Slattery were up to wrest the ball from a maul and Robbie McGrath sent Irwin away on the right and the centre timed his pass splendidly to Trevor Ringland, who scored a try with a most determined run and dive. But then came Holmes's try when Irwin was injured and the conversion left Ireland trailing 4–9.

But then, just before half-time, came a classic break and a series of dummies from Campbell and Finn was over in the left corner for his first try. And that left Wales just a point ahead (9–8) at half-time.

Johnny Murphy came on at half-time for Dean and then early in the half another superb break by Campbell, carried on by Murphy, gave Finn his pass for his second try which Campbell converted.

That put Ireland 14–9 ahead and the trend towards victory began. A marvellous movement by the forwards, which began with a burst by Phil Orr and was carried on by John O'Driscoll and Fergus Slattery, yielded an infringement by the sorely pressed Welsh who went offside in sheer desperation. Campbell, from twenty-eight yards, put Ireland 17–9 ahead. On an infrequent visit to the Irish half, Pearce dropped a goal for Wales, but Campbell had the last word with his second penalty goal to complete a very fine day for Campbell and Ireland.

From the *Irish Independent*, February 1982

Campbell Kicks Ireland into Triple Crown Glory

Edmund van Esbeck

One Crowded Hour of glorious life,
Is Worth an age without a name.

Now there is silent stillness all around, the great multitude has gone its diverse ways, the old, long of memory, the young, uninhibited by tradition, expectant, but no less appreciative, all with the warm and the satisfying glow of triumph in their hearts.

Lansdowne Road, a ground where, for a century and more, the drama, the excitement, and at times the frustrations too of international rugby, have been played out, has never known an occasion quite like last Saturday afternoon and Irish rugby no greater day in its long and honourable history.

For thirty-three years we have suffered and waited to acclaim a Triple Crown victory for Ireland, never in one hundred and seven years of international competition had Ireland won the Crown at Lansdowne Road. Never that is, until last Saturday afternoon when Ireland defeated Scotland by six penalty goals and a drop goal to a goal and two penalty goals and, by so doing, won the oldest and most cherished prize at stake in international rugby.

We have seen our dreams die often in the past, this time, before our eyes a dream came true, the collective triumph of fifteen men with the individual brilliance of one being written indelibly across the scene.

Campbell is the name and Campbell was the man who scored Ireland's twenty-one points, the greatest individual scoring feat achieved by an Irishman in international rugby, and how appropriate it should come to grace this occasion, Ireland's first Triple Crown triumph in Dublin.

It was not a great match, but it was an unforgettable occasion, one that will live for ever in the minds and hearts of all who saw it. The scenes at the end of the game as the crowd invaded the pitch to chair the Irish players shoulder high were shades of days of long ago in Belfast and Swansea, magic moments in Irish rugby history when most of those present last Saturday had not yet set out on life's erratic journey.

Here was the unbounded joy of people and the acclamation for a splendid endeavour that spelled out a message loud and clear, 'welcome back, Ireland, welcome back to the summit, after your period in the wilderness.' It was scene imperishable in memory and, in the days and the years ahead, we shall proudly proclaim 'Ah yes, I was there, I remember it well.'

The facility for performing the unexpected and fighting the good fight against the odds, may well be an Irish characteristic, in sport and in life. This time no freedom from the obligation of a nation's expectation of victory for the men in green. They discharged their burden in the spirit and the letter, the captain firm and steadfast on the bridge to steer a steady path along the plotted course.

Now an indelible entry has been inscribed in the rugby history books, gratitude for it will always be our memorial for the team of '82. No more must we travel back through the pages of history to find an Irish Triple Crown triumph. The year of 1982 is Ireland's year and Ireland's glory, there for the present generation to celebrate and for the future generations to investigate.

In good days and in bad, the Irish have never lacked vociferous exhortation and support at Lansdowne Road. Never in thirty-five years of patronage at the venue I heard anything to equal the support that came up from stands and terrace last Saturday. From the moment that Ciaran Fitzgerald led his side on to the field, it was evident that the Irish had come in expectation of bearing witness to a great event that would culminate in an Irish triumph.

And so it came to pass. Two years ago we had a new dimension added to the international occasion in Dublin, the singing of an enraptured gathering in acclamation. 'Cockles and Mussels' split the air at regular intervals and to it was added a slight variation on a familiar theme borrowed for the occasion from across the Irish Sea and the ample Kop at Anfield 'EE-Aye-Addio, we are going to win the crown.'

Win it the Irish did as Scotland wilted before the controlled fury of the Irish pack in the second half and Campbell, so cool, so composed, dictated the territorial location of where the game would primarily be fought out and his educated right foot ultimately fashioned the game's destiny, as he kicked six penalty goals and a dropped goal to score twenty-one points and break the record for an Irish player of nineteen points, a mark set by himself in Brisbane in 1979.

The day was cold and a vigorous wind blew a disconcerting path towards the Havelock Square end. It was a day when the most accurate of kickers could be pardoned for not finding the range. But Campbell compensated in the most delicate manner for the vagaries of the breeze, to kick six penalties, three of them truly splendid efforts.

I think it must be said that the game and its strategy, dictated by the elements and, no doubt, by the circumstances surrounding the match, did not tend towards extravagance in terms of fluid rugby. Yet, even in this respect, it had a few lusty moments, one in particular provided by the Scots which yielded six points and brought 50,000 back to the firm realization that the Scots had not come just to provide token opposition for an Irish carnival.

Indeed for a period before the interval, the Scots offered the Irish some considerable trouble and stretched the Irish defence as the visitors' forwards won some good possession and outside-half John Rutherford employed his attacking skills.

Although Ireland led at the interval by 15–6, it was not by any means an unassailable advantage and the Scots had performed reasonably well into the wind. Their big men Tomes and Cuthbertson did well out of touch where Donal Lenihan was Ireland's main ball winning agent, and Scotland also curbed Ireland effectively at the tail of the line.

In the scrums, however, Ireland always offered the better unit, but Scotland managed to get their own strike without too much stress being imposed and, in addition, in that first period, Ireland's most durable and tenacious scrum-half, Robbie McGrath, did not at all times seem in total accord with his hooker, Ciaran Fitzgerald, in the timing of the put-in.

Ireland, however, were always the better side in the loose and once more their speed to the ball and their facility for getting to it in greater numbers was evident and extremely beneficial.

Scotland had won the toss and elected to play into the wind and it was Campbell's task to kick off. The nervous anxieties so very evident in the early stages were clearly demonstrated when Campbell's kick-off landed over the Scotland dead ball line and so it was scrum back at half-way.

Vigour was not lacking in the Scottish pack's approach. Within three minutes, Campbell struck, a portent of things to come. He kicked a great penalty from forty yards out on the left, 3–0; six minutes later Ireland were awarded a penalty one yard inside their own half and Campbell, to the encouragement and obvious agreement of the crowd, indicated he was going to try his luck. He struck with unerring accuracy and Ireland led 6–0 – what a start.

Surely the Scots would not spoil the party? But they came not to bear witness to another's triumph, but to offer a worthy opposition and, after fifteen minutes, we got a demonstration of the possibilities contained in their back line. They won a line-out fifty yards from Ireland's line, Laidlaw broke right and made the essential initial breach in the Irish defence before transferring to John Rutherford who was clear and he scored near the posts. The conversion was a formality for Andy Irvine. Scotland had equalized.

There was a lot of loose and scrappy play as the Irish fought to re-establish their superiority. The line-out was a less than fertile area as the Irish varied their line-up in this vital area, Keane, Lenihan and Duggan switching positions. Lenihan got his hands to the ball more often than most, but Tomes too was giving Scotland some useful possession.

In the scrums, the Irish were comfortable, not yet dominant, and Scotland held their own ball without undue stress. Campbell went centre stage again and kicked his third penalty from thirty-two yards and well to the right to give Ireland a lead they would never again surrender, after nineteen minutes.

Then came a lovely movement that promised a try as Campbell broke free and transferred to Crossan but the young winger could not gather a difficult pass.

Slattery was in to offer the necessary support on the loose ball which was won and, with the coolness of the master craftsman, Campbell dropped a goal to give Ireland a 12–6 lead. Perhaps on the general balance it was a flattering lead.

There followed a few threatening Scottish moves and the Irish looked uneasy, but survived and, when Campbell kicked his fourth penalty in the thirty-second minute, Ireland led 15–6. Then, we learned that even the mighty Campbell was fallible, he missed one from a difficult angle, before Irvine had a great chance to cut Scotland's deficit from almost in front of the posts, but he kicked wide.

It was not to be Irvine's day and this was a display from the Scotland captain that made him look a very ordinary player indeed. He was vulnerable under the dropping ball and Campbell had kicked with great wisdom to give Ireland many fine attacking positions.

The Scotland line had survived tenuously enough on a few occasions. Yet a nine points lead, bearing in mind the wind, was by no means something that presented a measure of safety.

In the second half Ireland faced a test of character and how magnificently the pack rose to the occasion. After Irvine had missed two long-range penalty attempts, the Irish basically took over. The forwards, magnificently led by Fitzgerald, showed tremendous control as they ensured Irish territorial superiority.

The line-out was a more fertile area, the scrummaging got better by the minute. McGrath at times took the wrong decisions, but none the less made a signal contribution to give Campbell a good service; and Duggan was brilliant in the middle of the Irish back row. Slattery and O'Driscoll, two tremendous workers, and their colleagues combined to give the Scots a torrid second half experience.

Kiernan was almost through after Moss Finn had made the opening. Both played splendidly and behind them was Hugo MacHeill. His fielding of the high ball, when Rutherford or others tried this tactic, was positively magnificent and he made but one slight fielding error.

When the Scots ran at the Irish, the tackle went in and, as at Twickenham, Campbell was often the man to down the man who threatened danger. He elevated Ireland's lead to twelve points when he kicked his fifth penalty in the ninth minute of the second period before Jim Renwick took over such duties for Scotland and found the range from forty-three yards with sixteen minutes to go. But the pattern now was one of Irish supremacy in the forward exchanges and a try always looked a possibility as the Irish pair drove forward.

With ten minutes remaining, Campbell kicked his sixth goal, this time from thirty yards, and now armed with a twelve points lead that broke the heart of the Scotland challenge. Renwick got three points back with a few minutes remaining, but by then we all knew that nothing could now stand between Ireland and glory.

There are some statistics deeply impressive in themselves, but Campbell's achievement was the legend of accomplishment. His six penalties equalled the record in that regard at international level by any player. His general contribution was immense. He was the man of the hour.

There was a false alarm when the referee stopped play and some in the crowd thought it was the end and rushed to offer their acclaim. They had to wait yet awhile. What difference another few minutes.

A fierce light has focused on the Irish players over the past fortnight, but they learned to cope with it. They had captured the imagination of the young and the old and this time produced a performance that matched expectation.

There are few pictures in memory more sharply etched than the scenes that came at the end of the game. Some Irish players got the safety of the dressing-room early. Others, Campbell among them, were engulfed by the crowd.

Campbell got a torrid time before he could make his way to the dressing-rooms. They cheered him, they shook his hand, and at that moment he was the one man in Ireland who could have been certain to form a government. Lansdowne Road belonged to him and the Triple Crown, that mythical but, oh, so elusive trophy had been won at long last.

From the *Irish Times*, March 1982

Tours and Parlour Games

Sean Diffley

Although the Irish have been largely unsuccessful in the Five Nations Championship, their contributions to British Lions sides, as Sean Diffley points out, have often been crucial.

W.B.B.

Considering that from 1951 until that five-way share-out of the Championship in 1973 the Irish had won no titles and were, therefore, by statistical definition, undistinguished, their contribution to the Lions in that period has been of quite astonishing value. Particularly among the forwards, but often among the backs, the Irish have filled key roles. Willie John McBride still speaks in awe of Bill Mulcahy's second row lock play in South Africa in 1962, and any player like Willie John who has figured in a unique four Lions tours is qualified to speak with some authority on the subject.

Willie John's own contribution has been justly lauded, and if such estimates are admissible or have any real validity it is probably true that Willie John and Colin Meads of New Zealand have been the greatest locks of all time – and McBride is far from finished yet!

Syd Millar, McBride's Ballymena clubmate, had made three tours, the most notable being his part in that all-Irish front row in which his colleagues were Ronnie Dawson and Gordon Wood in New Zealand in 1959. Millar was in South Africa in 1962 but was considered a bit long in the tooth when the 1966 tour of New Zealand was being selected. Later it began to dawn on the rugby world that strong enough loosehead props were scarce and when they were available they generally improved – like good Irish whiskey – with age. So it came about that Millar, too old in 1966, was grabbed for the tour of South Africa in 1968 when he was thirty-three years old.

The part which Mike Gibson played in the Lions triumph in New Zealand in 1971 is well documented. It is significant that when Barry John's tremendous scoring feats are mentioned in the context of the tour New Zealand observers go to great pains to stress that Gibson's part should not be overlooked. The high and unselfish and thoroughly competent work of Gibson tends to be slightly overlooked by those viewing affairs a little superficially. What is implied is that the glamour surrounding Barry John was due, in large measure, to the dedicated support he received from the self-effacing Gibson who is not only one of the great players of the age but also a most conscientious team player.

The most spectacular contributions to the Lions, however, have come from Tony O'Reilly, David Hewitt and Tom Kiernan. O'Reilly, who tends to cause a stir wherever he goes or whatever he does, was on the Irish team in 1955, the year after he left school. Later that year he was the eighteen-year-old babe of the Lions team in South Africa and scored sixteen tries which is still the record for a Lions player in that country. Four years later he was in New Zealand and his seventeen tries there was another individual record (equalled by John Bevan of Wales in 1971). O'Reilly's scoring feats were never quite duplicated for the Irish team because of Irish midfield players' inability to create the openings to allow O'Reilly to use his speed, dash and strength to any great extent.

But there is many an Irishman who tends to view the difference of O'Reilly's performances for the Lions and for Ireland as some sort of flaw in the big fellow's game. Some years later when his selection for his country was not quite the automatic affair it had been a selector was said to have declaimed: 'O'Reilly would be my number one choice for a World XV to take on Mars . . . but I'm damned if I'd pick him for Ireland . . . '

O'Reilly gained his twenty-eighth cap in 1963 and then suffered a spate of injuries, disconcerting international business disruptions, and was the victim of some rather eccentric selection committees. There is no doubt but that he should have been chosen more often after 1963 but one felt that some selectors were more intent on displaying their total independence by leaving O'Reilly off the teams. All the glittering business and sporting success, the stories of offers of film parts in Hollywood – there was a suspicion that some selectors were more concerned to show how little impressed they were rather than judge the player on his merits as a player. Thus Tony O'Reilly was a figure of some controversy in those days.

His selection to play against England came as a great surprise to everybody. There had been no hint that he had even been in the running as a substitute when Bill Brown, the right wing, broke down on the Friday in London. Apparently Irish selectors pick the Irish team; pick a shadow team and also make a few provisions in case some of the reserves can only drive on the left-hand side or something like that. It was in that convoluted manner that Tony O'Reilly was drafted into the side. He had been asked to hold himself in readiness and then came the summons.

We were all there at the Honourable Artillery Company ground, somewhere east of Threadneedle Street – press, photographers, alickadoos – for the Irish practice on a grey Friday afternoon when the battleship grey limousine nosed its way soundlessly between the high wrought-iron gates of the H.A.C. ground. The chauffeur wore battleship grey too, with matching jacket and visored cap. O'Reilly, with us peasants gazing with round eyes and slack mouths, just managed to beat the chauffeur to the opening of the rear door and escape to the dressing-rooms before the salute. The rest of us took one pace backwards.

When we got to Twickenham the next day it transpired that before his late elevation O'Reilly had written the programme notes, producing another unique touch to that eighty-second encounter between Ireland and England. There was a telegram awaiting him at the ground. It was from Johnny Quirke, lately an Irish scrum-half, and it put matters in a certain perspective. It read: 'Heinz beanz are haz beanz!' The vice-president for All Europe enjoyed that one best of all.

In the match the right wing hadn't an awful lot to do. The ball did not run very fluently and he spent most of the afternoon either scrambling the ball away to touch or throwing it into the line-outs. But he got no chance to put the ball under his arm and run.

However, the final stages were interesting. Tony O'Reilly described them thus: 'I found myself at the last moment reduced to bravery. A long English footrush was terminated when – quite out of character – I dived at the feet of the England pack. . . . As I was emerging from momentary unconsciousness, I heard a loud (and, let me confess) Irish voice shouting from the popular terrace: " . . . and kick his bloody chauffeur while you're at it!"'

England won the match 9–3!

From *The Men in Green – The Story of Irish Rugby* by Sean Diffley
(Pelham Books, London, 1973)

Scared

John Robbie

Irish scrum-half John Robbie joined the 1980 Lions tour to South Africa, and later spent several years playing there. In 1976 he had toured New Zealand with Ireland, where the physical side of the game was as intense as in South Africa and Robbie makes no bones about admitting that he was sometimes scared. Ironically that admission takes a lot of bravery to make. Most players are scared at some time, either of opponents or of making a mistake that will cost their side the game; few have confessed it with Robbie's candour.

W.B.B.

We returned home, not quite as heroes but certainly having done better than anyone had expected, and with the makings of a useful side. The management and coaching had been excellent – far better in New Zealand than it was a few years later on the Irish tour to South Africa, but perhaps others would disagree. Overall, I had done well. Despite having an unexciting sort of Test, except for one really great catch under fierce pressure near my own line, the verdict was that I was one of the successes.

I had mixed feelings, though. Sure, I had been part of the only Irish side to have played in New Zealand, and we held our own in nearly all the games. It was also a big thing among my friends at home just to have been a rugby tourist, and to invoke the 'no stories from the tour' rule – all done with a knowing wink, as though I had now joined the ranks of the men about town (nudge nudge, wink wink, and so on). However, there were a number of things worrying me.

I knew that I was not running enough as a scrum-half. I was certainly fit enough, and when I was pushed into situations where there was no alternative, then I usually performed well. It was taking a conscious decision to run, and then seeing the breakthrough, that was the problem.

In every break there is that split-second where you commit yourself, after which you can no longer pass or kick – the point of no return. It is also the point where you leave yourself open to being tackled hard, often by someone you can't see. At this stage I would get away from the side of the scrum or ruck, and then – when I could have gone for the gap – I would angle in, draw the cover and give a pass to a man in support. Mind you, this was often the right thing to do; but there are times when a scrum-half (and indeed any back) has to evidence himself as a threat, make them tackle him, and I wasn't doing this. Looking back, I realize that I never really got over it. Sure, I learnt to conceal it well, and to recognize when there was a break on that did not involve that terrible second when the tackler makes his move. And by working with a good number eight, I made many good breaks where not a hand was laid on me.

It was the other kind of break I could never make, and the only conclusion is that I have always been scared. In fact, in those days I was often very scared on the field. Once, in our game against Canterbury, I displayed real cowardice. The very name 'Canterbury' meant dirty play to me. This was a result of the 1971 Lions tour to New Zealand, when there was a lot of thuggery. Although things had changed by 1976, I (being steeped in the game) had a subconscious terror of the province. Their pack was magnificent the day we played them.

At one stage, a few yards from our line, a scrappy ball was knocked back to me from a line-out. I had to make an instant decision: go forward, kill the ball and back into our pack; or stay back and hope it bounced to me. I chose the latter out of fear. One of their forwards came through, claimed the ball and his pack drove him over for a try.

After the game most people felt that it was in no way my fault: I had decided to wait for the bounce, and had been unlucky. I think I half-believed them. It was only later, when Mike Gibson and I were sharing a soft drink alone in the bar, that I really admitted the cowardice to myself. Quite matter-of-factly, Gibbo asked me if I had stayed back because I was scared. I lied to him, saying that it had been a calculated decision to wait for the bounce, and so on. He said nothing – but I think he knew.

From *The Game of My Life* by John Robbie
(Pelham Books, London, 1989)

A Sad Affair and a Happy Sequel

Edmund van Esbeck

The political troubles in Ireland led to a collective fright on the part of the Scottish and Welsh rugby authorities, who, for the best of motives, refused to allow their players to risk a game in Dublin during the 1972–73 season. Other nations were ready to take the risk, however, and were rewarded for their courage with a welcome they would always treasure.

W.B.B.

Even at the height of the political troubles and violence in Ireland after the 1914–18 war, the international rugby fixtures had been played. In this context, the failure of Scotland and Wales to come to Dublin occasioned great surprise and not a little resentment among Irish rugby supporters. For its part, the IRFU adopted a cool and dignified stance.

Friends are needed in times of stress, and in France Ireland found a friend with whom affinity had begun long after the forming of the old friendships between the home unions. France was willing to oblige one of the family of rugby nations and came to Dublin and met Ireland on 29 April, when the French team got the warm-hearted reception they deserved from the attendance of almost 30,000. It mattered little that Ireland won; it mattered a great deal that the game took place.

In view of the decisions of the Welsh and Scottish Unions and the refusal of British clubs to travel to Ireland, there was a lot of speculation about whether or not the Seventh All Blacks would travel to Ireland for the four games that were on their itinerary in the 1972–73 season. However, all doubts about the intentions of the New Zealanders were removed when their manager, Ernie Todd, announced that they intended to travel to Ireland and fulfil their programme, which was a two-part one, against Leinster and Ulster in November 1972 and against Ireland and Munster in January 1973.

The New Zealanders won a great match against Leinster in Dublin and the following day travelled to Belfast to prepare for the game against Ulster; if Ravenhill was forbidden territory to others, the New Zealanders saw no reason why they should not honour their commitment to play there. They duly arrived, were given a tremendous reception and won into the bargain.

They travelled back to the Republic in January, and Ireland achieved her best result against them by drawing 10–10 on 10 January. A draw was a fair result to a splendid game, but Ireland almost snatched an historic win in the closing minutes. Tom Grace scored a dramatic equalizing try in the right-hand corner within no more than an inch of the dead ball line, and Barry McGann's conversion was off target by inches. Four days previously a penalty goal in injury time had given the New Zealanders a 3–3 draw with Munster at Musgrave Park.

The All Blacks, like the Springboks before them, found rugby in the home countries a more highly organized exercise than at any time in history. In addition, they were perhaps not as good either as their illustrious predecessors, and their team had become noticeably unsettled by what they felt to be an unsympathetic attitude towards them during the early part of the tour. Ireland will, however, always remember the Seventh All Blacks with affection and gratitude. They lived up to the principles on which rugby was nurtured and has prospered. They came, they saw, and they came back again.

The president of the Rugby Union, Dick Kingswell, made it clear in January 1973 that it was his union's intention to bring a team to Dublin to play Ireland on 10 February 1973. Some feelings were expressed in England that the example of Scotland and Wales should be followed, and it was rumoured that some players had expressed doubts about playing in Dublin. The English Union was, however, unanimous in its resolve to play the match unless the Irish Union advised them otherwise, and they duly arrived at Lansdowne Road with their chosen team.

For over a century the happenings on the field of international rugby have stirred men's emotions, but it is doubtful if there was ever a more moving or emotional scene than that at Lansdowne Road when the English side ran on to the field. The entire concourse to a man stood and applauded the English team for five minutes. It was a wonderful sight and a wonderful sound. It was a great occasion for Dick Kingswell and his committee and an even greater one for rugby football. It was hardly material that Ireland won a close match in which England missed more chances than they took.

From *One Hundred Years of Irish Rugby* by Edmund van Esbeck
(Gill & Macmillan, Dublin, 1974)

10
GREAT NATIONS: FRANCE

The Dour French

Alan Watkins

Most neutrals would vote France the team they would most like to watch. The French side of the early 1980s, led by the incomparable Serge Blanco, abounded with world-class players capable of producing rugby of such audacity and skill that spectators and defenders were left open-mouthed in amazement. Sadly that Gallic flair was for some time stifled by the forward obsession of coach Jacques Fouroux, while French rugby has also always had a darker side.

W.B.B.

Tomorrow's encounter between France and England is undoubtedly the match of the Five Nations championship so far. How is it, I wonder, that I feel so little affection for the sides that are involved? This is not, I may say, a matter of pro-Welsh bias. Or I do not think it is. My fellow countrymen can be intolerable when they are on a winning streak, as they were in that most remote of ages, the day before yesterday. They can even be pretty tiresome when they are on a losing streak, as they are now.

In fact my favourite national sides have always been, in no particular order of preference, France, Australia and Ireland. I like France because they have usually tried to play entertaining football. I like Australia for the same reason, and because they have to contend with rival sports in their own land. And I like Ireland because they, too, have to compete for attention in their own country, because they are prepared to have a go and, not least, because they unite Protestant and Catholic, North and South, in one side. Incidentally, this laudable union does not seem to have had the slightest effect on relations between the communities in that country. I once asked Dr Conor Cruise O'Brien why this was so. He replied that rugby was played by the middle classes, soccer by the working classes, and that 'all the trouble' came from the latter.

My emotional preference will be for Ireland over Scotland tomorrow, though I shall not be putting any money on them. Emotionally I shall be neutral between England and France, whereas in the old days I should have been firm for France. What has happened? I have not changed, but the French have. In large French towns you may now see a McDonald's hamburger dispensary among the traditional cafés and restaurants, bistros and bars. The young crowd into the new place; understandably, in a way, because they wish to seem up-to-date. Jacques Fouroux, the French coach, has brought the philosophy of McDonald's to French rugby. He preaches the gospel of success, which is to be achieved through saturation coverage, through uniformity and through bulk.

Not all Fouroux's innovations have been bad. The scrum-half's throwing the ball into the line-out often succeeds in its aim, which is to drag opposing forwards in and to secure better possession. Apart from this, the hooker (a position put into temporary cold storage by Fouroux) has quite enough on his plate already, without having to throw in as well. Oddly enough, the French were the last country to persist with throwing-in by the wings. And many of them would still use the old-fashioned, two-handed, underarm scoop (the only kind of throw I ever mastered, and another reason for my former affection for the French).

How different it is today. And in other respects as well. Any national side that can consistently exclude backs of the class of Denis Charvet and Eric Bonneval must surely be governed more by political pressures than by rugby reason. The omission of these and other gifted players is not, however, Fouroux's chief fault, which is one of commission. French forward play was always rough and sometimes undisciplined. For robustness and occasional indiscipline, Fouroux has substituted organized brutality. I will refrain from naming names, not because I do not know them, but because among many failings of our law of libel is that foreigners can bring actions in our courts, as indeed they do.

This has nothing to do with the eight-man shove, which is a perfectly sensible piece of tactics to employ in certain circumstances – though dropping the hooker entirely, as Fouroux did until recently, raises different considerations. Nor is it a matter of laying down that only giraffes need apply for membership of the back row. No, Fouroux has coarsened and brutalized the national game. France have played attractive rugby this season, despite rather than because of him. It is good news that he will soon be relinquishing his post. Even so, I look forward with trepidation to tomorrow's match.

From *The Independent*, March 1989

An Hour with a Video is Worth a Century of Sweat

Denis Lalanne

Last season in Toulouse the French XV met a completely unknown team, that of the USSR. And this match, which seemed to be of only anecdotal interest, in reality opened our eyes to everything which inhibits and obstructs the pure expression of the game.

On the face of it, one did not give the novice Soviets any more chance of beating the French at Rugby football than one would have given them of beating the West Indies at cricket. It takes a long time to reach another planet, and still more time to conquer it. So imagine our surprise when we saw the Russians playing as if they had already played France a hundred times; as if they had spent the last fifty years perfecting the best ways of stopping the French from playing.

For more than an hour the Russian forwards exerted a well-planned and methodical pressure on every ball which reached the hands of the French half-backs. It was only in the final minutes of the match that the French were able to establish running as the basis of their attacks, and this culminated in two tries for the wings Guy Noves and Daniel Bustaffa. In the meantime, though, the USSR had even found time to score a try themselves. It was produced by an eighty-five-yard run, initiated by the Russian full-back, who intercepted when the French were attacking in his twenty-five.

On the day, the French forwards did not have a good match. Quite frankly the French pack was dominated in the rucks and mauls, partly because it was still suffering from the fatigue of a tour to Japan and Canada, but above all because it had underestimated the capability of its opponents. The fact is that the USSR XV, in its first match at this level, gave the impression of knowing more about the basics of the game than France did after thirty years in the International Championship, which was at about the time that another Russian, Prince Obolensky, caused something of a surprise on the green sward at Twickenham.

It is possible today for Soviet beginners to learn more about Rugby in a few months than the French did in thirty years of heroic exploration, and quite simply they can do it because of the development of modern means of disseminating information which make it possible to examine the strengths and tactics of the opposition in great detail and which make that information available to the whole world. It is not difficult then to make a most detailed match plan as a counter. The Russians probably played their first match against

France a hundred times before they actually went on to the pitch. All they needed was a good video-tape recorder to replay the most recent games played by France.

I do not know if this machine will allow us to reverse the history of the world until, for example, we can eliminate the surprise from such events as Trafalgar and Waterloo, but what I do know is that with it the French XV would not have had to wait until 1958 and the advent of Lucien Mias to discover the indispensable virtues of well-organized forward play – virtues which had to be explored in the heat of battle and not in the cool and well-ordered study of film evidence. Until then the French had learned their Rugby back to front. They had neglected what might be called the bricks and mortar, and here I am thinking of scrummaging, and instead had poured the whole of their talent into Rugby football's equivalent of the decoration, by which I mean the great handling code. They enchanted the public, but they were very badly marked indeed by the examiners.

Today, a good session with a video replaces a century of patience, of sweat, and of tradition. The French game was no stranger to the Russians; they already knew it and all its culture, just as Armstrong knew exactly what he was doing when he stepped on to the moon. But if one transposes this phenomenon to the level of the countries who are members of the International Rugby Football Board, one quickly understands why Rugby has fallen into the hands of the counter-espionage service. World-wide television has reduced the entire world of Rugby to the dimensions of a village where everyone knows everyone else's business. The Rugby field is a sky swept by all the radars of the squad system; a new ploy by the centre three-quarters represents a surprise as big as an Unidentified Flying Object.

Nowadays one can no longer imagine an army like the one of Lucien Mias storming the beaches of South Africa to the stupefaction of the whole country. But the progress in question is not evolution in the best sense. It has only driven the rules of the game into a state of almost total blockage on the chessboard of the pitch, because such scientific study of the strengths of the opposition is only carried out with the object of destroying them. How can one talk of progress when the fundamental concept of carrying the ball is in such decline?

From 1971 until 1978 one team dominated the French club Championship, and it did so by bringing to perfection the understanding of the small print of the law. The team was Béziers, and it was unequalled in swallowing and digesting the ball in the mauls, hiding it for eighty minutes from the view and the appetite of the opposition. It is actually true that in the course of a recent match between Béziers and Auch, an Argentine forward freshly enrolled in the Auch pack ended by crying out, 'What has happened to the ball?'

This cry of despair made his captain almost die laughing. The captain in question was none other than Jacques Fouroux, but in that phrase was summed up the dilemma of the true Rugby game. Jacques Fouroux made light of it and, with his team in opposition to Béziers, put up with everything that the French XV, of which he was then captain, was making others endure. I cannot recall that the pack of mastodons driven by Fouroux earned much in the way of sympathy. It even encountered a lot of hostility, exactly the same hostility that Béziers encountered in France. This proved simply that Rugby which is brought to this degree of organization, strength and rigidity cuts itself off completely from its origins. It must therefore discover another freshness to make its faithful sing.

In this situation the French team have often been accused of sins which are not theirs, because after all the French were the last of the great Rugby nations to realize that one could win a match without scoring a single try and without attacking once through the three-quarters. One morning in 1968 on our way back from New Zealand I was in an Australian television studio surrounded by a pack of interviewers, who fired questions at me off the cuff as surprising as the following: 'Why do French players kick their opponents in the guts?' 'Why does General de Gaulle pay the French International players?'

That was a bit like asking me, 'When did you stop beating your wife?' and I must admit, my breath was taken away by it all. Only the players could make the correct responses to questions like those and they did it on the turf of Sydney Cricket Ground. They did it beautifully, too, with all the gallantry and style associated with players like Villepreux, Maso, Trillo, Cester and Spanghero. Mind you, this did not prevent other players in the French team from being drowned under a shower of penalties for kicks in the guts, even if those kicks did miss.

Similarly, only the players can answer the problems of Rugby today, despite the calculations of the generals of the video. Only the players can dig out the ball buried in the tomb of the mauls. They have to go beyond the knowledge which is now public property and explore again the originality and folly that William Webb Ellis displayed when he found himself confronted by the same problem of blocked play and a buried ball.

I confess that I have great hopes that our own JPR, Jean-Pierre Rives, will turn out to be the revolutionary, generous and slightly mad sportsman who will provide this positive approach that we need so badly. One evening at the beginning of last season, in a street in Tokyo, our JPR said to me, 'It is said that everything has happened before, but I believe that the most important things will happen last.' He was speaking as a simple soldier, as a simple amateur, as sensitive to the wafts of the old-fashioned spirit of the game which blew over our meetings with the best players in Hong Kong and British Columbia. Fate without doubt has had a most felicitous hand in recently giving us Rives first as an improvised captain and now as a most thoroughly deserved appointment. Against Wales last season he breathed new life into his team and into the Championship. In him you see France, newly elected to the International Board, and poised to give back to Rugby football everything which Rugby football has given to France in the last eighty years.

From the *Wales v. France programme*
(Match Publications Ltd, 1980)

Gallic Folly Outweighs Flair

Geoffrey Nicholson

The criticism of England for playing too narrow a game, for relying on Simon Hodgkinson's place-kicking, for running things too close in every sense – that is all academic now. The Grand Slam is theirs again after eleven years and champions don't have to make excuses for themselves.

It is the French who need to make the explanations. In particular, why did they allow the opportunities to slip away through lack of discipline?

Leslie Peard is not the most draconian of referees: he was especially lenient with Xavier Blond, who might well have been sent off for grabbing the official's jersey when he was already pacing out an extra ten metres for dissent to a penalty. But neither is Peard a soft touch, and the French inflicted their own troubles.

The atmosphere was vibrant from the start. The cheering for Serge Blanco as he led out France for his last Five Nations appearance was warm and generous.

But it was nothing to the blast of encouragement that greeted the white jerseys as they filtered out from under the West Stand, and when Hodgkinson put them ahead with three points in the opening minute, England's supporters were prepared to be charmed by every move they made.

The match was crystallized in the opening period. For ten minutes after that first penalty, which looked like confirmation of all that England hoped for, Hodgkinson went wide with his next kick at goal. Saint-André caught the ball behind his line and Blanco ran it out from his posts, setting up a movement which carried the length of the field, with Lafond and Sella running into the spaces to develop the momentum, and Camberabero handling twice before kicking inside for Saint-André to deliver the *coup de grâce*.

By his exacting standards Blanco had an indifferent match, but that one piece of opportunism – the very antithesis of England's methodical approach – left one final, lasting impression of a magnificent career.

After Andrew's drop-goal levelled the scores and another exchange of penalties extended the stalemate, England introduced some panache of their own. With Hodgkinson coming into the attack and Guscott missed out, Underwood was left with the narrowest of passages to the French line. But in running round Lafond with blistering pace, he scored one of his finest tries.

By all the evidence England looked totally in control, but they had still not piled up a big enough score to give them an insurance against possible setbacks. The last two French tries put them under unnecessary pressure in the final quarter, but for all that it added to the enjoyment of a magnificently tense match.

To which criticism, of course, England have every right to reply that a win's a win, and a Grand Slam does not come every decade.

From the *Observer*, 17 March 1991

Captain Courageous

Peter Bills

Jean-Pierre Rives is one French player who is above all criticism, one of the finest and bravest wing-forwards I have seen. Instantly recognizable by his flowing mane of blond hair, Rives always led by example and was always to be found at the heart of the action.

W.B.B.

The eyes were glazed, not through the blood which had almost become his trademark, rather with the mist of emotion which caused a slight twitching of his body, as though it were being subjected to electronic stimulus. Half a dozen injections, administered as an antidote to the stabbing pain he felt at each movement, had been scarcely more effective than aspirin.

We all knew his face well enough; and the blond hair, hanging soaked and dank on a wet rugby afternoon, had already been a rallying sight to the youth of rugby for some six years or more. And yet, it seemed, nothing could have prepared us for the appearance of this man now as he stood at the top of the pavilion steps contemplating the arena like the infantryman his killing ground.

His body quivered with adrenalin, and the muscles tightened. Jean-Pierre Rives, France's captain, understood what was at stake: he knew that a physical nightmare, an afternoon of unremitting agony, lay before him. Thus, even the slightest mental preparation that was calculated to block, at least partially, the worst of the physical torture from his mind was a valuable medicine for him that day.

And yet Rives was not alone. Other men had stood at these steps steeling their muscles and nerves against the torment they knew confronted them. Almost exactly fifty years earlier the cream of Australia's cricketers had to walk through the white wicker gate to face the challenge of 'Bodyline'.

So here we now were, beneath the green tin roof of the old stand, a structure which epitomized the days of Empire if ever a building told of Commonwealth and history. This was Sydney; home of the Strine accent, and playground for a thousand tilting cans of beer. Yet the battle Rives was waging with his own conscience and emotions was a new experience for a man who had epitomized the laid-back, cool, apparently uninterested approach to major sport and its singular demands; the blond-haired flank forward of whom his fellow Frenchmen would tell one after another of humorous anecdotes.

Rives's predecessor as leader of the French national team, Jean-Pierre Bastiat, used to joke: 'At two o'clock in the afternoon, you wouldn't give him ten years to live, he would be so lethargic. But at three o'clock, he would come to life. I have seen him broken, knees demolished, bandaged up, but still he would go on.'

This time it was different. For only fourteen days earlier Rives had dislocated his shoulder four times, an injury which was to cause him physical pain even five years later. The absurdity of the challenge before him was to play and survive a major Test match against the Australians with only one arm of any use. The other hung limp at his side, lifeless and useless. It was a handicap few sane men would have contemplated, still less accepted. But by his action in taking up the gauntlet as best he still could, maintaining all the while his classically Corinthian sporting attitude, Rives revealed the core of his character.

Corinthian? Certainly, a throwback to a bygone age; a man still in love with that era of true sportsmanship, with its close friendships with adversaries; a romanticist of sorts, a complex character who was destined to become the greatest sporting attraction France had seen in decades.

Rives, trapped at the bottom of a ruck in an earlier match at Sydney, against New South Wales, had hissed in pain through clenched teeth, as a rogue boot disfigured his shoulder bone. Of course, rugby men see such things the world over, like the New Zealander raking studs down J.P.R. Williams' face at Bridgend, coolly cutting open the skin almost like some abattoir worker about his trade. The trick, so they tell you, is to get up with a grin, and bound off to the next confrontation. Is it, or should it, be so? Should men like Phil Bennett, captain of the British Lions, 'Benny' to his friends, lie squashed under bodies on a New Zealand tour and feel boots driving like sledgehammers into his body and neck?

As Rives was helped away from Sydney that day, his shoulder bone grotesquely twisted out of position and threatening to burst through the skin, his shrewd, calculating mind had no time for feelings of retribution. The Test match, at Brisbane's colonial style Ballymore ground, lay only eight days away. And France, infected by injuries, was facing major problems.

Bravely as Rives had played all through his career, this was a serious worry. Rives, to his friends, was a man in love with humour. What was the joke he told about himself of a match he played against Romania, a few seasons earlier? 'I took a punch,' he recounted, 'my god, what a punch. It caught me close to my kidneys. I could not move. I said to Jean-Claude Skrela, who was playing on the other flank, "I cannot walk. I cannot stay on the field." And do you know what Skrela said to me? "Why do you want to go off? It does not matter if you cannot walk. You should be running. Stay where you are."'

And the little fellow, with the grappling-arm power of a mechanical scoop and short, scuttling legs which revved almost to danger point when he smelt a whiff of his prey, stayed exactly where he was, playing on in agony. Not much seemed to worry Rives on the rugby field. Even the seriousness inherent in some horrific injuries he incurred left him undaunted.

For Rives, pain was no stranger. In the first, overtly physical encounter with Queensland, France's captain had suffered hideous punishment, as he sacrificed his personal safety for the sake of his team's first victory on the tour.

Loane, No. 8 on that day too, conceded Rives was a man who would willingly endure personal agonies for the benefit of his side: 'That match between Queensland and France was a very physical game. Queensland had never beaten the French and, late in that game, trailed 18–15 with a few minutes remaining. At least twice, we had the French pinned on their own line and probably only needed the ball to make the winning score. But Rives buried himself on that ball to prevent us winning it. He took the consequences and they were pretty severe. We needed a try to win but we lost. Rives took some real punishment to stop that try being scored – the boots were going in and they weren't treading carefully. But he never let go of that damned ball.'

Loane knew his subject. A rugby player of renown, and esteemed in his profession, Loane explored new ground in assessing Rives, a player he faced and played alongside in a career spanning almost a decade. 'Rives,' he reflected, 'took punishment all his career but he seemed impervious to pain. Some guys are like that – Willie Duggan, of Ireland and the British Lions, was another. He seemed to enjoy a physical mauling. I was in South Africa, working, when the French toured there in 1980. It was obvious on that tour how the French players had so much respect for Rives because, in France, to go down on the ball at all is to risk being maimed.

'It's absolutely terrible over there. No one goes on the ground because you get your head kicked in. But here was a guy who spent hours of his rugby life on the ground, taking the treatment. Rives took that bravery too far at times. It is not possible, no matter how much your heart is willing, to contribute fully to a match with a busted shoulder joint.'

Yet here was Jean-Pierre Rives, treading cautiously as he shepherded his side out into Sydney's sunshine. Even to appear was magnificent; to play the entire game, injured as he was, bordered on lunacy.

His appearance brought gasps of disbelief from the French supporters, decked out, quite incongruously in the Australian city, in black berets, and carrying baguettes of French bread. Australians murmured in astonishment or roared with laughter.

Rives's straw-coloured hair tumbled down on to shoulders which resembled a monster's. Heaps of padding, strapping and protection for the damaged shoulder had built the top of the Frenchman's torso into a figure more suited to American football. His protection was almost obscene, hideous on a field of supposed sportsmanship. What place had he here, why this ridiculous charade, of going through the motions simply to get on to the field?

Loane, as amazed as anyone else in the 42,000 crowd, said: 'I was staggered he tried to take on the game, let alone finish it. It was bravery to the point of insanity. OK, the French were running out of players because of injuries. And Rives always led from the front. Perhaps all rugby is folly in the end. But I certainly would have found it impossible to play with that.

'He could not tackle but he tried to take the ball off players several times. It made me think of Napoleon's troops bravely retreating from Moscow. Battered and beaten but still attempting to make a contest of it.'

Battered and eventually beaten, Rives was – but not bowed. And his appearance at Sydney, sustained as it was in the main by sheer will-power, revealed a side of the man his closest acquaintances would come to regard as crucial.

Rives himself said: 'Maybe I should not have played that day. But I did so because on tours there is a special spirit and to know that is to understand these decisions. We were in the same boat that day – and what a boat! So many injuries. The players asked me if I would play and I said "OK". I wanted to be together with them. Everyone knew before the game I could not play very well. But they wanted me with them and that was a great compliment to me.'

That was it; for the boys, for comradeship! The personal honour was superfluous. Rives played because close friends, colleagues, had asked. That old colonial spirit flourished in the mind of France's romantic captain!

Rives tried to explain it thus, 'It is the spirit – l'esprit. Somewhere, something happens. I don't know. Maybe I should not have played, but I don't regret my decision because it was good for the spirit. I was with my friends in the team.'

France's coach, Jacques Fouroux, a small figure cast in the Napoleonic mould, was to reflect at the end of the affair: 'It was madness for Jean-Pierre to play. But as I shared his madness, I was just as mad as he was. It was mad because it didn't change anything. It only accentuated the seriousness of the injury.

'When I was a player myself, I often played with injuries and fractures. You are unconscious of it in the game usually, and I believe you recognize the great player at times like that. But it was not playing with that one serious injury that showed Jean-Pierre's courage. He was always hurt somewhere on his body. The manner in which he played meant that he was hurt every time in some way or another. But he always rose above the pain. That was his great courage, his No. 1 quality. It was fantastic courage.'

From *Jean-Pierre Rives – Romantic or Revolutionary?* by Peter Bills
(Allen & Unwin, London, 1986)

11
GREAT NATIONS: SOUTH AFRICA

Muller + Geffin = Grand Slam

Fred Labuschange

The Fourth Springboks would rank alongside any of the other great teams I have mentioned. Magnificent forwards, including a devastating back row and a slick, well-organized back division, were more than a match for their British opponents, but the foundations for that all-conquering tour were laid in the home series against New Zealand in 1949.

W.B.B.

Ever hear of a pack of forwards being selected by the pound?

Nonsense?

Not at all. I can tell you that the 1949 All Black selectors virtually picked the fifteen forwards for the South African tour, by the simple expedient of putting them on the scale and then selecting the heaviest of the bunch!

From trial match to trial match, they humped their portable scales, and the dressing-rooms afterwards must have resembled the Chicago stockyards, as they weighed and graded the beef on the hoof.

Such was this fixation to ensure that the Springbok giants (mostly imagined) must be matched in size and weight, that at least two of New Zealand's most dynamic forwards of the time were ignored.

Avoirdupois was king in New Zealand rugby thinking, and anybody weighing less than 200 pounds was dead in a touring sense.

Thus an automatic selection like K. Arnold, for instance, found that his weight of 175 pounds was viewed with scorn by the selectors, whose whole horizon was crowded with visions of the 1937 All Blacks being ground into mincemeat by Philip Nel's pack of 'Iron men'. Size and more size was the watchword, and in the end the pack picked averaged a record, for New Zealand, of 210 pounds.

If only the All Black selectors had known at the time the two major mistakes they were in the act of making! Firstly this weight-watchers hang-up; and secondly picking the team the year before the actual tour! Combined, these blunders meant that, not only were the selected All Blacks psychologically affected – knowing they were in the team they relaxed and accepted the fêtes and adulation automatically bestowed on them in that rugby-mad country – but they were also unable to keep to any kind of training schedule.

Thus, in the eight months between selection and the first match of the tour, a lot of that avoirdupois turned into flab. The result was an acute case of adiposis among a number of the All Black heavyweights.

But when the side arrived at Hermanus in the Cape Province a full three weeks before the tour started, South Africans rubbed their eyes in amazement.

These slab sided All Blacks could not scrum worth a halfpenny! Not Springbok style, anyway. This fact was to give rise to a controversy which can be settled right now.

Was it Dr Danie Craven or Bo Wintle who took the visitors in hand, and taught them the rudiments of 3–4–1 scrumming? The All Blacks were overweight, but they were not stupid.

It was soon apparent to the props, like Auckland's terrifically strong Johnny Simpson, that New Zealand had no chance of beating the Springboks to the ball in the set scrums, if they continued to pack in the outmoded and mainly disorganized All Black pattern.

There was only one thing to do and Simpson did it – he asked for assistance from a former Western Province prop forward, Bo Wintle, who was acting as South African tour manager for the first half of the trip.

The story goes that Simpson's request came after the sixth game of the tour against Natal. Another version is that Dr Craven gave the All Blacks their first lessons before the first Test in Cape Town.

However, it is quite clear that Wintle had already started giving the All Blacks some pointers at Hermanus, and then, later, acceded to Simpson's request via Fred Allen, the All Black captain in Durban for more comprehensive coaching.

This incredible fact (there would be a riot in both New Zealand and South Africa today if the local experts were to coach the enemy!) led to a marked improvement in the scrumming technique of the visitors. Three matches later, in Kroonstad, they decided to try and get in a session with the best man in the business – Danie Craven.

Now, at that time Craven was not only a national selector, he was also the appointed Springbok coach for the Test series.

When the request reached him he was sharing a room with another famous Springbok, Gerry Brand. Dr Craven recalls that he consulted with Brand on his dilemma, and together they decided that he should coach the All Blacks. 'We had decided to help them because I was convinced that if their scrumming was not radically changed the tour would be a flop, and they would lose all the Tests,' Craven told me recently.

'So I called them together right there, and in their stockinged feet they scrummed down in the hotel's lounge.' Ironically, the All Blacks did lose all the Tests, anyway, but at least it can never be said it was because they could not scrum.

In fact, they learnt their lesson so well that they were beating the Boks by the time the third Test came round. There is an interesting twist to the scrumming story, however, which Dr Craven recalls in a somewhat wry manner. Apparently when he got to New Zealand seven years later as manager of the ill-fated 1956 Springboks, he found himself accused of having used the knowledge, which he of necessity must have had, of the All Blacks scrumming technique, to beat the New Zealanders in the Tests!

I suppose had Fred Allen's side won the series, Dr Danie Craven would today be a Freeman of the City of Wellington (New Zealand)! Such is gratitude.

But getting to know the 3–4–1 scrum technique was simply not enough to save the great

New Zealand crusade to avenge the 1937 defeats. At it turned out the 1949 tour was fated to become to the shocked New Zealand public what the 1956 débâcle became to the equally stunned South Africans.

Something akin to a blot on the national image, and therefore to be wiped out at the first available opportunity.

But what did happen to the 'Fortyniners?' Why did they fail to strike rugby gold in South Africa? There can, of course, be no single answer, but to put it in a nutshell, the South Africans won because they were, on the year, the better side.

And strange as it may seem, the most virulent critics of that tour, and one in particular, mellowed to such an extent over two decades that credit is at last being given in New Zealand to the actual playing ability of the Springboks, as well as the brilliant, and astute, tactical planning of Danie Craven.

> From *Goodbye Newlands, Farewell Eden Park* Fred Labuschange
> (Howard Timmins, Cape Town, 1974)

A Question of Attitude

John Reason

Bleddyn Williams is in no doubt that the 1951 Springboks were the best side he played against.

'They were fully equipped. They were superb up front, with forwards like Jaap Bekker, Chris Koch, "Salty" du Rand, Ernst Dinkelmann and that great back row of Basie van Wyk, Stephen Fry and Hennie Muller and they had a very sound player at fly-half in Hannes Brewis. They also had Tjol Lategan in the centre, a marvellous player, and Ryk van Schoor, who could tackle like a ton of bricks. "Chum" Ochse on the wing scored some wonderful tries, and Johnny Buchler at full-back was as safe as houses.

'Even more important than that, of course, was that the Springboks were prepared to use all the equipment that they had at their disposal, whereas the All Blacks were not. South Africa had good backs and they used them. It has always remained a mystery to me that the All Blacks never really tried to develop their back play until comparatively recently, when they found that their forwards no longer had the advantages of superior organization which they always used to have over British packs.

'The Springboks showed the modern world how to scrummage and whatever may have happened in the 'Thirties when Bennie Osler was playing for them, they showed us how to use that ball in the first two series after the war. The All Black forwards could match the Springboks with their play in the loose, particularly in their own country, and in "Tiny" White they had a line-out forward who could beat anybody, but they never really used the ball they won. The Springboks did and that was basically the difference between the two teams. It was a question of attitude, and as a midfield back, I saw the difference very clearly.'

Williams himself certainly impressed the 1951 Springboks. He was such an absolute master of centre three-quarter play that Ken Jones, an Olympic sprinter as well as the winner of a record number of caps for Wales as a winger, even felt tempted to leave Newport and join Cardiff! The Springboks thought that there were only two players in Britain who might have got into their team, and Bleddyn Williams was one of them. The other was Roy John, also of Wales.

Hennie Muller made an equal impression on his hosts. He ranged the country demonstrating just why he was the most significant number eight to play in international Rugby since Wavell Wakefield. By the time he had finished, he had any number of British players saying 'Amen' to the admiring and rueful judgement of Bob Scott, the New Zealand full-back, at the end of the All Blacks' tour of South Africa in 1949. 'I would say unhesitatingly that he was the greatest loose forward I have ever seen. He had great speed – he was very nearly as fast as our Peter Henderson, who was an Empire Games sprinter. His hands were good. He could kick well. He was always alert and he could last out a test match on a hard ground and a warm day without visible difficulty. As if all that wasn't enough, he was completely fearless and quite ruthless.'

The Springboks returned to their country to look forward to what would obviously be a much less demanding home series against Australia in 1953. Hennie Muller went through that series as captain of South Africa but he retired at the end of it. Muller's health had been of concern to Danie Craven for some time. The picture of his drawn, exhausted face as he received the congratulations of the Australian captain, John Solomon, after South Africa had won the third test at Durban gave some idea of the depths of the reserves that he drained with the mercilessly sustained running he did for his country. He died of a heart attack in middle age. Looking at that face, it is not difficult to see why.

From *The World of Rugby* by John Reason and Carwyn James
(BBC, London, 1979)

The Fourth Springboks

R.K. Stent

A popular summary of two different attitudes, supposed to exist in the British Isles and South Africa, is that, in Britain, rugby football is played for the purpose of keeping fit, whereas in the Union, the purpose of keeping fit is to play rugby.

Judging from what we saw and heard on the tour just ended, the generalization about attitudes may be a fallacious one. In many parts of Britain there is no less an ardent approach to the game than that which exists in South Africa. But circumstances and conditions are very different. Early darkness in winter-time means that it is not possible for clubs to hold mid-week practices – at least not along the lines that they are held in South Africa, where, practically every evening, a full-scale game is held for one team or another. And, apart from the international and county championships, there are no recognized competitions. Unofficial 'merit tables' are published regularly by the news-papers, but there are no such things as leagues or logs.

Public interest is not minimized by their absence in Wales, for instance, as inter-club rivalry is traditionally beyond what any competition could create, but in other parts there may be a more casual interest in the results of the matches which, in turn, has some effect on the general outlook.

At all events there was much surprise, and even an occasional raised eyebrow, at the seriousness and the vigour with which the Springboks got down to their training programme during their first fortnight in England, when they were quartered at Bournemouth. They read this view in a home newspaper: 'It seems that galloping up and down the field nearly forty times, in addition to hopping across it on alternate legs, with a full-blown practice thrown in, is too much.'

But Danie Craven's training plan had been carefully considered and its influence on the ultimate success of the tour was as great as any one other factor. Their great fitness helped the Springboks win many matches with a storming finish, and the fact that there were so few serious injuries in the heavy programme of thirty-one matches was not just luck.

Danie had explained his plans to the players soon after they sailed from Cape Town in the *Pretoria Castle*. He would keep them in trim on the voyage with a mild but regular PT routine, concentrating on exercises which were designed to strengthen the muscles and protect places susceptible to injury – the knee-joints, shoulders, wrists, hips, hamstrings.

He also had exercises to ginger up general alertness, shaped to keep the players, as baseball players say, 'aware', so that snapping up a pass, slipping through a gap, diving at a chance try and other split-second matters would become instinctive things when they were once again on a rugby field.

The next stage of the Craven Plan was to shake off the effects of the voyage with a series of loosening-up runabouts at Bournemouth. During this time the players used a ball, made in the four-panelled English style, rubbed in mud manufactured on the spot (no rain fell at all during this period), to give them some notion as to what it would be like in unaccustomed conditions ahead (they had also thrown it about, after it had been freely rubbed with grease and wet soap, on the ship).

The tempo was then speeded up with full-pace handling movements by the backs, serious scrumming by the two packs and some combined operations, when dribbling rushes had to be stopped by a player nominated by a sudden shout.

Craven spent a long time on the scrums. He was not satisfied, at first, that all were pushing and pulling with their arms at the same moment. Others, he advised to straighten their legs as they heaved forward. I recall his calling out: 'The buttocks of the flanks and the number eight must disappear, pull those hips down!'

The 'first shove' has been as potent a reason as any why the Springbok scrumming developed into the great force it did. Synchronizing all efforts to achieve this was another matter, which took a lot of the time at these trial runs, and various words and signs were used to indicate when it was wanted.

Line-out technique was another main source of concentration. It may not have been known then how severely anything approaching a barge would be penalized and what small importance, by contrast, would be given to throwing the ball in straight (it seems, in the Union, the seriousness of these two offences is regarded in an inverse ratio, but I would not say that the referees in the British Isles are not right!). However, a first instruction was to avoid lunging and at all events never to hit out.

General tackling efficiency was examined and each man had to show that it was second nature for him to take off on one foot and have both feet off the ground at the time of the tackle. Punting and fielding high kicks, a rolling ball, a diagonal kick were matters not left only to the backs. And hand-to-hand movements, in which a change of direction was a frequent theme, were tried again and again.

On the specialist side, scrum-halves were kept busy streamlining their dives; centres and wings were polishing up their inter-passing; drop- and place-kicking experts tried all manner of distances and angles – all under the vigilant eye of Craven, who seemed from the comprehensive way in which he reviewed every occasion never to miss the slightest incident.

It was the basic, rudimentary things, then, that were concentrated on first – that, and the building up of match fitness and stamina. As the day for the first game appeared, more advanced lessons were scheduled, more sophisticated movements tried. All possible conditions were considered and the players had to go out early one morning so as to get a 'natural' feel of a wet ball – there was still dew about at that hour. With this Craven demonstrated his semi-lob pass, which he had found so useful when he had toured the United Kingdom with the 1931 Springboks. 'There is less chance of its slipping away if this method is used,' he explained, and showed that the technique involved a shorter follow-through.

His tip that a wet ball should also be caught against the body was remembered by the team when they did strike rainy weather and, strangely enough, when this came, their handling was even better than it had been under fine conditions – Neath and Aberavon was an example.

Danie timed this training plan for the first match so that it reached its peak with a full-scale practice a couple of days before the game against South-Eastern Counties. This was in order that the players could ease off and be relaxed before they had to play. And those familiar with the training routines used by most athletes and boxers will not consider the system used here to have been either novel or too rigorous.

Meanwhile, in the pre-match team talks, Craven had been discussing the side's general style of play and the application of particular tactics.

He told the players in the course of one discussion: 'Rugby is a house supported by four main pillars, and these pillars are: (i) handling, and all forms of passing; (ii) kicking in its various uses – touch-kicking, short punts, cross-kicks, diagonal kicks, grubber kicks, dropping for goal, place-kicking; (iii) scrumming, both tight and loose scrumming and its close associations such as wheeling, and (iv) line-out play.'

Under each of these four heads, he discussed attacks developing from them both through an individual and through a team effort. Defensive plans were discussed on the same basis.

When the time came for the first match to start there was a harmony of ideas that could hardly have been anticipated. It was obvious that with thirty players sufficiently experienced to be chosen as internationals there would be different notions about various phases of the game. One of Craven's tasks was to mould these into one. He went a long way towards achieving this in those days in Bournemouth – and the matches did the rest.

I recall Danie telling a group of Welsh enthusiasts whom he addressed towards the end of the tour: 'We may not have any great stars in this side, but that fact has helped towards enabling everyone to fit into the machine. Every man knew what was expected of him as a *team player*.'

From *The Fourth Springboks* by R.K. Stent
(Longmans, London, 1952)

The Terrible-tempered Mr Mark

Chris Greyvenstein

If Danie Craven's coaching played a big part in the success of the Springboks, Craven himself learned much from an even more indomitable figure, 'Oubaas Mark'.

W.B.B.

He would stalk along the touchlines of the rugby grounds at Stellenbosch. His hat, pulled down over the broad, white forehead, hid the sparse hair and added to his forbidding appearance. The bushy eyebrows almost met as he frowned angrily at the snorting, straining young players training before him.

He was August Friedrick Markötter, known as Mr Mark and Oubaas Mark to the rugby world as he was certainly one of the most unique characters ever to lift a sport out of the doldrums of dullness. In his lifetime Mr Mark was more than just a brilliant coach and amazingly discerning selector. For more than half a century he was the dictator who ruled South African rugby from his shooting stick throne. He stood no nonsense from anyone and it took more courage to oppose him than to tease a Bengal tiger.

One Saturday afternoon, for instance, he turned up at Newlands as usual without his member's pass. A new and keen gatekeeper stopped him.

The old man withered him with a stern glare and rapped out: 'Get out of my way, young fellow! This place belongs to me.' And through the gates he went.

But it was seldom he wasted his ire on officious gatekeepers. The highest officials in rugby and the vast army of players were really his favourite targets. And whatever he did, he always did with the singleminded purpose of improving the game and the player.

During one practice at Coetzenburg he got particularly annoyed with a certain player and he rounded off a scathing verbal assault with a resounding kick to the offender's hindquarters. The highly indignant student walked off the field. The next afternoon he was back and as he prepared to take his place, Oubaas Mark called him.

'Look laddies,' he said. 'I never kick a man down. I always kick him up. I don't kick fools.'

And that was his philosophy. He was not interested in the mediocre player but heaven help the man with rich potential. Over the years it became the highest honour for a player to collect a kick on the pants or a crack over the back with his famous stick. It was interpreted, and correctly so, as painful but definite proof that you were a player to watch!

Sif Loots, who was deprived of Springbok colours by a knee injury, had a shattering first meeting with Mr Mark. In practice he missed a certain try by attempting too much on his own and the blast from Mr Mark's whistle echoed from the surrounding mountains.

'Get me a cane,' Loots was ordered and not suspecting anything he cut a sturdy branch from a nearby tree.

'Put your head into the scrum!' was the next order and then and there Loots, later, incidentally, to become a minister of religion, got the hiding of his life.

Dr Danie Craven, who grew to understand Mr Mark better than perhaps anybody else ever did, had an even more puzzling introduction. The night before an important match he was summoned from his bed to go immediately to Mr Mark's house. When he arrived there Mr Mark, hat on his head, was busy explaining tactics to several first team players with the aid of a few coins.

Craven could not make head or tail of what was going on. Suddenly Mr Mark looked piercingly at him. 'Get me?' he asked.

Startled, Craven answered in the affirmative.

'Explain,' Mr Mark ordered.

Completely flabbergasted, Craven kept quiet and was then told exactly what Mr Mark thought of him.

'When I finally escaped I was convinced of two things,' Dr Craven said later. 'The first, that I knew absolutely nothing about rugby and the second, that Mr Mark was a mighty dangerous man!'

Oubaas Mark hated to see mistakes made on the rugby field and he never hesitated to correct players of other clubs.

Once walking along the touchline at Newlands he saw a Gardens wing make a bad mistake and without further ado he trotted on to the field, snorted 'You bloody fool!' through his bristling moustache, and then lashed out at the surprised player with his ever present walking stick. Everybody on the stand and all the players burst out laughing but, without a glance at them, the irascible Oubaas carried on with his constitutional.

As a selector he never thought it much of an art to spot potential backline stars, but he was fascinated by forwards. He made the selection of forwards a mathematical affair. He once showed Cyril Medworth how he selected packs first on a weight basis, then to balance heights and finally how to blend the eight men with all the best qualities he could find in them. He preferred strong and tough forwards and always used to describe light forwards as 'chicken feed'. The old boxing adage of a 'good big 'un' better than a 'good little 'un' meant a lot to him.

Earlier in his career he regarded the full-back as the most important man among the backs. 'Get your best man and put him at full-back,' he would say. 'Then pick your halves and centres, and put any bloody fool who can run on the wing.' Later in life he regarded the centres as the most important players. 'Pick them first,' he said. 'They must be born.'

Cyril Medworth summed up Mr Mark's attitude as a selector very well when he wrote: 'He would make up his mind instantly about a back or a loose forward. But he was far more cautious with a tight forward. His attitude was that locks and front-rankers proved themselves in the last ten minutes of a hard game.'

Dr Danie Craven asked him once to list the duties of a forward. His answer was: 'First duty is to push. Second duty is to push. Third duty is to push.'

Mr Mark stood no nonsense when he wanted something done his way during committee meetings.

At one meeting André McDonald, the famous Springbok loose forward, was proposed as captain and the Oubaas immediately got up and said: 'McDonald has been proposed. Who will dare to propose anyone else?'

And that was that.

Although it was no secret that Mr Mark was fond of a drink, he was against players partaking of the stronger forms of liquid refreshment. It was his invariable custom to walk into a bar with a few players and then to order the barman to bring 'orange for the players and the usual for myself'. Any players found drinking on weekdays were invariably punished and he never forgot or completely forgave them their indiscretions.

One night on a rugby visit to Johannesburg he spotted two of his players buying whiskies in a nightclub. He promptly walked up to them, drank both whiskies himself and then ordered shandies for them. After a game he saw to it that his players received a shandy each in the dressing-room immediately after the showering.

He abhorred professionalism in rugby in any form. His last appearance at a meeting of the Western Province Rugby Union took place when Stellenbosch and several other clubs decided to break away because they would not play for war funds during the last war. That night he made a touching declaration of faith during his speech when he said: 'Mr Chairman, I have no religion and I have no politics. My religion and my politics are rugby. The students are my children. No father will forsake his children. I am going with my children.'

And then, with the old belligerence showing for a fleeting few seconds, he looked straight at the chairman and the men flanking him and said: 'And when we come back I hope some of you won't be here!'

From 'The South African Sportsmen' in The Rugby Companion by Wallace Reyburn
(Stanley Paul, London, 1969)

Pale Shadow

Fred Labuschange

Another victorious series for the Springboks, this time against the 1970 All Blacks, saw the end of the Test career of the great Colin Meads. South African writer Fred Labuschange saw the great man's injury and subsequent loss of form as one of the crucial factors in the result of the series.

W.B.B.

Would Burk and Vodanovich have failed had Colin Meads not been injured? I put it this way because failure on a rugby tour is, after all, losing the Test series.

My personal opinion is that the Springboks would still have won; but it would have been a far closer thing than it eventually turned out to be.

Meads was in terrific form right from the start of the tour. In fact, although, as we've seen earlier, he was a mighty player on his previous visit here as far back as 1960, he seemed not to have lost any of his edge ten years later. If anything, experience had added a dash of cunning to his tremendous talent, and granite-like physique. This enabled him to not only inspire the younger players in the side, but also save himself a lot of running around, and unnecessary effort.

With Lochore on the injured list from the start of the tour (following a wrist fracture in Perth on the way over) Meads took over the captaincy with obvious pride. And he led by superb example whenever he captained the side. Ironically, the first match in which Brian Lochore took over his side from Meads, the great King Country player received his broken forearm which was to have such a decided effect on the series.

The injury occurred during the 'brawl' of a match at Springs against Eastern Transvaal where no less than five All Blacks were placed on the casualty list.

Meads' injury did not, at first, seem to make too much difference to the efficiency of the ruthless All Black machine. They had, up to the time when Meads was injured, compiled the astonishing record of playing six provincial games without conceding a single try!

They did so in the next match – against the highly touted Transvaal – but still won handsomely by 34–17. Transvaal notched two tries, but the one was touched down after an obvious knock-on. By the time the first Test came round in Pretoria, the New

Zealanders had, in ten matches, conceded only six tries – but against these half-dozen they had notched an incredible fifty-six of their own!

It would seem, therefore, that Meads was, at first, not sorely missed, as Alan Sutherland blossomed into a fine lock-forward, and the big Taranaki man, Alan Smith, joined Sam Strahan in jockeying for Meads' spot in the first Test.

Subsequent events showed, however, that even in the second, and only, victorious All Black Test, the drive, strength and actual presence on the field of Colin Meads were sorely needed.

When I say this, I mean the fully fit, utterly fearless Meads of the pre-Eastern Transvaal match, where he was injured, presumably by accidentally hitting the local hooker on the head. With his forearm?

Be that as it may, Meads was persuaded, not that he needed much persuasion, to play in the third Test in Port Elizabeth with his arm in a leather guard.

It happened to be his fiftieth Test match for the All Blacks, and, predictably, it was his worst.

I had seen Meads in action in every rugby-playing country belonging to the International Rugby Board, except Australia. In New Zealand – his first Test against the Australian Wallabies – England, Wales, Ireland, Scotland, South Africa and even in France. This is not name dropping – others have also been there – but is only to illustrate why I felt so absolutely heartsore that day in the Boet Erasmus stadium.

Even though I was understandably bucked by the splendid Springbok victory, my joy was clouded at the sight of Meads – or rather the pale shadow of the Meads who became a legend in his playing days, and who will continue to grow in stature as the years go by.

Colin Meads passed from the South African Test scene that day, although he did, in fact, play in the final Test at Ellis Park. His performance in the Port Elizabeth Test was enough to leave one with the undoubted knowledge that, even should Meads' arm knit completely, the spark was gone – for ever.

From *Goodbye Newlands, Farewell Eden Park* by Fred Labuschange
(Howard Timmins, Cape Town, 1974)

Danie Gerber

Gareth Edwards

South Africa's political troubles during the 1970s and 1980s prevented their players from testing themselves against top-class international opposition. There is no doubt, however, that players of the calibre of Danie Gerber would have been great international rugby stars without their country's years of sporting isolation.

W.B.B.

Had it not been for the political shadow cast over rugby in South Africa for the past two decades and thus the limitation of her sporting contacts with other nations, I have no doubt that Danie Gerber would have proved himself one of the century's best midfield players. Even though, as I write, his cap total is a mere nineteen, both opponents and onlookers at matches in which he has been involved acknowledge that the Eastern Province centre is a player of extra quality.

Take, for a start, New Zealand, whose one failure in world rugby has been their inability to win a series in South Africa. Ten minutes from the close of the third unofficial 'Test' of 1986, the Cavaliers were all square at 18–18 and looked hopeful of reaching Ellis Park, Johannesburg, for a final shoot-out with everything still to play for in the rubber. The Springboks desperately needed a decisive, morale-bashing score to snatch victory and put the series out of the tourists' reach. It was Gerber who provided it, capitalizing on good approach work by Carel du Plessis, to elude the defence and scorch thirty-five metres for a try that broke the Cavaliers' spirit. When the whistle went for time, they were 33–18 adrift!

What about England? Well, they will think back miserably to 1984, when Gerber gave them a real run-around. Before his own people in the First Test at Port Elizabeth, he gave the tourists a foretaste of what was to come with a single try before shattering them in the first half of the Second Test at Ellis Park with a hat trick – which took him only eighteen minutes!

Ireland? Yes. Danie Gerber has done them some damage too, scoring a couple of tries at Cape Town in the First Test the Irish played on their short tour of 1981. When Scotland opened their new stand at Murrayfield, the South African centre crossed for two tries for the invitation Barbarians XV. And he scored four tries (including a First Test hat trick) against the South Americans in 1982.

And Wales? Well, he hasn't had a chance to play against the national XV, but there was a marvellous Easter Saturday at the club ground, Cardiff Arms Park, when Danie was in the Barbarians side that met my old club: on that occasion, his contribution was four tries, one of them begun deep inside the tourists' twenty-two and ranking with the most memorable ever seen at Cardiff. I understand he describes the Arms Park as his favourite ground . . . well, I'm not surprised at that.

I've set down those statistics carefully because they do demonstrate his consistency. That kind of scoring is beyond the reach of the ordinary player and suggests great gifts and natural ability. Gerber possesses the perfect build for a centre, six feet tall and weighing thirteen stones twelve pounds. His hands are good and you'll see from action pictures that he holds the ball before him when he's on the move – that's the way to invite defenders to buy a dummy. His tackling is in the firm, fearless tradition of the best Springbok midfield men.

Apparently he is a fitness fiend, a tendency helped by the job he does as a sports administrator, which allows him to put in a two-hour training schedule each day. This starts with a quick 300 sit-ups! For purely sporting reasons, it was a shame the Springboks were not represented at the World Cup. For example, how would Danie Gerber have fared against that other great centre of the 'Eighties, Philippe Sella? What a riveting contest that would have been!

From *100 Great Rugby Players* by Gareth Edwards
(MacDonald Queen Anne Press, London, 1987)

12
GREAT NATIONS: AUSTRALIA

Waltzing Wallabies

Stephen Jones

The Australians have produced two great sides and two absolutely outstanding individuals in the last decade. The 1991 Wallabies, inspired by the brilliance of David Campese, were worthy winners of the World Cup, but for me, the 1984 Grand Slam Wallabies, with a back line superbly orchestrated by Mark Ella, made an even greater impact, showing skills that none of the Five Nations could match.

W.B.B.

The first priority is to give a tumultuous welcome to the return of artistry to international rugby. Australia disappeared over the horizon in the last quarter, in a blaze of skills and pace and with three superlative tries. It was all in remarkable contrast with the bogged-down trench warfare of recent rugby history.

But if the artists killed England off, then the artisans supplied all the weapons. Australia have spent their tour so far watching Steve Cutler, their line-out giant, soaring off into a shambles of loose tapping and general flippancy. Yesterday, they stopped spectating and piled in.

When Cutler or Tuynman tapped the ball, there was always someone around to sweep up. Therefore Australia were in such unchallenged control at the line-out that the pressure on the other parts of their team never became a factor.

Add to this the fact that the Australian scrum was never in trouble and that Poidevin was so superbly hungry at the breakdown, and suddenly all chinks of light for untried, inexperienced, anguished England were blacked out.

England did have a few teeth sunk into the game at half-time, when they turned to play downwind at 3–3. But that was the limit of their aspiration.

The fact that England's front five was given such a thorough roasting made the performance of their half-backs and back row as individuals even more remarkable. The calmness of Melville and Barnes and the exuberance of Butcher and Rees were truly remarkable. Stringer, too, was generally assured at full-back. But the rest of England's effort was painfully short of international class.

Nothing at all is going to happen for them until they put together a competitive scrum and line-out, and nothing they produced yesterday suggested that they are on the point of doing so.

The Australian midfield had lacked conviction in the first half but all that changed very quickly, and all the pretty patterns carried the hallmark of genius. Ella scored the first try when a loop with Lynagh sent him gliding through to the posts.

It definitely seemed to me that the Australian centres ran out in front of Ella in an innocent but nevertheless illegal blocking manoeuvre. Slack had already been penalized on the tour under the same circumstances. But Ella scored, and legal or not it was lovely to watch.

By the time Burke arrived to replace the injured Moon, Australia were playing basketball. With his first touch, Burke released Gould and the full-back with languid movements but electric reactions sent Lynagh overlapping outside him to score.

In fact, this sealed a remarkable afternoon for Lynagh. He had been brought in to kick goals but proceeded to fire almost every kick wide of the posts. At the same time he provided the rich compensation of an authoritative performance in the centre.

Lynagh's try made it 13–3 deep into the last quarter and even the English supporters sunk back in their seats in gloom simply had to sit up and enjoy the waves of Australian attacks.

The best try was the last, by Poidevin. Gould picked up a loose ball under pressure but he managed to fire away a long pass to Ella. The ball was at toenail height when it reached Ella but he picked it up at top pace and sent Campese away down the left wing. Poidevin, supporting faithfully, scored near the posts.

Only the perseverance of Butcher and Rees in defence kept the score down. A crushing tackle by Butcher on Gould saved a certain try and the ability of both England wings to ward off their opposite numbers was another feature of the England defence.

England's attacking achievements can be briefly summarized as an occasional, unsupported run by Carleton, an occasional, unsupported charge by Butcher, and a lone break-out by Underwood.

Their prospect of scoring otherwise rested solely on Barnes and his goal-kicking, and even that was sub-standard.

From the *Sunday Times*, 4 November 1984

Like Giants Among Pygmies

Stephen Jones

Half an hour before the match at Pontypool, the Australians emerged in their track suits to warm up. They formed a circle to perform exercises. Inside the circle, pacing around with a justifiable swagger, was Alan Jones, the coach. As the players circled him, stretching and tuning themselves mentally, Jones flourished a rolled umbrella, looking for all the world like a circus ringmaster. The image was apt. Jones has proved a superbly clever coach, and he produced a stylish team, but I still have the feeling that we have not seen what we think we have seen.

The style is undeniable. Australia's back play, orchestrated by the uniquely brilliant Mark Ella, was a fascinating collection of loops, mass-moves and flipped passes, often setting up a runner bursting into the line. The basic skills came naturally, the reactions of the players were razor-sharp, then support play came in waves. Bravely, they scored dazzling tries at important stages of each international match. It was usually Ella, Gould and Campese who provided the brilliance, but there were dependable players from the bog-standard ranks – Lynagh, Stack – to carry it through. If the ball went loose, all the backs became ball-grabbing flankers.

There are some qualifications. There were days in which all the moves came to nothing, and in any case, one of the foundations of their game was nothing more mystical than a great big hoof into the air which everyone chased after. Another rule of the tour was, 'no Ella, no effect'. But beyond doubt, the Australians were virtuosi. Now everyone is insisting that we British have been taught the lesson that we must totally rethink our back play, our ambitions, that we are boring.

In fact, the lesson was nothing of the sort. The real value of the tour was that it showed us how far back our forward game has gone. Everybody knew that we no longer play a dazzling game. But on the evidence of the tour matches, we are now incompetent at playing our narrow game as well.

We were until recently a nation of scrummagers, because if you scrummage well, the rest of the game is five times easier to play. After Cardiff had scrummaged powerfully against Australia, the outstanding Tom Lawton and his tight forwards went unchallenged for fourteen matches. It was only when Graham Price of Pontypool took hold of Rodriguez, lowered him into the position he wanted him and, with his colleagues, drove Australia back fifteen yards in one scrum, that we realized what we were missing. It was only when Jeff Squire, visibly lacking fitness, put the finger on the Australian back row all round the field at Pontypool, that we discovered the extent of the decline in our back-row play.

Added to that, kicking of British teams in support of their forwards was staggeringly bad. Roger Gould is a tremendous full-back. He catches everything you kick at him. But he is a big man. No one varied the kicks to make him turn, everyone kicked up and unders too long, so that he was given time. Wyllie of Scotland, Ker of the South of Scotland, Barnes of England, Dean of Ireland, Davies of London, Cusworth of the Midlands, Goldsworthy of Pontypool, Dacey of Wales – you name them, they kicked it straight down the throat of the Australian full-back. The tour was never under sustained pressure. Think about that before you bemoan the absence of thrills and spills. Until we rebuild the foundations, we can forget about the dazzle.

Now that we are all settled in the correct classroom for the Australian lessons, we can consider the question I have heard asked so often during the past week. Just how good are the Australians? Answer: very good indeed.

For one thing, they maintained their fitness. Whereas recent British touring teams have dropped like flies, the Australians remained superbly fit and well, so the obvious lack of cover in so many positions, which made their midweek team so vulnerable, never showed on Saturdays.

Australia also negotiated cunningly what I felt would be the major barrier, the harshness of the fixture list, by caring only for the international matches. If this meant that the second XV were cast to the wolves, so be it. If they lost, so be it. Every touring coach says he is there to win the big ones. Alan Jones was the first really to mean it.

So let us praise a team that played wisely, fairly, attractively. But let us not go along with the starry-eyed euphoria which has greeted them this week. Remember that the combined efforts of the four international teams ranged against them never amounted to more than a rabble.

England and Ireland are trying to recover from a period of total collapse. Wales are emerging slowly from such a period, yet on the day they played Australia it didn't look like it. They were dreadful. They will be back. Scotland were unrecognizable as the championship team of last season.

OK, so Australia won a Grand Slam. So, in the prevailing circumstances, would Romania, Cardiff, Pontypool, the second XVs of South Africa and New Zealand. Old Rottinghamians would have stood a chance, too.

From the *Sunday Times*, 16 December 1984

The Mark of Magic

Greg Campbell

No scriptwriter or composer could have written or arranged such a fitting finale to a rugby career. Mark Ella, the former celebrated Wallaby fly-half and captain, ended his playing days in exactly the same manner in which he completed his international career six years earlier against Scotland at Murrayfield – with a try.

It was fitting on two accounts that Ella should end his career in such a fairytale fashion when his Sydney club Randwick disposed of champion English club Bath 20–3. Firstly, Ella's playing philosophy was firmly committed to attack and using the ball intelligently and positively. Secondly, because of this unbending philosophy, Ella gave the world rugby public from Dublin to Dunedin immense pleasure. Therefore it was typical of his unselfish nature that he should score Randwick's last try only five minutes from full-time to allow the 7,500 spectators to leave Coogee Oval with broad grins and warmth in their rugby souls.

The try itself was typical Ella. Bath lost the ball on the Randwick quarter, Ella hacked clear a few metres, regathered the ball and almost instantaneously he slipped the ball to his half-back Adrian McDonald who found open country. Outside McDonald in support was full-back David Knox who carried play to near the Bath quarter. He lobbed the ball inside to no. 8 Michael Cheika and, as the Bath cover defence converged, there was the man who started the whole movement himself, Mark Ella. Needless to say the 7,500 crowd cheered wildly like a 75,000-strong throng.

Ella was pleased with the manner in which the try was scored. 'Typical Randwick effort out of defence,' he remarked. But his modesty surfaced again as he said that McDonald was the one responsible for the try. 'As always, I just took the easy option of running down the middle', he said.

But it really wasn't a matter of taking the easy option. It was more than that. It was typical of his vision – a vision which could see around the corners of the field, a vision which could thread a pass through an almost impossible hole, a vision which could sense when a defender was tiring or unsure what to do. It is these qualities Ella will be trying to introduce into the Milan team in Italy when their championship kicks off. It will be his first step into coaching and there will be more than a passing interest from top level Australian rugby authorities as results filter back.

It was Ella's visionary talents which resulted in the grandest individual slam of all when he scored a try in each of the 1984 Wallaby tour victories. There was the clever loop move against England, the support on David Campese's outside shoulder at Lansdowne Road, the intercept against Wales and the inside support pass when the Grand Slam was secured over Scotland at Murrayfield.

Ella retired after that historic team and individual conquest but made a comeback at club level for his beloved Randwick club last year. Randwick qualified for their thirteenth successive grand-final and won their ninth title in that period with Ella playing no little role in their triumph.

Now thirty-one, Ella says he has finished for good except for the odd social or fundraising match. 'When I retired back in 1984, I had youth on my side. Now it's six years on. At this age, it's for good.

'When I made my comeback last year, it was just to have a bit of fun and to try and lose some weight. It wasn't a comeback with a thought that I would play for New South Wales and make myself available for Australia,' he said.

But there would have been several coaches, including Wallaby coach Bob Dwyer, who would have loved to have Ella back in peak condition and eager to wear the green and gold once again. He said: 'The selectors and the coaches never really pressured me into anything which I am unhappy about. It was a comeback for the rugby but Randwick rugby is more like social rugby'.

During the recent Wallaby tour of New Zealand where Michael Lynagh struggled for form right up until the final Third Test, the thought of Mark Ella coming back into the Australian team for the *World Cup* crossed the mind of many. Back at home, Ella, slimmer after playing the closed season with Milan alongside David Campese, was back to his best dazzling opponents with his vast arrays of gifted skills.

Why was he so gifted? 'I didn't have a great fend and I wasn't fast. I suppose it comes down to having a knowledge of the game and reading what will happen quicker than your opponents,' he answered.

Ella was twice offered huge money to switch to rugby league by the Eastern Suburbs and St George clubs. He stayed in rugby because of his loyalty to the game. There are those, such as Australian rugby league captain Wally Lewis, a team-mate in the invincible 1977 Australian Schoolboy team, who firmly believe that Ella would have been a huge success in the professional game. Lewis, who is known as 'King Wally' in his native Queensland, himself claimed he would have been forced to abdicate had Ella defected.

While Lewis is known as 'King Wally', down at Coogee Oval Ella was simply referred to as 'God'. After scoring his try, Ella attempted a tackle on powerhouse Bath winger Adedayo Adebayo and injured his arm in the process. After regaining his feet, the ground announcer said: 'It just goes to show that you can't hurt God.'

The game itself was an unspectacular match until Ella's final fling. Stuart Barnes dropped a goal for Bath after only twenty seconds and soon after Randwick began to take control chiefly through the scrum. Testimony to that scrum supremacy came midway through the second half when Randwick scored a push-over try against the head.

But it wasn't push-over tries the crowd had come to see. It was Ella and he wasn't about to let the spectators down. As full-time was whistled, Ella was besieged by photographers, cameramen and autograph hunters. Then suddenly flankers Simon Poidevin and Gavin Boneham hoisted Ella high on their shoulders to chair a remarkable player off the playing field for the last time.

There are many in Australia believe that Ella could have still played a significant role in the Wallabies' World Cup destiny next year. His tally of twenty-five Tests could have only been the tip of the iceberg.

These sentiments were best expressed by Poidevin who said: 'I still can't believe in my own mind that he's finished. If he was broken down and struggling I could understand it.

'But, the way he is playing now, he could go on for another ten years. If he put his mind to it, he could still be the best fly-half in the world.'

From *Rugby World and Post*, 1990

Campo, Campo, Campionissimo

Stephen Jones

He is addicted to the adrenalin rush of risk-taking. Only rarely does he take the first, easiest choice of play. He is a glorious crowd-pleaser and impish entertainer and beyond any doubt the personality of the 1991 World Cup.

He has been allowed to indulge himself, playing around the calendar in his beloved Italy and Australia. He has been allowed to express all his talent.

Many British players will go into retirement with the long reaches of their ability untapped and will lack final fulfilment. Not David Campese. He has thrown away the odd game through vaulting ambition but he has always been forgiven quickly.

He has been allowed to be singular and his coaches at club and Test level have embraced his philosophy; perhaps through gritted teeth, but if you take the rough with Campese's smooth, then the smooth is velvet.

Last week, the Australians staged a photo opportunity at their training. A bunch of them posed with arms draped around each other's shoulders. The central figure in the picture was Campese, beaming in the heart of his team in the essential one-for-all team game, apparently at peace with himself. It was a strong image. Several newspapers used the picture.

It was also severely incongruous. To encapsulate better the nature of the man you would need a wide shot of the All Blacks' haka before the marvellous semi-final in Dublin last Sunday.

The haka has now become a contest within a contest. The opposition have to decide whether to stare back or appear loftily unconcerned or even, as Ireland once did, to advance menacingly.

Yet as fourteen Australians stared back from close range, Campese was forty yards away, happily fooling around with the ball by himself while he waited for the kick-off; archetypal Campese.

Campese is a singular man, studiously so and sometimes stroppily so. He calls a chapter in his autobiography (*On a Wing and a Prayer*, Queen Anne Press) The Loner.

The vast majority of Test rugby players have an unquestioning, desperate loyalty to their team which blinds them to all faults for the common good. Not so Campese.

And a man at peace? The autobiography is fascinating. Here is a consummate rugby player, the most outrageous all-round talent the game has seen, a man fast in deed but lightning in thought. It often takes three seconds to catch up with his train of thought.

You see the possibilities he sees, and the option he takes, just when you are asking yourself what on earth he is up to this time.

Yet amazingly, and almost tragically, the autobiography is not the story of a man at peace or in a state of fulfilment. Perhaps it does not represent his true feelings, but he is bridling throughout.

In the book, he rails against every aspect of the game: his Australian team-mates, Alan Jones, Bob Dwyer and other coaches, British Lions, British rugby, British grounds, Carling, Guscott, New Zealand, rules, regulations, administrators and just about anyone who failed to pass the ball to him on a regular basis.

You have to wait till the very last paragraph of the book to find Campese reflecting on the countless moments of brilliance and elation which his career has brought, for some insight into his feelings when he puts up the twinkling feet. After you have put the book down, you feel like pleading with him: 'Campo, you did it all. You made us love you. It must have felt better than *that*.'

Perhaps it did and perhaps he was simply unable to reach inside himself to express it. Yet if he does decide to leave the Test rugby scene in six months' time as he hinted yesterday, then Campese as a character will remain, to all but his team-mates and even to some of them, as a vivid enigma.

Admittedly, the public perception of Campese that he is a man to be loved is correct. He is the sort of player you stand and cheer when he has scored a try against your own team.

When he scored a searing individual try against the Barbarians at Cardiff in 1988, in the final match of the tour, the crowd stood and roared him all the way back to halfway. The Dublin crowd cheered him for scoring a try against Ireland two weeks ago. It is a rare feat to transcend nationalism in rugby.

How many times has he endeared himself to youngsters over the seasons? He is always last from the field, having arranged the swarms of autograph hunters into an orderly queue, signed every proffered book and posed for every click of an Instamatic.

At Leicester one Christmas, after he had played for the Barbarians, he was out in a darkening stadium still surrounded while his team-mates were long out of the shower and on their second drink. He has earned the adulation of the followers of world rugby.

In any case, you simply cannot feel other than bereft that he is apparently leaving the international scene, robbing us of rich entertainment and box office, and robbing us too of that rising crescendo of sound and expectation as the ball moves towards his wing.

And there is another perception about Campese, another supposed enigma, that can be utterly dismissed. You still find people who regard him as a frivolous accessory, a goose-stepping clown to enliven the game's dull moments, a colourful nothing.

Then you remember that he has scored forty-six Test tries and that only Serge Blanco is within sixteen of him. You remember the games he has won by clinical finishing, the times he has turned games at the critical stage.

He has also been an all-rounder. He is an explosive, rifling kicker of a dead ball, and though he can be fallible under the high kick, he is one of the outstanding defensive tacklers. How many times, when seemingly outnumbered three to one, have we seen him shadow one attacker, then another, then tackle the third?

How do you pick the best memory? You have forty-six tries and a thousand other moments to choose from. Certainly, the most painful memory for Campese will be from the third Test against the Lions in 1989 in Sydney.

The series was level 1–1, the match was in the balance and Rob Andrew had missed a drop-goal attempt by miles. Campese caught it, sought the adrenalin surge and ran the ball from behind his line.

He flung out a hopeless pass to Greg Martin, and Ieuan Evans, the Lions' wing, stole in and scored. The Lions won, though not solely because of that try, and Campese still shudders.

He should not. He is so much in credit. The first track on my Best of Campo would probably be the hat trick he scored against England B in 1988.

The first try came when Dean Ryan, the massive England No. 8, drove at him. Ryan hit Campese, and the other England forwards prepared to drive with him; except that, in the instant of contact, Campese had stolen the ball and was already clear at the touch-line.

The second was a typical individual effort, with those slashing side-steps. The third came when he hung way out on his wing, apparently forlorn, and made the extra-sensory connection with Nick Farr-Jones, who kicked flat across field. Campese picked the ball up and almost walked over the line.

The freshest memory is of him bewitching New Zealand with his try last Sunday in the semi-final, then again with a sublime pass with which he gave a try to Tim Horan.

That was Campese. I hope we shall see him again. A man in love with theatre and audience and sensation will surely miss it all too much. Fervently, let us pray for it.

Whichever planet you came from, Campo, I wish I could watch rugby there all the time.

From the *Sunday Times*, 3 November 1991

13

GREAT NATIONS:
NEW ZEALAND

The Native Team

John Sinclair

A tour by the All Blacks is one of the highlights of anyone's rugby calendar. The First All Blacks toured Britain in 1905, of course, culminating in the famous (or infamous in New Zealand) match at Cardiff Arms Park. Sixteen years before those First All Blacks, however, another rugby team had left the shores of New Zealand.

W.B.B.

A hundred years ago saw the start of a Rugby tour right from the pages of Ripley's *Believe It Or Not*. In the European winter months of 1888–89 Great Britain was toured by the strangest rugby touring side the world has ever seen.

And it was a WORLD FIRST.

First time the Home country had been toured by any overseas rugby side. From any country. Let alone a self-styled New Zealand Maori team . . . playing 108 games on a world trip that lasted fourteen months . . . and seventy-four games in Britain in six months. (Well nearly four as two months were lost in travel.)

Mocked as being not much better than a social side because of mates rates and nepotism in selection (nearly one-third of the team came from two families . . . there were three Wynyard brothers and five Warbricks).

Despite predictions like the Otago Rugby Union's 'they won't win a single game' and the Hawke's Bay journalist's 'they couldn't beat English schoolboys' . . . they won 70 per cent of their games . . . in a punishing games schedule that today's match secretaries would nightmare over.

The team started out as The Maoris . . . but short in four positions before departure press-ganged four ring-in Pakehas.

No longer the Maoris, they switched their name to THE NATIVE TEAM.

Ice and snow playing conditions were something Polynesians hadn't even read about. At one game the opposition were so cold and numb they couldn't continue. But the Maori back line had the improvised answer for that . . . when they were shivering cold once and presumably their own forwards controlled the game . . . the Maori back line wore overcoats. One or two of the Maoris weren't at all comfortable playing in boots. With only one set of playing gear, frequently still wet or damp, they sometimes turned out in composite attire. Part football gear, part street clothing. Once their landlady got the laundry baskets mixed and left them women's clothing.

The Native Team games schedule for November 1888 was . . . playing on the 3rd, 5th, 7th, 10th, 12th, 14th, 17th, 20th, 22nd, 23rd, 24th (that's three days on end), 26th, 28th then over to beat Ireland 13–4 in the first ever Rugby International. Even World Cup winning All Blacks would run for cover from those dates. Yet The Native Team was only warming up. In March 1889 they were to play fourteen games in twenty-five days.

You gotta have heart. No team before or since has ever played with such heart and soul and fire in the belly. Or stretched it so thin.

Liniment was bought by the bottle. Then by the case. With so many legitimate claims for sprained ankles, dislocated shoulders and injured limbs, the Insurance Company exercised an escape clause and backed off. The Maoris had to play from sick beds. Having flu was no excuse. Forwards had to play as backs and vice versa. Often players couldn't go in hard for tackles in case they worsened the injury they already had. Because there were no replacements. On one occasion four players got crocked and a team of eleven had to soldier on. But at least they had started that day with a full team. Another time only fourteen men took the field. The Maoris couldn't raise a full team that day. It's said they were the only Rugby team that ever limped going *on* to the field. They rarely had more than a dozen completely fit players. One seeming malingerer was told to get stuck in. He did. He had TB and died shortly after returning to New Zealand. Two of the players finished up in mental homes. The poundings they took on the tour weren't necessarily a contributing factor . . . but it was no bloody help . . . I'll tell yer that for free.

Talk about a clash of cultures, the unsophisticated up-country boys had no experience of wine sipping. It was just a table drink. One day, playing too soon after a special luncheon, when it came to the composite team photo before the game some of the Maoris had locals crouched down behind them holding on to their jerseys to keep them more or less upright.

Once playing at a garden fête after a champagne party the boys didn't score a single point. They might have come right by half-time if it had been the usual scungy orange. But at half-time liveried footmen trooped on to the field and from silver salvers proffered hothouse grapes and more champagne.

(They must have got their signals wrong. On one of the tours to Australia, after a long train journey, the All Blacks were well behind at half-time. In the second spell they won going away. Sports writers praised the Captain's team talk at the interval. Years later it was admitted that it wasn't so much his sense of urgency. It was the water bottle being passed around. It contained almost neat gin.)

As Bully Williams observed 'those in the team were exceedingly temperate until the banqueting evil took hold of them'.

Always being pressed with drinks was Arthur (definitely not Martha) Warbrick. Squat, powerfully built in physique, he had a seventeen-inch calf. Constantly being backed into a corner by the ladies with the polite incredulous request Mr Warbrick-may-we-have-a-quick-peep. At social occasions after he had a few stings . . . to make it easy for everyone he wasn't above standing around with one trouser leg rolled up.

Jimmy Duncan, who always played in a cap as was customary at the turn of the century, once worked the blindside, and went through to score. Knowing he was masked from the ref by the scrum he passed his cap which the opposing defence bought. Charming. Coming from an All Black Captain and one of New Zealand's greatest coaches. Perhaps he was just working on ideas for his initiative talk.

All touring sides suffer strange decisions. Mind you The Maoris asked for some of it. Those at Home weren't accustomed to Colonials' inherent suspicion of unchallenged authority and British refs were backchatted too much. It has been said that if the ten-yard rule had applied then, The Maoris would have played all their games in their own dead-ball area.

But in one important game they ran up against a real hometowner. He was never off their backs and when a British player tore his strides, play stopped. The Maoris were part of the courteous screening. An opposing player picked up the dead ball, dotted down for a try and had it allowed. That did it. Three of the Maoris said 'well stuff it' and walked off the field. It took some placating to get them to resume play later.

Rugger was an English Public School game. There were raised eyebrows when The Maoris said they kept fit on the boat coming over by stoking the ship's boilers. When their ship got blocked in the Suez Canal . . . they got off and played a game with such ferocity spectators winced.

It was probably the first time Rugby was played in Egypt. There is certainly no mention of it in ancient history.

Everywhere they were made most welcome. A leading article wrote: 'The spectacle of the noble Maori coming from distant parts of the earth to play an English game against English players is essentially a phenomenon of our times. It is one of our proud boasts that wherever we go, whatever lands we conquer, we found the great national instinct of playing games. Now the olive brown descendants, with their well shaped intellectual heads and fine muscular development, of those migrated from Hawaii some 500 years ago in outrigger canoes come to play football and we gladly join in the welcome which the Rugby Union proffers them'.

From the *New Zealand Rugby Museum Newsletter*, October 1988

The End Was Not All

Terry McLean

Of all the subsequent tours of Great Britain by New Zealand rugby teams, none has lingered in the memory like that of the 1963–64 All Blacks. Wilson Whineray's side won many admirers, if rather fewer friends, for their clinical, efficient rugby during the tour, but they captivated the whole nation with the manner of their farewell at Cardiff Arms Park.

W.B.B.

All great Rugby tours produce some unusual matches of which the principal feature is some spark which ignites every one of the thousands present and turns them into active participants. Such a match was the fourth test between New Zealand and South Africa at Auckland in 1956 when thousands upon thousands chanted 'Black! Black!' to urge on the All Blacks to the victory that won the rubber. It was on the same ground, only three years later, that as many thousands, some of them assuredly the same folk as in '56, cried 'Red! Red!' to urge the British Lions to defeat the All Blacks. At Wellington, in 1950, the spectators were transported by the struggle of thirteen effective All Blacks to defeat the Lions, as they did, by six points to three, and as by some atavistic impulse respectable patrons of both sexes *screamed* encouragement when Elvidge of the All Blacks, though all but broken by injuries, dived over a tackle to score the winning try.

One's mind flits back over the years – to, as examples, the First Test against the South Africans in 1937, when fourteen All Blacks won the day, to the First Test of 1930, when Ivor Jones and Jack Morley, two Welshmen of the British team, between them scored the winning try to beat the All Blacks, 6–3, on the call of time – to these many extraordinary encounters which within an hour of no side are elevated to fables the truth of which no one would seriously attempt to question and the stature of which grows until, over the years, they achieve an Homeric quality.

There have been many such; but none, surely, will ever equal the fixture between Whineray's men and the Barbarians at Cardiff Arms Park on 15 February 1964. There were 58,500 present and they *all* screamed, at least for most of the second half. Such were the circumstances after Whineray himself, by the most delectable of dummies, had scored the last of the eight tries, that most of the thousands, united by the unique feeling of the match, wept, or at the least had suspiciously runny eyes. As by some electric impulse, the song, 'For He's a Jolly Good Fellow', swept around the ground; and was sung again, at the end. In all the long history of Arms Park, no one could remember such scenes, such enthusiasm; and it may be that in all Rugby history, this was the unique occasion, the supreme expression of total enjoyment.

It was in concert with the mood of the crowd that the match itself was turned into an occasion of riotous splendour, full of unbelievable skills and totally magnificent in the way attack was succeeded by counter-attack and thrust was answered by riposte. If there is a Rugby heaven, the All Blacks of the second half were made angels of it, so faultless that when Whineray once and Graham another time failed to hold passes, and Gray in a long attack threw a ball forward, the crimes were serious enough to be ranked by the perpetrators as next to treason and bloody murder.

Whineray! Whineray! Whineray! They all kept shouting Whineray. Not, as it happened, without cause. Never in the history of the Arms Park, never, perhaps, in the history of first-class Rugby, had there been scenes to compare with this spontaneous gesture of affection – the singing to him of 'For He's a Jolly Good Fellow' because he had scored a try, the incessant cheering of him, the lifting shoulder-high, the singing again. First his team-mates rushed upon him to congratulate him, then at the final whistle the reserves poured on to the field to grasp at him. And all of the time, for minutes on end, the crowd – and there were 58,000 of them – were singing and cheering and placing the man, the captain of New Zealand, the soul of 'Willie Away', on a pinnacle as tall as Nelson's Column. It was not possible for a New Zealander, be he chauvinist or world citizen, to look upon these scenes except in a mood of the most intense emotion. The pride of a great game, of a country's great contribution to that game, was involved in the tributes to one who, fitly, was called a great player and a greater captain. So it was Whineray! Whineray! Whineray! In the olden days, they would have rung out the bells. In the Navy, they would have spliced the mainbrace. In Rugby, they could only sing, and cheer, and raise a fantastic clamour of Whineray! Whineray! Whineray! In each case, the emotion was the same: Ecstasy.

No one who saw the overwhelming of the Barbarians, in person or on the television screen, can ever think of the occasion except in the personal terms of Wilson James Whineray, the first man in Rugby to become, instantaneously, a legend, a storybook hero.

The first five minutes of the second half and two brilliant pieces of play by Graham and Nathan settled the issue and principally were responsible for making the match a myth and a legend to hand down through the generations. At a scrum on the goal-line, Barbarians' put-in, Dawson heeled. The ball travelled back through the scrum. The instant it reached the goal-line, Graham dived upon it. A try. A D.B. Clarke goal. Three minutes later, again on the goal-line, again from a scrum, Simon Clarke threw a pass at Sharp. His aim was awkward. The ball pitched in front of Sharp. Before he could reach it, there, diving, was '*la panthère* Maori'. Clarke goaled again. From 6–3 the score had proceeded, in five minutes, to 16–3.

After this, the dam burst. Four more tries, all of them turned into goals by Clarke, were scored. The All Blacks might have been the Marx Brothers playing *A Day at the Rugby*. The zaniest of moves and movements were attempted and completed. Forwards passed the ball as if they were Harlem Globetrotters. Backs jinked and cut, speeding players rushed about with the alert efficiency of traffic officers. All was madcap merriment. Young's short little legs, though pumping furiously, were just too short to carry him to the line. So Dick was there to complete the try. 'More, More, More,' shouted the crowd. Nathan rushed to a second try after Tremain had charged a kick-down. Caulton went in after Dick had intervened from the other wing and Little, Don Clarke, Whineray and Graham had co-operated by various means to put the ball into Caulton's arms. The crowd were singing now, from the joy of it all, 'Now Is the Hour' and 'When You Come Home Again to Wales'. Time was passing and still the merriment went on. There never had been anything like it on the Arms Park. There never could be again.

And then Little and Graham cut through and suddenly, twenty yards from the posts, there was Whineray, going hell for leather, Meads alongside him and Flynn flashing across from the right to make the tackle. The three neared the posts. The Tower of Babel was a quiet country pub at an off-hour compared with the Arms Park.

Amid the fantastic noise, Whineray passed. Or so it seemed. His arms moved out towards Meads. Coincidentally, he side-stepped the other way. It was the dummy pass to end all dummy passes. Hook, line and sinker, Flynn bought it. Whineray, so it seemed, slackened to a trot as he carried the few more yards to the posts and the final try of the tour of Europe.

They sang to him then. The All Blacks crowded upon him. The television camera picked him out, at halfway, hands on his knees, bald head gleaming, waving now and again in response to the noise. In a minute or two, after a tremendous run by Dick, the game was over. And they sang again. 'Whineray! Whineray! Whineray!' The mood carried on into the newspapers, the radio, the television. At the celebratory dinner, Brigadier Glyn Hughes, president of the Barbarians, said that when the crowd chanted, 'More, more, more,' all that the Baa-Baas could think of was 'Yeah, yeah, yeah.' There never had been such a thing before. There never could be again.

From *Willie Away* by T. McLean
(Herbert Jenkins, London, 1964)

Team Talk

Fred Allen

Great teams are often produced by great coaches. Two of New Zealand's finest were Fred Allen and Jack Gleeson.

W.B.B.

I suppose it is because, where Rugby is concerned, I am a pretty nervous character, that I am in favour of team talks. As a player, I used to get all sorts of jitters. As a coach, I still get them. I can't eat lunch, I can't stand around talking to people. More and more, as the hours pass, the match tensions come into my mind. I try to think of all the possibilities. I make notes. My mind whirls about. And then, as I come to make the talk – which ought to be staged as close as is convenient to the start of the game, but before the team has changed – I find I know exactly what points I want to make. The fewer of these, the better. I wouldn't have any truck with blackboards to illustrate a point in a pre-match team talk, or with bringing in officials or other people from outside the team-group to offer inspiring words. A team talk is essentially a private matter between players and the coach, whoever the coach might be. At best, outsiders are a distraction. At worst, they are a damned nuisance.

It has been said that team talks are bad things. British sources imputed, a year or two ago, that the New Zealand team talk generated foul Rugby because during it the players were brainwashed into believing that they must win *at all costs*. This comes under the heading of remarks better left unsaid. When it has been said to me, I have copied the Virginian by saying, 'Next time you say that to me, son . . . Smile!' I take leave to doubt that people who make this sort of remark have ever strapped on a boot, at least in first-class Rugby. If a team of fifteen intelligent men were to be *ordered* to win no matter how, most of them, Rugby players being what they are, would refuse to carry out the order. Under refereeing of any standing whatsoever – and the remark has mostly been made about play at international level – the remainder would soon be found out. And if it happened that a *team* was committed to such a policy, there is a precedent for total remedial action. I don't think it ought ever be forgotten how close the tiny and capable Welsh referee, Mr Gwynne Walters, came to abandoning the international between France and South Africa in Paris in 1961 after the French, by deliberate intent, had set about the wrecking of the Springboks team in the first few minutes. This is no place for discussing rough Rugby. We can't overlook that it has been a factor in the game ever since William Webb Ellis first picked up the ball and ran with it. But I will say this: If there are coaches who talk of or preach absolute warfare on the Rugby field, they are not of my acquaintance. Nor do I think they would last very long in the game.

Team talks have not this intent at all. Far too often it is forgotten that Rugby is a young man's game; and most young men, no matter how hard they may try to convey a different impression, are nervous before the big tests. The big tests are not necessarily the All Blacks playing the Springboks for any so-called world championship. The big tests are to be found in any kind of Rugby at any level you like to mention. One of the inexhaustible fascinations of Rugby is that it is never less than a gruelling, demanding test of the body and the spirit of a player. The small boy who flings himself on the ball at the feet of a raging pack composed of other small boys will not have to suffer many more severe demands on his mental and physical courage during the rest of his life. If, because of training, he can do this unpleasant task without flinching and, what is more, can check the rush, he will have added a cubit to the stature of his manhood.

So it seems to me that if, before the test, some agency can steady the mind of the team, then that agency is worth while. This agency, in my experience, is the team talk.

It is important in a team talk that the players should think rather about the game *they* are going to play than about the game they are going to have to combat. The business of playing only as well as the other side will let you is bosh. Your team's business is to play as *your team* can. You set the tune. Let the other side dance to *it*.

The coach who sets about a team talk is faced with a number of problems. Some of the group – not necessarily the older, more experienced players – will be calm and unmoved. Others, in the rough language of the game, will be on the verge of having a 'touch of the Hollywoods'. The coach must seek to bring calm to the temperament of this player and uplift that of another, all through the team. He must construct a united, single-minded effort from the disparate elements in his team. The thought of hanging, according to Dr Johnson, concentrates a man's mind quite wonderfully. The thought of winning, in my experience, concentrates a team's mind.

I am a decisive man by nature. When I have resolved on such and such a course, I do not easily divert from it. Nor am I embarrassed about speaking bluntly to players. Because of this I have always found directness to be a great help in team talks. If one is candid to players, they will, after a time, be candid with you, and this, take it from me, is a great help to any coach. But candour is not the whole answer. Some of your team, you may be sure, will to start with be too shy or diffident to react favourably to the plain statement. So you must be subtle, too. Somewhere along the line, I invented what the members of the Auckland team I had so much to do with came to call 'Fred's White Lies'. If I wanted to ginger them up, I might say: 'Well, I just met their coach. He tells me his boys think they are sitters to win.' Some of my team might think: 'Old "Needle's" having us on again.' But they could never be quite sure, while the others, you could bet, would be saying, 'Sitters, eh? Just let 'em wait. We'll see who is a sitter when the time comes.' Between them the doubters and the doers would end by thinking the same thing, and they would all be just a little more determined.

Sometimes, of course, Providence plays into your hands. During the Lions tour of New Zealand in 1959, a terrible brouhaha developed about the practice of some All Blacks wearing, as was then permitted, canvas or leather shoulder-pads. Alf Wilson, the fiery manager of the Lions, shot off rockets all over the place. On the day before the third Test in Christchurch, Vivian Jenkins wrote a preview for the *Christchurch Star*. The All Blacks, Vivian declared roundly, were 'softies'. Softies! The remark must have cost the Lions at least five, possibly ten points, in the match proper. On the morning of our second Test with the French at Wellington in 1968, Alex Veysey, the correspondent of the *Dominion*, concluded after weighing the evidence that the All Blacks were about to be defeated. His newspaper made a bold poster of this, 'FRANCE SHOULD WIN – Veysey', or something of the sort. Somehow one got into the room where the All Blacks were assembled for their team talk. When I arrived, I started in horror at the sight of the poster, but went into my talk, glancing nervously from time to time at the placard. I wound up my peroration, full of steam. Then I glared around at the poster and blazed, 'Now, tear that bloody thing down.' If I may modestly say so, the effect was pretty stimulating; and if, as I am bound to add, that Test turned into so dirty an affair that the Governor-General of New Zealand, Sir Arthur Porritt, later declared there should be an end to karate in Rugby, the seeds were not planted in my team talk. The first punches – worse, the first kicks – were delivered by the other side!

For that is one thing I would never countenance in any team I coached. I have always given the firmest instruction that under no circumstances was anyone to indulge in rough stuff. Nothing could be more disastrous than to encourage men to commit mayhem. I discouraged it and denounced it; and some of the straightest talking I have ever done has been to players who indulged in play which passed from robustness, which is legitimate, into dirt, which is not.

I do not believe in long team talks. Short, pungent, strong – that's the form I like. You have to sense the will building up in the players and bring them up to the point where they are all thinking as a team, as one. In the great days with Auckland, we had with us Mack Herewini and Albert Pryor. Herewini was remarkably and sometimes excessively brilliant. Pryor, though a lock- or prop-forward, had an instinct for the loose. He hungered for the ball so that he could make runs – and, in his time, he scored tries that no other forward of the time in the world could have emulated. But it was often necessary for me to remind these two exuberant characters that they must curb their extraordinary individual abilities for the sake of the team. The point is that you can't build team-play on to individualism. You build individualism on to team-play – and there's a world of difference between the two. So I would coax, command or cajole this pair to see their duty to the team as the first requirement. When they had done this, they could play hob with the opposition. I must say it worked, too. They both contributed wonderfully to Auckland's record.

It has been said, not least in New Zealand, that a coach with his team talks can command too much influence, and that it would be better if he were seen but not too often heard. Otherwise, so it is said, he is bound to diminish the prestige and powers of the captain. On the face of it, this seems a pretty hard one to argue against. But I can quote one of New Zealand's best-loved soldiers of the Second World War. This was Howard Kippenberger, a Territorial Army officer who rose from a half-colonelcy in command of a battalion to become a major-general in charge, for a time, of the New Zealand Division at the Battle of Cassino. 'Kipp's' orders groups for battle while he was a brigadier became famous. He was meticulous in his planning and every possible contingency was discussed. But as he closed his remarks, he would say to his battalion commanders and senior officers: 'Well, gentlemen, the battle is yours. There is nothing more I can do.' Rugby is not war, nor ever should be. But what General Kippenberger said about war applies to Rugby. From the moment of the first whistle, the coach is completely without power. The captain is the sole director, and that is as it should be. In my view, the coach, as such, does not diminish the stature of the captain. In his role as guide, helpmeet and friend, the coach should be of great assistance to the captain, just as he should be to the lowliest player in the team. A coach plus a captain should equal confidence; and if you have confidence within the team, a confidence born of well-trained individuals who have moulded their undiminished talents into a unit, then to my mind you have achieved the possible. You have no need to worry about the qualities of the other side, no need to *get* the brilliant opponents, no need to indulge in anything remotely unsavoury. You have a team, in the finest sense of the word.

From *Fred Allen on Rugby*
(Cassell, London, 1970)

The Team That Jack Built

John Hopkins

Mourners came by bus and plane, car and train. Four hundred of them squeezed into the wooden pews in St Brigid's Catholic church in Derby Street, Fielding, and 800 more gathered on the grass outside. The funeral service included the 23rd Psalm and the hymn 'How Dear Thou Art'. Peter Gleeson, the only son, read from the Book of Wisdom ('The just man, though he die early, shall be at rest'), and from the back of the church a Maori schoolboy choir sang 'Now Is The Hour' as the congregation filed past a guard of honour from Fielding Rugby Club and out into the warm sunshine.

Gleeson was buried at the top of the highest knoll in the cemetery. They placed a crucifix in his hands, and his wife unstitched the silver fern from his All Blacks evening-dress suit and lovingly placed it amid the roses, carnations and gladioli on top of the coffin before it was lowered into the ground. The grave was marked with a simple white wooden cross and the words 'John (Jack) Gleeson'.

In the 760 days Jack Gleeson was coach to the All Blacks, his teams beat the Lions 3–1 and the Australians 2–1 at home. On foreign tours they drew with the French before achieving a unique set of victories over Ireland, Wales, England and Scotland, a special sort of Grand Slam. Gleeson masterminded those victories with an integrity and gentleness that earned him respect and admiration that bordered on love from his players.

He first suspected he was ill at Leicester in November 1978, when he felt back pains while hunched on a bed watching television. But it wasn't until January this year, back in Fielding, that exploratory surgery revealed growths half as big as tennis balls in his liver.

In his eulogy at the funeral, Father McDonald spoke of Gleeson's not knowing when to quit, and this was never more true than during the past year. He resigned as All Blacks coach, yet remained a selector and travelled by plane or car to twenty-nine matches last season, accompanied by his devoted wife, Ida. Growing more gaunt and frail, and unable to stand more than a few minutes, he also went about the sombre business of settling his estate and making sure of the future for Ida, their daughter Geraldine, and Peter. 'Are you sure you're clear about that, Ida?' he would ask as an accountant or lawyer unravelled a legal knot or interpreted some financial quirk in long, often complicated, meetings.

He implanted that sort of will-power in his teams. 'I built up the pace of the party so the opposition couldn't match us,' he said in an interview with New Zealand's TV One station shortly before he died. 'We were playing for eighty minutes – they were finished at sixty.'

Time and again his method worked, tries coming in injury time to beat the Lions in the fourth Test in 1977, and Ireland in November 1978. Then the All Blacks crawled back from 4–12 against Wales to that controversial 13–12 victory, the crucial penalty coming in the seventy-eighth minute. Eddie Dunn kicked the match-winning drop-goal against the Barbarians at Cardiff in the second minute of injury time.

Outside New Zealand, those narrow squeaks and the brevity of his reign as coach prevented him from receiving the acclaim he got at home for his achievements. Including a hectic, nine-match internal tour of New Zealand in 1972, and an All Blacks' tour of Argentina in 1976, Gleeson's teams won forty-eight of their fifty-two games.

'His teams were very hard to score against, and you made mistakes at your peril,' says J.J. Stewart, a former New Zealand selector and Gleeson's predecessor as coach. 'But personally I felt more could be constructed, particularly by his backs, than by putting pressure on opponents and waiting for them to make mistakes. He was bloody lucky against Wales, and if Ian McGeechan's drop-goal attempt had gone over for Scotland instead of being charged down, then the scores would have been level.'

Yet Stewart also believes Gleeson's teams were unlucky to lose the second Test against the Lions in 1977 and, later that year, the first Test against France. It may well be that, attack-minded as Gleeson said he was, his legacy will be the discipline he brought to defence. In the twelve Tests they played from May 1977 to December last year, the All Blacks conceded only eleven tries – and five of those came in one cathartic game against the Australians.

Jack Gleeson had a gift for drawing out the thoughts of his players and knowing when to use these thoughts to underpin his own tactical strategies. 'I think he was never 100 per cent confident of himself, and neither was I,' says Stewart. 'We knew enough about the game to recognize that we could both be wrong, and maybe this helped him recognize the limitations in his players and construct a plan that was suitable for them. He never asked them to do anything he knew they couldn't do.'

Another former All Black coach, Vodanovich, burly and black-browed, talks of Gleeson's 'fine tuning, his absolute, entire ability to get on with men.'

His approach was different from the barrack-square roars of Fred Allen and Vodanovich and other All Black coaches, recalls Bill Freeman, New Zealand's director of coaching in Wellington. 'If I saw a player take the wrong option during training, I'd be on the pitch shouting and sticking a pin in his arse telling him what was wrong. Jack just stood there and watched it all.'

In his last days, Gleeson watched more and more television (*The Good Life* and *Rumpole of the Bailey* were two favourites) on a set in his bedroom. His biggest comfort, though, was his religion. He kept some holy water from Lourdes on a bedside table, and often he would dip his hands into it before blessing himself. For a time his stomach was swollen, so that his family joked that he was pregnant. When it subsided, the reason was clear for him: 'Father McDonald gave me communion.'

Last week, Mrs Gleeson busied herself around the comfortable new home they moved into two years ago. She still hadn't had time to sort out her husband's clothes, which hung in a cupboard just off the bedroom, and twice a day the post brought piles of telegrams and letters which she stored in a cardboard box by her chair. Showing some will-power of her own, she expressed her determination to answer each one, no matter how long it took.

'I think Jack did believe in an after life,' she said at supper one evening. 'Some nuns who had nursed him in hospital called to see him just near the end. As they left, they bent over the bed to kiss him and say goodbye. He told them, "It's not goodbye, it's *au revoir*."'

Gleeson often said he hoped he could live longer. But he died, aged fifty-two, at 11.30 in the evening of Friday, 2 November, three days before his twenty-fourth wedding anniversary. A few hours later in Leicester, the All Blacks he should have coached scored five tries in a second-half salute. 'That was for Jack,' remarked his great friend, Graham Mourie, the captain. But they conceded one try. And Jack Gleeson would have been worried about that.

From the *Sunday Times*, 18 November 1979

Mourie the Magnificent

Ron Palenski

Gleeson was fortunate in having Graham Mourie as his captain, a great back-row forward, fine tactician and a superb All Black captain, both on and off the field.

W.B.B.

For the New Zealanders, it had been one of the good days. An autumn sun provided a comfortable warmth and Brive was one of those quiet, tree-girt French towns which make rural France a delight. The All Blacks were there for their first game in France in 1977, following a fortuitously won series against the Lions at home and a scraped win against an Italian scratch team in Padua, an ancient northern Italian city where New Zealanders first made their mark in the twilight stages of the Second World War. Brive was where Graham Mourie played his first full game of rugby as captain of New Zealand – he'd played about half of the Italian game (replacing injured Kevin Eveleigh) and had captained the All Blacks in the Argentine the year before. But Brive was the first time he led the full, first-choice New Zealand side on to a field. The rugby that followed befitted the style of captaincy and play that was to mark the Mourie years. A French side chosen by the national selectors and called, as were all the non-test opposition on that tour, a French Selection, was beaten 45–3. French rugby journalists, as excitable and volubly articulate as any of their nationals, were both enraptured and apprehensive about the awesome All Black display. Le tout noir, they said, like a black wave . . . inexorably pushing back the pride of French rugby, then riding high in Europe. Even New Zealand journalists, some of them cynical of the All Black chances after the chill of the Lions' winter, reached for the flowery phrases inspired both by the effervescent and welcome rugby and the intoxicating Gallic atmosphere.

But for some New Zealand supporters in the crowd, it wasn't the atmosphere that was intoxicating. Wearing kiwi T-shirts which seem to bloom overseas but are seldom seen at home, they pushed a supermarket trolley full of vin ordinaire – purchased, no doubt, at insignificant prices on the way to the ground – around the touchline, searching for the ideal seating. They found it, with a helping hand from some of the Brive gendarmerie, and settled down to their wine and their rugby. The latter was without doubt of greater quality than the former.

Each had its effect, however. Later that night, as the All Blacks sat quietly in the dining room of their new, open-plan Mercure hotel on the outskirts of Brive, the supporters took their bravado and their flagons in hand and decided to seek out the All Blacks, show them a little back-home appreciation. En masse they came, a flying wedge of pot-bellied patriotism, determined to seek out the men in black who, at that stage, were listening to the urbane cosmopolitan, Andy Haden, translate the menu for them. The hotel manager, a young, personable man obviously destined for higher honours in the hotel chain which paid his francs, saw the approaching bonhomie and mistook it for mayhem. A swift call to the gendarmes was made. New Zealand journalists at the bar saw the supporters clamouring and gathering at the door, saw their state, and saw the manager dialling and rolling his eyes. It was potential dynamite. French police do not take kindly to drunken, shouting rugby supporters, however well-intentioned they may be. The police arrived and the talking . . . the shoving in the chest . . . the fist-waving, ensued.

Someone slipped into the dining room and told the players. Without a word, Mourie rose from his sole meunière and walked out into the foyer. All stopped. At a look from Mourie, the police stepped back. He went up to the closest of the supporters and said: 'G'day, where you from?' They sat down, a couple of other supporters joined them. They chatted for a couple of minutes and Mourie told them he'd go back and finish his meal and if the supporters went to a nearby brasserie, he'd make sure some of the team went there when they'd finished their dinner. The supporters shook the Mourie hand and left, happy. The hotel manager smiled. The police smiled and left. Mourie went back to his sole. The journalists turned back to the bar and some of them, who had been on other tours in other countries, reflected on what might have been with similar circumstances at another time. Violence? Perhaps. Disrespect and a turning-away from chance contact? Almost certainly.

In context, years later, it was seemingly only an insignificant moment of time, an insignificant incident, barely surfacing on the sea of memories that rugby touring engenders. But was it?

It seemed to epitomize the style that Mourie brought to All Black rugby. The commanding but not loud presence, the alert, inquiring mind, the gift of diplomacy that not even all diplomats are endowed with, the gentle gesture well timed and well executed.

There are similar incidents, on and off the rugby field, which have shown the Mourie touch. In 1978 in Swansea, the All Blacks played West Wales. It was the second match in Wales on the Grand Slam tour and, being the third game of the tour, was reckoned to be the first stiff test of the All Blacks' mettle, with only Cambridge University and a surprisingly weak Cardiff behind them. If Welsh fervour comes in degrees, it was well up the scale that day at the old St Helens ground, the forbidding terraced houses on one touchline and the Bristol Channel on the other. About 20,000 were packed into the ground, most of them Welsh, most of them loud, most of them in tune. It can be a daunting experience for a young rugby player unused to the rarefied atmospheric heights of Welsh rugby. The mind-tingling emotion of 'Land of My Fathers' began to echo around the ground, the lines overlapping as the packed terraces caught up with the sound from the main stand. The West Wales team stood in a circle, led by Ray Gravell in their own singing. Across the halfway line, the All Blacks stood, also in a circle, looking at their captain. Mourie was tracing his right index finger around the silver fern on the left side of his jersey . . . not saying anything, just reminding his players in a chauvinistic but effective way who they were playing for that day, and what they had to do.

Mourie's teams were not always winners and the All Blacks can have had fewer, more comprehensive beatings than that by Munster in 1978. The score was only 12–0 and Australians would immediately say some of their recent wins over the All Blacks represent greater hidings, but it was the manner of the All Blacks' loss – or, fairly, Munster's win – which stuck in the mind. There was a feeling among spectators even before the game that this could be the All Blacks' first tour loss. Once the game started, there seemed little doubt. The men of Munster, playing with a ferocious dedication and intensity, blocked every All Black move and retaliated with the unblockable. The tiny, intimate Thomond Road ground could not hold any more people – and all of them willed Munster on. It was eerie. When Tony Ward kicked one of his penalties, you could hear the sole of his boot scuff the grass before contact. And you could certainly hear instep against ball. The roar began a millisecond later.

After the game, half the crowd seemed to be waiting around the back of the small stand to greet the Munstermen. Still in their seats, Irish, British and New Zealand journalists tapped away the news in the fading light and increasing cold. As the players exited out the back, Mourie went out the front, walked briefly back on the turf, then ran up the steps to the press benches, a broad smile signalling his mood. 'You guys want anything?' he asked. 'Get all the quotes you wanted?' Terry O'Connor, the long-serving and respected rugby and athletics writer for the London *Daily Mail*, was amazed. 'No one's done that before,' he said. 'Most of them try to avoid you. That Mourie's magnificent.'

At the centenary dinner in Cardiff's city hall, Cliff Morgan, the artful Welsh fly-half of the 1950s, rose and said: 'If I now meet my maker, I don't mind because I have watched what I consider to have been the greatest back row play by Graham Mourie.' When you've just beaten Morgan's Wales by twenty-three points to three, that's praise indeed.

For most of Mourie's career, these have been the two principal factors – the style of his play and of his captaincy. After Wales, a third dimension of Mourie's life was dramatically made public – his sense of right, his morality. The decision not to play against South Africa came as little surprise to those who knew him, and that included most of the managers, coaches and players with whom he had been associated as an All Black. But it was a surprise to the wider public of New Zealand. All Blacks before had stated a case against South Africa, some after touring there, some not. But there was no precedent for an All Black captain declaring his unavailability for a home series because of his own conscience. The decision elevated Mourie from the purely rugby publicity which hitherto had accompanied him.

From *Graham Mourie – Captain* by Graham Mourie and Ron Palensky
(Arthur Barker, London, 1982)

The Conductor

Gareth Edwards

Dave Loveridge was a member of Mourie's 1977 All Blacks. I rate him as one of the finest scrum-halves of his era, but he never seemed to get the praise he merited. Perhaps he was too much under the shadow of his predecessor Sid Going, or perhaps, as Gareth Edwards suggests, his supreme skill lay in organizing his side and playing his own game so unobtrusively.

W.B.B.

One afternoon in 1977, while in action for Taranaki against the British Lions, the young Loveridge's body became jammed in a rolling maul, his foot trapped beneath another player. The movement had such a horrific effect on his knee-cap that those close at hand had to look away – it had been twisted so severely that it was pointing sideways from his leg. He was indeed fortunate that there was an ambulance at hand with a doctor in attendance who understood sports injuries, and he received prompt, expert attention in hospital in New Plymouth which allowed him not only to resume his career, but to become one of the best half-backs his country has produced. In 1978 he came on the British tour as understudy to Mark Donaldson and reached Test status against Wales when the latter was injured.

That comeback from injury alone, demonstrating tremendous courage and determination, almost qualifies him for this book without other considerations. But the fact is that, although I missed direct confrontation with him on the field, I rate him as a great player too. His skills included a short, snappy pass that was more effective than that of his great predecessor Sid Going, whose prime task, of course, was not so much to pass as to use the boot to keep the ball ahead of his forwards. But, like Going, Dave Loveridge was always at the heels of his pack, ready to accept the gilt-edged possession offered by men like Mexted and Mourie. Then everything would start buzzing again: maybe with a wristy flick to a first or second five-eighth; maybe with a few strides and a planting of the ball securely in the grasp of a supporting flanker. It's clear to me, too, that he understood the importance of a well-balanced posture: legs braced and wide apart to prevent back row opponents from unbalancing and dispossessing him.

All of that makes me think of Loveridge as a 'conductor' of the play. In Europe that role is usually filled by the stand-off half, but the All Blacks' tactical emphasis is different.

The scrum-half can go through a game almost without being noticed, but if he is as good as Dave Loveridge, then the men around him are doing fine!

From *100 Great Rugby Players* by Gareth Edwards
(MacDonald Queen Anne Press, London, 1987)

The Big Game

A.P. Gaskell

While the All Blacks have dominated the world stage, like every other rugby nation, New Zealand has a thriving club and provincial competition, where, to the participants, their games are every bit as important as an All Black Test. A.P. Gaskell's short story superbly captures the feel of the build-up to a big match.

W.B.B.

I was dumping my togs in the bag as the caretaker put his head round the door. 'You boys ready? I'm waiting to lock up.'

We went out with him. 'Think you can hold the Southern?' he asked. He called them 'Southeren'.

'We'll give them a good fight for it,' said Mac. He was our spokesman on occasions like these.

'They've got a fine team. You'll need all your luck to beat those forwards of their – man!'

'We're going to play fifteen backs and run them off the paddock,' said Bob.

'Are you now? Ay? Well, I'll be watching you, but I'll no say which side I'll be barracking for. Goodnight.' He locked the gate after us.

It was quite dark now and all the street-lights were on. The air was keen and frosty. We went up under the railway bridge and stood in front of the lighted shops waiting for a tram. I was beginning to feel cold and stiff and tired now that the excitement was over.

'You know,' I said, 'football would be a good game if we could just play it on Saturday.'

'Come up to date, boy,' said Bob. 'This is Saturday. You remember yesterday? Well, that was Friday. Today we've just beaten Kaikorai.'

'I bet he carries a calendar,' grinned Mac to me.

'No, fair go,' said Bob seriously. 'It's just general knowledge.'

'I mean it,' I said. 'It would be good if we could just play it on a Saturday. I've just been thinking, here we are just after slogging through one hard game and before we're off the ground even, everyone wants to play next week's game with us. Why can't they give us a spell?'

'I suppose they're greedy,' said Mac. 'They just get over one sensation and they're greedy for the next. They don't like having nothing to look forward to.'

'Hero worship, too,' said Bob. 'They like to air their views in front of the well-known Varsity skipper. It makes them feel big. Or perhaps they think we don't bother about much else, we just live for football.'

'We will be for the next week,' I said. 'We'll be playing Southern all the week and by the time Saturday comes we'll be so nervous we can't eat. It's one hell of a caper in a way. I'll be glad when the season's over and I can relax.'

'Did you get any knocks?'

'No worse than usual. The knee's pretty sore.'

The tram came along. It was good to sit down again. The conductor evidently recognized Mac. 'They'll make you run around next week,' he said. 'The Southern, I mean. Be a good game.'

'How did they get on today?'

'Against Taieri? 46–3,' he said. 'How do you feel now?' He laughed and went to the back of the car. He came past us again later. '46–3,' he said again and winked.

The next Saturday morning I woke early in the digs and looked out the window. The sky was right down on the hills and there was a thick drizzle. Oh hell, I stretched down under the blankets again and tried to sleep but the thought of the match kept me awake. It had been a tough week as we were getting close to the exams and I'd had a good deal of swot to do but I felt very fit. We'd been for a run every night after finishing our swot, usually about midnight, and on Wednesday there had been a really hard practice. The coach kept us packing lower and lower, scrum after scrum, and kept us down there with the strain on for so long that my muscles were all quivering and Buck who locked with me was groaning under the pressure, and when we stood up I felt dizzy and queer little lights slid down across my vision. It felt a good scrum though, very compact. The line-outs afterwards were plain hell. And then, of course, the team-talk on Friday night. We used to hold it in a lecture room in the School of Mines. All around us on the wall were wooden models of pieces of machinery and charts of mines and geological strata. They made you realize the earth is very big and old, and goes down a long way. The coach would stand on the platform and start on his old game of building us up to fighting pitch. He was an artist at it, he could mould us just the way he wanted us. He spoke for a while about the traditions of the Club and then about the honour of playing off for the championship. 'Tomorrow,' he said, 'we'll start as usual by taking them on in the forwards. Here I am in the line-out. I look at my opposite number and think, "You're a good man, but by Jesus I'm better. Today you've got no show."' His voice takes on a stirring note. He moves about on the platform suiting actions to his words. 'Into them! Dominate them! And every man when he sees where the ball goes, he thinks "There's Buck in. I'm in, too." Into them! And every man is thinking the same and we're all animated with the same spirit, we're going in to dominate them and we pack it tight and we're giving all our weight and strength and we're thinking together and working together and no one lets up. Dominate them.' And he goes on acting the part, words pouring out of him in that stirring tone and we watch him mesmerized, so that he takes us with him and we're there in the game too playing with him, working as a team. We leave the lecture room with a feeling of exaltation.

Then, on the other hand there were the football notes in the paper. I know it was silly to take much notice of them, but I always read them. Referring to the Kaikorai game, the reporter said that I 'went a solid game but lacked the fire and dash that would make all the difference to his play'. The best thing I'd done, the movement where, to my mind, I had shown fire and dash was credited to Buck as 'one of his typical dashes'. Of course we are very much alike in build, but all the same I felt disappointed. The papers make people think that we are a sort of entertainment troupe, a public possession. Actually, I suppose, we'd go on playing if there were no public; we'd relax and enjoy our football much more.

It's one hell of a caper really, I thought, stretching out under the sheets. I was lucky to have a girl like Betty who was keen on football. Some of the girls used to go very snooty when the blokes couldn't take them to the Friday-night hops.

Well, this is the day. A few hours and it will be all over. This is it. It's funny how time comes around. For ages you talk of something and think of it and prepare for it, and it's still a long way off. You keep thinking how good it will be, and then suddenly, bang, it's there, you're doing it and it's not so enjoyable after all. I think football's like that, better before and after the game than in it.

Well, the day had come. I wasn't keen to get up and face it but anything was better than lying in bed and thinking a lot of rubbish. I put on a dressing-gown and slippers and padded around to Bob's room. He was still asleep. 'You won't look so peaceful in eight hours' time,' I said. 'They're queuing up at Carisbrook already.'

He raised his head from the pillow with a start. 'Eh?' He rubbed his eyes. 'What's wrong?'

'Jackie Hore just rang up to see how you are. He said their forwards are going to break very fast today, so he probably won't have an opportunity to ask you after the game because you'll be in hospital.'

He grinned. 'Then it's all bluff? I thought it was.'

'What?'

'About you forwards dominating them. I didn't think you could. I've never seen you do it yet. Just a bunch of big good-natured guys.'

'Not us,' I said. 'A pack of wolves just a-howling for prey. That's how we'll be today.'

Bob yawned and stretched his arms above his head. 'I must watch you. It would be interesting for a change. Have you eaten yet?'

So we went down for breakfast. Afterwards I cleaned my footy boots and packed my gear, and there was nothing to do but wait. I had no lectures on Saturday morning and I couldn't settle down to swot. The weather began to clear and a watery sun showed through the clouds as Bob and I went for a stroll. The town would be full of football talk and trams placarded, 'Big Game Today, Carisbrook 3 p.m., Varsity v. Southern', so to get away from it we went down to Logan Park and climbed up above the quarry. It wasn't so cold in the sun and the harbour looked glassy. There was no one about. We threw stones down into the quarry. It was good watching them. They dropped away from us, slowly getting smaller and smaller, then suddenly they struck the bottom and exploded, shooting fragments out sideways, starlike.

At twelve we went back to the digs for an early lunch. I didn't feel very hungry, and while we were waiting for the food, Bob kept tapping with his knife on the table. We caught the quarter past one tram out to the ground. Everybody looked very jolly and expectant. We saw Buck and Mac on the tram and that cheered us up a bit. It was good to realize that there were others who had to go through with it too. Buck didn't care a hoot about it all.

'Think you can win?' an old man said to him.

'Win?' Buck seized the old fellow's hand. 'Be the first to congratulate us on winning the championship. Get in early. Do it now. Be the very first.'

The old chap pulled his hand away looking a bit silly.

At Carisbrook we joined the crowd around the gates and pushed through to the players' entrance. I could see people nudging one another and nodding towards Mac. We showed our passes and went in along behind the stand and in underneath to the dressing-rooms. Most of the boys were early, there were other bags lying on the seats.

'Shall we go up for a while?' said Mac. We went out in front of the stand to see the final of the Junior Competition. The stand was packed and the bank opposite was dark with people. We stood about watching the boys playing with a sort of detached interest and then at half-time we went underneath to change. The strain was getting to me a little – I'd take things off and then forget where I'd put them. I had to undo my pants to see whether I'd put on my jockstrap. Most of the chaps were pretty quiet, but Buck kept going and we were pleased we had him to listen to. Mac was roaming round in his underpants looking for his glasses.

'Like to make a statement before the match?' I asked him.

He just looked at me. 'I can't find my bloody glasses. I suppose some bastard will tread on them.'

'Just a picture of confidence,' said Bob. My face felt very tight when I tried to grin.

Soon the trainer came in and started to rub us down. The room was filled with the smell of eucalyptus and the rapid slap slap slap of his hands. It was a great feeling being done, he made us feel nice and loose and warm and free-moving. Then Jackie Hore, the Southern skipper, came in to toss and we looked at him. There he was, the man we had been talking about all the week. He lost the toss and laughed. He looked a good deal smaller than I'd been imagining him. Of course we had played against him before but the strain makes you think silly things. We felt better after he'd gone.

'He doesn't look so soft,' said Bob to me.

'Poor old Jackie. I'll try and bump him again today and you just watch.'

'Never mind,' he said, 'unless you do it from the other side and straighten your nose up.'

I strapped up my weak knee and when the Vaseline came round plastered it on my face to prevent scratches. The coach came in and we packed a scrum for him.

'That looks all right,' he said. 'Well now listen, boys. Remember you're going out now as the Varsity boys have done for many years now to play off for the championship, and a lot of those old players are out there today watching to see how good you are. Don't let them down. Remember the first ten minutes in the forwards. Hard!' He punched his open hand. 'Go in there and dominate . . . ' But the referee was in the room to inspect the boots and the coach's exhortation was lost in the movement.

'Righto, boys. One minute to go,' said the ref.

We took off our coats and handed round chewing gum. Buck and I put on our ear-guards. Mac found the ball and we lined up in the passage. The Southern players were there already, skipping about and rubbing their hands. They felt the cold, too. The whistle blew, there was a glare of sunlight, and we were outside going out on to the field, right out in the open. A roar from the crowd rolled all round, enveloping us. A cold easterly breeze blew through our jerseys as we lined up for the photographers, squinting into the low sun. The Southern players looked broad and compact in their black and white jerseys. We gave three cheers and trotted into the middle. The turf felt fine and springy. We spaced ourselves out. I took some deep breaths to get charged up with oxygen for the first ten minutes. A Southern player dug a hole with his heel and placed the ball.

'All right Southern? All right Varsity?' called the referee. Both captains nodded. He blew the whistle. The Southern man ran up to kick.

'Thank Christ,' I thought. 'The game at last.'

From *New Zealand Short Stories*
(Oxford University Press, Auckland)

14
GREAT TOURS

Colin Meads and the 1971 Lions

John Reason

The 1971 Lions were the finest rugby team I have seen, a collection of supremely gifted and dedicated players, led by an inspirational captain and with one of the great coaches of the modern game in charge. The 1971 Tour of New Zealand brought my two great second-row heroes, Colin Meads and Willie John MacBride, into opposition. In 1966 Meads had been at the heart of an All Black side that had overwhelmed the Lions. In 1971 the Lions were to emerge triumphant.

W.B.B.

Meads featured large in the Lions' planning. By then, he had acceded to the captaincy of the All Blacks, but even before Meads' appointment was confirmed, the Lions' coach felt that he would be the key figure in the psychology of the series. Accordingly, he studied Meads closely in the games which had been arranged so conveniently to celebrate the Rugby Union's centenary. Meads was frightened of no one. He revelled in taking on opposing forwards to find out how hard they were. He used physical pressure to the point of intimidation. He only respected those who could stand up to him. He truly was the Godfather, an analogy to the Mafia made even more compelling by the all black playing uniform worn by his country.

He had an inbuilt resistance to those who tried to impose law on the game. His presence was such that he effectively refereed many of the games in which he played, or he did if he could. He took on the referee in the same way that he took on the opposition, and he probably did it for the same reasons, and enjoyed it as much.

Meads was always superbly fit. He was a good handler and a great rucker. He was nothing extraordinary as a line-out jumper, or even as a scrummager, because his own instincts were halfway between being a tight forward and a loose forward, but it was significant that the opponents he always respected most were not forwards of brilliant talent like Frik du Preez, in whom he might have seen something of himself, but the really tight forwards, like Johan Claassen and Rhys Williams. When you looked at him, either as a coach or an opponent, you knew you were looking at a unique figure. He was utterly uncompromising. It was as if God had distilled in him the essence of competition. He accepted the Adam in himself and admitted that there were moments in his career which he regretted.

He was the product of a unique environment. Boys in Wales wanted to be Barry John. Boys in New Zealand wanted to be Colin Meads. He came from a breed of hard men, of farmers, like the South Africans, for whom he has such respect. He gloried in being a part of that breed. He always had a mind to Rugby when he set about the daunting physical work on his farm. That work meant that he spent hours on his own in conditions of absolute solitude and it gave him a great deal of time to think.

Colin Meads had tremendous pride in his country, tremendous pride in being an All Black. His views on the game were conservative and as a member of a team, he had a natural acceptance of the authority of his coach and his captain. His relationship with Wilson Whineray was revealing for its absolute obedience to playing authority. Meads was the last of the great forwards who had this acceptance.

He was an implacable opponent, but in no way a small man. Deep down, he is warm and sincere. No one tried harder on the field, but when the day was done, he was generous in defeat, and even more important, he was sensible and restrained in victory. Even then, it was evident that he represented the essence of 'us' to all New Zealanders against the 'them' of the rest of the world. He was larger than life. He still is. Even then, it was apparent that we would not see his like again.

The refereeing of any country mirrors the strengths and the weaknesses of the game in that country. New Zealand refereed the ruck well, so their players rucked well. New Zealand did not referee the scrum at all, so their players scrummaged abysmally. Their foot-placing, their binding, and their scrum-feeding were all wrong.

The scrum therefore became the area of physical contact that was the hub of the Lions' planning with regard to the forward play, and because of the quality of British props then available, it was possible to achieve domination. This was vitally important, because one of the beauties of the scrummage in Rugby football is that it is primeval. It is an eyeball to eyeball contest. Therefore, the sight of Colin Meads and his scrum in retreat in the second match of the tour, against the symbolically named King Country, was a tremendous encouragement to the Lions psychologically. So was the sight and feel of Meads and the All Black pack almost running backwards in the second test. New Zealand won that test by the most decisive score of the series, but to the Lions' coach it was immeasurably more encouraging than the first test, which the Lions won. He felt that New Zealand were fifteen points the better team in the first test, even though they lost it, and it was hard to see how they could be outmanoeuvred. The Lions' scrummage domination in the second test gave them a platform off which they could build. All they had to do was fill up the holes.

In other areas of the game, though, the Lions had to face realities. They were fighting a tradition of All Black pride. They were fighting a tradition of nice guys coming second. According to Meads himself, in an interview with Terry McLean of the *New Zealand Herald* which produced perhaps the most memorable remark of the tour, Lions forwards in the past had given New Zealand's captain the impression that they believed in fairy tales. The Lions had to correct that impression as well.

Remembering the line-out play of the 1967 All Blacks, and remembering Meads' methods in the Rugby Union's centenary games, the Lions' coach decided to make such a mockery of the illegal practices as to make the All Blacks' continued use of them both embarrassing and difficult. He knew that the Lions could not really compete with the All

Blacks in the line-out, except through Mervyn Davies in that vital area at the back, so they had to conduct a holding operation, with all the assistance they could get from propaganda. Hence the expression 'get your retaliation in first'. Hence the careful attention drawn at all the early Press conferences to the fact that as the Lions were in the line-out of Rome, they intended not only to do as the Romans did, but even to practise it. The stratagem worked so well that in the end, the International Rugby Football Board rushed to re-write the line-out laws. They made a mess of it in the process, but we will come to that later.

The Lions also had to fill up the holes in their defence at the side of the scrummage, and at the same time provide the support essential behind the middle jumper in the line-out. For these reasons, they chose a big man to play as a blind side flanker, and they chose a fast, outstanding tackler to play on the open side. The Lions were fortunate to have a choice between Derek Quinnell and Peter Dixon on the blind side and John Taylor and Fergus Slattery on the open.

The realities of dealing with the situation as it existed in New Zealand in 1971 shaped the rest of the Lions' play. The last thing the Lions' coach wanted was second phase play, whether artificially created or otherwise, because the All Blacks were supreme at that phase of the game. Accordingly, the ball had to be moved as wide as possible and as fast as possible from the New Zealand forwards. This did not apply only to the test matches. It applied with just as much force to the provincial games, because all the powerful New Zealand provinces were capable of outrucking the Lions.

This was what made the contribution of the Lions' midfield and full-back so crucial. It is all very well having the notion of moving the ball rapidly from A to F, but it will not bear much fruit if B, C, D and E cannot pass. Happily, both John Dawes and Mike Gibson were supreme passers of the ball and J.P.R. Williams came into the line so well from full-back that Gerald Davies and David Duckham were able to make use of their skill on the wings.

Similarly, the Lions had to make use of any ball that New Zealand kicked away. They had to develop the counter-attack and they had to develop the confidence to use it under pressure. The All Blacks and the provincial teams had a tendency to overkick when trying to hoist the ball into the box behind the forwards on the blind side wing, and so the Lions' wings had to stand deep so that they were in effect playing as three full-backs. Then they could support each other in their counter-attacks. This had its greatest moment in the match against Hawke's Bay, when J.P.R. Williams caught a narrowly missed kick at goal behind his own posts and launched a surging counter-attack which ended with Gerald Davies scoring a try between the posts at the other end of the field.

Carwyn James treasured him, as he did all his other gifted backs, but he knew that if those gifted backs were to have the chance to express their skills, the Lions' forwards would have to come to terms with the realities of rescuing every scrap of possession, often from a position of weakness. He knew that on many occasions, the Lions would not be rucking in the ideal situation of going forward. Frequently, they would have to ruck or maul in retreat, and so it was important that they should know how to do it and that they should practise it regularly. That practice alone paid dividends in the first test, when the All Blacks were so much the better side, and yet the Lions got away with a victory.

Finally, the Lions were helped by the fact that there were players in the team who had been to New Zealand and who knew what it was all about. Gareth Edwards and Barry John had toured New Zealand in 1969 and had been rated as nonentities. Their coach was delighted. He knew that two years later, Edwards and John would want to prove themselves, and they did. By the seventh match, when the team played quite beautifully and destroyed Wellington, the Lions felt that they were capable of a genuine roar. Even the brutal match against Canterbury a fortnight later, in which they lost their two test props for the rest of the tour because of injury, did something for the Lions. In one way it was a disaster, the low point of the tour, but after darkness there has to be light, and that match made the Lions more determined than ever to prevail. 'We shall overcome,' they sang. And they did.

From *The World of Rugby* by John Reason
(BBC, London, 1979)

Believing in Victory

Terry O'Connor

Before leaving England James had pencilled in his first five teams for the New Zealand tour. It was all part of his plan to develop the side early into a Test combination, and he was rewarded with one of the most breathtaking displays of rugby, including nine glorious tries in the fifth game against Wellington. As a province Wellington have always ranked in the top flight and had known victories over the Lions, but this time they were a supporting cast in one of the finest games I have ever seen.

The Lions won 47–9 and John Bevan, the Welsh wing with the strength of a forward, scored four of the tries, one memorably, where he finished off a dazzling movement started by J.P.R. Williams near his own line. It came when Wellington were launching one of their own rare attacks. They had reached the Lions' twenty-five when their full-back kicked straight to Williams. Strange characters, these Kiwis, Williams must have thought as he ran the ball out, linking up with Mike Gibson. Gibson then passed out to Bevan, who, running from his wing to the centre of the field and from there to the try-line finished off a movement of more than eighty yards. Accolades by the thousand were heaped on the tourists, but for James the psychological aspect was even more important. The New Zealanders now had reason to worry about the Tests, while the Lions' confidence soared. A 21–9 victory over Otago, another premier province, left the Lions ready for the 'fifth Test' against Ranfurly Shield winners Canterbury.

While the match at Wellington had illustrated all the beauty of rugby the Canterbury affair at Christchurch revealed the brutal, vicious and unhealthy side of the game. *The Times* was moved to report: 'They bayed for the blood of the Poms.' Canterbury were determined to win by any means and the punching in the front row spread to every part of the field. It ended the tour for Sandy Carmichael and Ray McLoughlin. Carmichael was pummelled unmercifully in the front row, suffering a depressed cheek bone, and McLoughlin broke a thumb hitting Alex Wyllie in one of the many punch-ups which punctuated a game soured by such taunts as 'Come on, you soft Pommy bastards.' In addition Fergus Slattery was smashed in the face when standing in the line-out, and was concussed for most of the game; Gareth Edwards was repeatedly kicked, often from behind.

The Lions won 14–3 because they did at least try to play the ball; and the courage of Bevan was magnificently displayed when he swept through two men and dived through another three who appeared to be defending their line with their fists, like soldiers in a trench. Barry John was deliberately excluded from this game for fear he might be injured.

Mike Gibson played fly-half and his tackling destroyed Canterbury's favourite move of bringing Fergie McCormick in from full-back to run at the opposition like a tank.

Teams are really tested in adversity and this was the case with the 1971 Lions. During the week that followed Sean Lynch and Ian McLauchlan were transformed into Test props. For me the opening stages a week later of the first Test at Carisbrook, Dunedin, was a nightmare. The tidal wave of attacks launched by the All Blacks' forwards was so reminiscent of the scene I had witnessed on the same ground in the first 1966 Test match that I feared the Lions would be swamped. Repeatedly it seemed the thin red line which represented the Lions' defence would be broken, but the courage shown in resisting those attacks determined the fate of the tour.

It was also fortunate that Barry John had conversed with Colin Meads on the subject of how he dealt with fly-halves. John remembered an incident during the 1966 tour when Meads had floored another small Welshman, Dai Watkins. Meads told John that after that he had decided not to hit backs. 'I believed him, and therefore thought it was safe to hang on to his jersey as he came crashing through at me from a line-out,' said John. It worked, because even the 16-stone Meads could not carry the 11½-stone John for long, and was brought tumbling down.

After that first mighty wave of New Zealand attacks the Lions settled down, their better scrummaging gave them more control, and John was able to torture full-back McCormick with long rolling kicks to touch. This proved to be the last game McCormick played in the series, and he must have learned to hate the name of John. Worse still for McCormick, he was off target with his kicks and could land only one penalty goal, while John collected two and Ian McLauchlan scored a try after charging down a poor clearance by Alan Sutherland. So the Lions won, 9–3.

With the All Blacks needing to win the last Test to square the series, MacBride realized they would be prepared to take extreme measures. He feared the game might degenerate into a rough-house, and on the eve of the Test he warned the team of his fears. It did not take long for MacBride to be proved right, as in the third line-out Gordon Brown was knocked out by the explosive fist of Peter Whiting. The referee saw the incident but confined his punishment to a penalty. Such is Test rugby, and some officials wonder why leading rugby players cheat.

MacBride had been worried that, even with two substitutes, the Lions would be lucky to finish with fifteen players. He decided to create a fight and force the referee to warn the captains, so he broke up a scrum near the opposition line and finished with raised fists while Tom Lister retreated. It worked because referee Pring called Dawes and Meads together and told them to control the temper of their players. Unfortunately this had little effect on the All Black prop Jas Muller, who deliberately kicked Brown early in the second half. Brown needed eighteen stitches in his leg for this injury and a further six for the Whiting punch; he was forced to retire from the game, and was replaced by Delme Thomas.

These incidents and the tenseness of the occasion prevented play flowing and led to a game of poor quality. But the character of the Lions, which had been an underlying feature of the tour, emerged when they pulled back from an eight-point deficit. It was also intoxicating to see the joy in the face of J.P.R. Williams when he kicked a rare dropped goal to gain a 14–11 lead. However, a Laurie Mains penalty squared the scores, and the game finished 14–14. The Lions had achieved their ambition, and Dr Smith's 2–1 prognosis had been proved right. The All Blacks had taken earlier defeats well but were sour at losing the series. It was another indication that rugby had assumed too much importance in New Zealand. Yet it seemed fitting that the game's original pioneers should be back on top at a time when rugby football had entered its second century.

From *How the Lions Won* edited by Terry O'Connor
(Collins, London, 1975)

The Lions in New Zealand

Colin Meads

If I were to relate the performances of the 1971 Lions in New Zealand with others of those composite British Isles teams against whom I played I could not do better than to repeat what I said to those Lions: 'You are the greatest touring team I have played against. You are great because you have stopped believing in fairy tales.' That judgement was received with comment good and bad yet it was not made without thought, nor do I believe it to be an over-simplification. Through the Lions of 1971 and the men who inspired them British rugby became adult – in the sense that the team and those who supported them realized that Test matches are to be won, and that it is difficult to win them without realistic planning. To achieve success there had to be a new mental and physical attitude to the business of winning parity, at least in that area of rugby where matches are won, always have been and ever will be: in the forwards, in those pieces of play from which possession is won. It was in this that the 1971 Lions succeeded most dramatically.

When all the praise – and it is justified – has been given to men like Carwyn James and Ray McLoughlin and Dougie Smith we must come again to the essential ingredient, the players of the game. I do not except Ray McLoughlin from them but it was in the planning and technical sense that Ray had such an influence on the players. The injury which disqualified him from participation in the Tests was, in an ironic way, one of the reasons why they won the series, because he concentrated his attention, almost fanatically, on the techniques he knew the Lions must perfect to win.

Where the Lions of 1959 and 1966 set out to attack, they did so too often from positions which were not controlled, from positions where the opposition was not committed and, therefore, where the defences were set and in depth. There were fine players in these teams, but the conception of what had to be achieved before they could express their talents was not of the same standard. The 1971 team had players of brilliance in the backs and they were given their head in many of the provincial matches. But when it came to the Tests the head ruled the heart, and these Lions played the sort of utilitarian rugby which, allied with magnificent defence and stout forward play, is terribly difficult to beat.

If I have a qualification about the development of this new spirit it would be that, having achieved the techniques to scrum with the best, to contest possession from all sources, British rugby should not allow itself to become top-heavy. It appears in danger of doing so. By that I mean that Britain should not now cut its backs out of the game. The new forward power and skill should have given the British the platform from which – with devastating effectiveness – they can play total rugby better than any other nation in the world. It would be a great pity were traditional brilliance in one area of the game now to be squandered because Britain has found such quality in another.

My first experience with the Lions was in 1959 when as a reserve at Carisbrook, Dunedin, I watched Don Clarke kick six penalty goals to give New Zealand an 18–17 victory against a Lions team which scored four tries. That sort of defeat would upset me, too. Yet with the laws as they were then the referee was right, and scoring tries was not necessarily enough to win a game against a team kicking penalty goals. My observation that day was that the Lions had only themselves to blame for losing what could so easily and deservedly have been a slashing victory. I am aware that though they were beaten in the series the Lions of 1959 believed deeply they were the better team. The same story could have been true in 1971. I believe New Zealand, with constant goal-kicking, would have beaten the Lions. But this is all hypothetical. The facts of wins and losses are straightforward enough.

The year 1971 saw the great awakening of British rugby. For years they had watched their teams being beaten by All Blacks who used their possession with stiff-necked utilitarianism, who spread their wings only rarely – and then when it seemed it was safe to do so from positions of control. While the All Blacks were doing this, the Lions, receiving much less controlled possession, and often as they were moving back, or without the New Zealanders having committed themselves, would launch uninhibited attacks which were doomed before they started. In 1971 the roles were reversed. The British and, I suspect, Carwyn James in particular, had worked out their priorities and had decided that there was a great deal to be said for winning – even in the game of rugger.

Yes, the Lions of 1971 stopped believing in those old fairy tales. But I wonder whether another fairy tale is not already born – that because you have developed strength forward then, *ipso facto*, you can forget your old strengths. That could be as damaging to British rugby in the long run as the proposition that you can muck about with poor forward play as long as you have brilliant backs. I see Britain as being in a unique position in world rugby, but I wonder if the British themselves appreciate it. New strength in the forwards has not automatically cancelled out brilliance in the backs. So why not use the new to exploit the traditional? That seems to make a lot of rugby sense to me.

From *How the Lions Won* edited by Terry O'Connor
(Collins, London, 1975)

There *was* a Lot of Kicking

John Reason

Some people argue that the achievements of the 1974 Lions in South Africa eclipsed even the proud record of the 1971 Lions. John Reason is among those who beg to differ, largely because of the style of rugby which the 1974 Lions chose to play.

W.B.B.

With that pool of forwards established in 1971, and with world-class players in the key positions of half-back and full-back, the Lions could afford to make an indifferent team selection and to leave three world-class backs at home as well as three of their best forwards and still beat South Africa with something to spare.

Indeed, granted the same pool of props, the same half-backs, the same full-back and possibly the same number eight, British Rugby could have permutated any nine or ten players from forty and still have beaten South Africa. It was not even a contest. It was the men versus the boys.

Yet even with that sort of an advantage, the Lions played such a desperately unambitious game that many of the hundreds of supporters who had flocked out to see the second half of the tour were so bored with the football that they did not even bother to watch the midweek games. It was a forwards' tour. The backs were there just to make up the number. They had no significant influence in the councils of war and the team was the poorer for it.

This was the inevitable consequence of appointing a coach and a captain who were both tight forwards and who both came from the same club and the same country. Their vision of the game was restricted to the scrummage and to the tighter aspects of forward play. The work they did in this area was both thorough and effective and they sustained it until the end of the tour, but scrummaging ought to be a means to an end, and not an end in itself. Their view of the contribution of the backs was strongly influenced by their desire to keep the ball close to the forwards and they did not have the flexibility to expand their approach when they saw that such a cautious approach was no longer necessary. It was miserly stuff compared with the visions of grandeur of the 1971 tour, visions which were realized on that unforgettable day in Cardiff when the Barbarians played the All Blacks in 1973. The 1971 tour embraced the aspirations and the philosophies of Llanelli, London Welsh and Wales at that time. They were the clubs and the national team of Carwyn

James, the coach, and John Dawes, the captain. The 1974 tour embraced the aspirations and the philosophies of Ballymena, Ballymena and Ireland. There was a world of difference between the two concepts of the game.

South Africa will never know how lucky they were. Had the Lions played them on their merits or had the Lions used their backs with the confidence of the 1971 team, the Springboks would have suffered at least two defeats even bigger than the 44–0 thrashing they gave Scotland in 1951.

For years, British Rugby had worked to improve its forward organization so that it could release the skills of its backs. The pot of gold at the end of the rainbow was always 50 per cent of the ball. 'If only we can win 50 per cent of the ball.' Our coaches said it so many times, and they said it so wistfully.

In South Africa in 1974, the British Lions won more than 70 per cent of the ball. And what did they do with it? They played like the 1963 All Blacks, but you cannot possibly criticize the All Blacks and the Springboks for playing that sort of game and then say that it is all right for the Lions to play it.

The sad thing was that it was all so unnecessary. It was no good arguing that the Lions had to play as they did because their leading backs were not available to tour. The backs who went in their place may not have been the greatest defenders in the world and some of them may not have been the greatest footballers either but they were all a lot better than anything in South Africa.

In any case, the Lions' forwards were so much in command that the backs never had to do much defending anyway, and on the wings, they had runners in Andy Irvine and J.J. Williams who could have cut South Africa to pieces if J.P.R. Williams had been encouraged to set them up.

To some people, the end justified the means. They did not care how the Lions won, just as long as they *did* win. They did not stop to think of the implications for the future of British back play contained in the way the Lions played the game. They shut their minds to the fact that British back play would have no future if that style of play was adopted. They were not remotely concerned about the battle for the hearts and the minds of the young, and of the enthusiasm of all those selfless people who teach the young how to play. Winning was all that mattered.

John Dawes went to New Zealand as captain of the Lions in 1971 convinced that he was leading a missionary expedition to save a whole country from the burning. He said then, 'Look at the changes we have seen since we were here two years ago with Wales. Soccer is on the increase everywhere. Look at what is happening in the schools.

'Everywhere we go, our players see the same thing – more and more soccer and less and less Rugby. Schoolmasters are not supporting Rugby in the way they did, and who can blame them? Rugby in this country is no fun for a schoolboy. He has no freedom of expression. He has to conform to a pattern, the same dull pattern which you see right through the game. It is efficient, I grant you, but because it is so dull it contains the seeds of its own destruction.

'Look at the teams we have played so far. They all play in the same way and they all train in the same way. Who would want to be a back in New Zealand? He is only there to stop the other side and return the ball to the forwards. They all look as if they have come out of a machine.

'We must show them here that our way is so much more interesting than theirs. I really do believe that if the All Blacks win this series playing ten man Rugby, it will do irreparable damage to the game in New Zealand. It is for their own good that we must win.'

John Dawes needed to continue his missionary work in South Africa in 1974 – with the British Lions. That was exactly the way the Lions played and only a hypocrite or someone very ignorant of Rugby football would have pretended otherwise.

Of course, if you are playing against a team which is beating you consistently for possession, as the Lions were in 1971, then you have to live off your wits as John Dawes and Barry John did, but if you are playing against a team which has nothing to offer either fore or aft, as the Lions were in 1974, then you can play the game on any terms you choose.

The Lions chose to use their backs to stop the other side and to return the ball to the forwards. It was efficient, I grant you, but it was dull, and because it was so dull it contained the seeds of its own destruction, or at any rate, the destruction of British back play.

Fortunately, those seeds are unlikely to flower, because each of the four home countries which make up a Lions team has its own way of playing the game. No doubt Ireland will go on playing the same sort of Rugby as that played by the Lions in 1974, and perhaps Scotland will be tempted to do the same, but it is hard to imagine Wales or England presiding over the demise of the three-quarter. Most of the supporters who watched the second half of the Lions tour were Welsh, and those who had also been in New Zealand in 1971 had no doubt of their preference.

Syd Millar justified his choice of tactics by saying, 'It's winning Rugby.'

Indeed it was, but England had played winning Rugby in 1972, and they had played it with infinitely more style.

From *The Unbeaten Lions* by John Reason
(Rugby Books, London, 1974)

Injured Pride

Chris Rea

My own tour of South Africa with the 1980 Lions was much less successful – we lost the Test series 3–1, but we regained a lot of pride with the manner of our victory in the fourth Test at one of my favourite grounds, the Loftus Stadium in Pretoria.

W.B.B.

Few people outside the Lions' camp thought they had much chance of winning the fourth and final Test in Pretoria. No other Lions' team had done it in South Africa; even the highly successful 1974 side could only draw the last match of the series after winning the first three. Of the other major touring sides to visit South Africa, New Zealand had won the fourth Test on their 1928 tour, and in 1933 Australia won the fifth Test in a five-match series. The usual reasons advanced for the extreme difficulty of winning this last game are that the visiting players' thoughts are turned towards home, that they are occupied with buying presents, saying 'Good-bye' to the large numbers of new friends they have made, and generally preparing for the journey home. They have little time to think of Rugby Football. Dr Danie Craven said quite frankly that it was wrong to end a tour with an international match. Yet it has always been done, and probably always will be, for the event must finish with a climax. One or two minor matches after the last Test would be useless.

However, inside the Lions' camp, in spite of all the distractions, far from there being a despondent mood as to the outcome of the game, there was an air of determination, a resolution that there should be no 'whitewash'. It was quite amazing how the general state of mind of the individuals in the party, which for want of a better word we call 'team spirit', remained buoyant to the end in spite of every setback. Maybe that was one of the reasons why these Lions were such popular tourists. They had suffered many bitter blows and disappointments, and perhaps they knew in their silent thoughtful moments that they might inadvertently commit again some of those Rugby sins that had beset them. Yet they refused to show it, and they went into the game with a confident air.

Perhaps it was their confidence and determination, more than anything else, that enabled them to achieve the seemingly impossible; particularly the determination of the forwards, for there were times during the match when the old troubles of the backs returned. They beat South Africa 17–13, showing at last what could and should have been done in the other Tests. However it is of little use to reflect afterwards on what might have been; we must deal with facts.

The splendid Loftus Stadium in Pretoria was packed with a capacity crowd of sixty-eight thousand, all seated. There had been a tremendous scramble for tickets, and for the first time on the tour the touts had done a roaring trade. All South Africa wanted to be there to see, as they anticipated, the Springboks achieve the series grand slam in the sunshine of Pretoria. For their captain, Morne du Plessis, such an outcome on this ground was essential to obliterate his memory of the match played there six years earlier. On that occasion he had been in the Springbok side who had lost to the Lions by a record margin, and he had been dropped for the remainder of the series. A final victory here would have erased that memory, but it was not to be.

If ever a pack of forwards was completely outplayed and mastered in an international match, it was the pack in which Morne du Plessis was captain that day. The Lions won overwhelming possession, and for most of the game had the Springboks in constant retreat. By half-time they ought to have held such a commanding lead that the South Africans could not possibly have caught them. In fact they led by four points. There had been a few moments here and there when it seemed that the Lions were back in the old rut. Ollie Campbell's goal-kicking, for instance, was erratic again. In the home championship he had hardly ever missed; in the Tests in South Africa his performance was quite the reverse. He missed with important kicks at Bloemfontein, at Port Elizabeth, and again at Loftus Versfeld, where in the whole match he succeeded with only two kicks from eight attempts. Late in the game Andy Irvine ignored an overlap and a try was lost, but this time there was compensation for these errors.

Campbell may have been off target with the boot, but his running was much more effective, and he played an important part in the Lions' first try. Irvine began the move in his own half, fastening on to a poor kick and giving Campbell the chance to show himself as an elusive runner. John O'Driscoll, the outstanding player in a magnificent pack, was up with Campbell and drove on twenty-five metres, tantalizingly near the Springboks' line. Van Heerden stopped him, but O'Driscoll made sure the ball was available for Clive Williams, who was shoved over by his fellow forwards for the try. By then Campbell had missed four penalty kicks, so Irvine was called upon to make the conversion attempt, and he also missed. So, Campbell and Botha each having kicked a penalty goal earlier, the Lions led by 7–3.

The Springboks had hardly been in the game, but as before they were quite capable of hanging on in the hope that eventually the Lions would give enough away to be beaten. It was a coincidence, and perhaps ominous, that the Lions had also led 7–3 at Port Elizabeth. On that occasion the Springboks had followed up by scoring three times. This time it became frighteningly apparent that they might do the same thing again. Botha set up a try for them, picking up a loose ball and making a lot of ground before passing to Willie du Plessis who swerved past a couple of Lions with tantalizing ease and touched down near the posts. Botha's conversion attempt hardly got off the ground. At this point, though, the Springboks enjoyed their one period of domination. Botha had been jeered by the crowd for his kicking failures, and Gysie Pienaar was given the kick from fifty-two metres when the Lions got off-side. With all the confidence of a man at his peak, he kicked a beautiful goal. Two minutes later the Lions again were off-side and again Pienaar, from a much narrower angle, kicked the penalty goal. It was not the first time in the series that the Springboks had been able to look at the scoreboard and wonder why they were six points up in a match that ought to have spelt for them comprehensive defeat.

The Lions' forwards, however, fought back as they had so often done before, and for a short time that determination with which they had gone into the match became apparent not only in the pack but among the backs as well. While the forwards maintained complete and utter control, the backs, perhaps out of embarrassment, began to move the ball with some resolution. They handled it out to Bruce Hay on the left wing – not at a great pace – but Irvine got up in support, and when Hay was tackled Irvine gathered the ball quickly and got over in the corner. There was a suspicion that Irvine was off-side, but the referee was up with the play and saw nothing wrong. After a moment's hesitation he awarded the try which gave Irvine the four points he needed to equal the world record of 210 set by Phil Bennett in thirty-seven internationals. Irvine had played in forty-six.

The try which won the match came soon afterwards when Irvine, having failed to give John Carleton the ball with the Springbok line wide open, was ankle-tapped by Pienaar. The Lions recaptured the ball, Tucker and Squire rolled it, O'Driscoll supported, and with several Springboks on his back scored the try so close in that Campbell could not possibly miss the conversion.

There were a few minutes still to go, but the Lions had their tails up by then and maintained command, while John Robbie kept the ball tight. At last the Lions had won! Certainly they deserved to do so this time. They had destroyed the Springbok pack, and even the experienced Morne du Plessis was near to panic. Only Willie du Plessis and Pienaar behind the scrum played with anything like the skill expected at the top level. Had there been a fifth Test the South African selectors must have made changes, because they could not have returned to the fray with that side. For the first time in the series their mediocrity had been thoroughly exposed by the Lions, whose forwards had never played better. Syd Millar said he had never seen a better pack, which was praise indeed for he had coached the 1974 forwards to a new peak of efficiency.

From *Injured Pride: the Lions in South Africa* by Carwyn James and Chris Rea
(Arthur Barker, London, 1980)

A Deep Sense of Relief

Carwyn James

At the final whistle of the last Test I felt a deep sense of relief because the Lions had survived after once again showing an infinite capacity to destroy themselves. Somehow they had seemed to defy the age-long principles of the game, including the basic one that the side which wins the most possession should win. With the amount of the ball they won in the first half they should have led by five times the four-point margin which the scoreboard showed. The pack, hunting together with power and pride, were yards too quick for their opponents, and with so much pressure inflicted on Morne's men the tries surely ought to have come. Yet in that glorious first half of power play they scored only one try, initiated by their backs and finished off by Clive Williams, who was the epitome of the saying that props should never be seen.

At half-time I had the uneasy feeling that I had seen this many times before: power play resulting in little actual reward, and the inevitable boost it gives to the opposition, who know that if they can stem attack upon attack, then surely, most surely, their moment will come. And it came. Botha did the approach work, and Willie du Plessis finished off the movement with a brilliant piece of running. Pienaar, unquestionably the man of the series, did the kicking that mattered, and the Lions were six points adrift – two knock-out punches, and both beautifully timed.

While the Lions' fight-back earned them eternal credit, even when Irvine scored – if he did – the passing was still shoddy, and it was a near miracle that the ball got that far. Then Irvine had the Springboks, their line, and the silent crowd at his mercy, but he stuttered and fell, and failed to pass to Carleton. Irvine, more than anyone, I am sure, must have been relieved when O'Driscoll scored the all-important try for his team to win the match. O'Driscoll, I thought, was the most improved player in the Lions' squad.

There is no doubt that the Lions deserved their victory; a victory which only underlined the fact that they were the better side in the series but applied their talents to mediocre effect.

From *Injured Pride: the Lions in South Africa* by Carwyn James and Chris Rea
(Arthur Barker, London, 1980)

Touring is Fun?

Phil Bennett

Rugby tours, whether at international or Extra B level, can be the happiest days of their lives for some and unremitting nightmares for others. Welshman Phil Bennett and David Frost of the *Guardian* have differing views on the joys of touring.

W.B.B.

You need the bad times to appreciate the good 'uns, and you need bad tours to make you appreciate the enjoyable ones. As the memories fade, it's interesting to find that the humorous highlights are the ones that stay. Nevertheless, the Welsh tour of New Zealand in 1969 still haunts me and I'm not too enthusiastic about recalling journeys to Japan or Argentina either.

It is only now that administrators are beginning to realize what meticulous preparation is needed before embarking on international rugby tours. Acknowledging an itinerary as being acceptable without first-hand knowledge of the country's venues and the local circumstances, is nothing short of criminal. The Welsh administrators were guilty in all three of the countries that I've mentioned. The team was confined to a country house stuck in the middle of nowhere in Argentina; they were given the same hotel for the whole stay in Japan; and whoever planned the tour of New Zealand should have been lined up outside Cardiff Castle in a medieval stocks.

I wonder if it is asking too much of the overseers of such money-making tours to ponder a little before committing their gladiators to the arduous timetables. Though Wales went to New Zealand as conquerors of Europe and Home International champions in 1969, they were totally destroyed by a magnificent All Blacks team – helped by our own suicidal schedule. We had hardly recovered from a forty-two-hour flight when we were thrown into a hard provincial match against Taranaki. To make matters worse, four days after that we had to face New Zealand. The history books will tell you that we were taken to the cleaners; though no excuses should be offered, despite the best will in the world, the commitment needed was absent because of genuine tiredness.

The Welsh have acquired a reputation of being lousy travellers, an introspective lot given to homesickness and cliquish formation. I personally plead guilty to all charges of *hiraeth*, but on the two Lions tours that I've been on, I haven't seen any evidence to support the theory. I wonder, however, how many could withstand the boredom of same hotel and same routine that the Welsh players had to endure in Argentina. Goodness knows, I'm grateful for the opportunity of seeing the world and doing what I enjoy best, playing rugby, and it might seem less than charitable to criticize the people who spend a great deal of time organizing the tours. Nevertheless, there was little to do in the Argentinian country club except train, play golf and eat steaks. To those who would hold up their hands in horror at such ingratitude, there is a little saying in Welsh, '*Gormod o bwdin dagiff gi*,' which literally translated means 'Too much pudding will make even a dog sick'!

From *Everywhere for Wales* by Phil Bennett
(Stanley Paul, London, 1983)

Anyone Can Tour

David Frost

It cannot be emphasized too strongly that going on a rugby tour is not an activity limited to the elite. The great tours are the ones which make the headlines throughout the world. But anyone can get on to a rugby tour of some sort simply by joining a rugby club.

The first type of tour you may get an invitation for when you come into senior rugby is an Easter one. It is one of the firmest customs in the game that clubs go on tour at Easter. Lots of English clubs great and small, for instance, go on tour to South Wales or the West Country at Easter, and most of them play at least two games over the holiday period. These are usually on Easter Saturday and Easter Monday with an additional match thrown in perhaps on Good Friday.

Always accept the invitation if you possibly can. It quite often happens that two or three senior players cannot get away for the tour, and their absence provides an ambitious young player with a chance to play for the first team for the first time. Travelling is likely to be less well organized than for a normal away match because some players may be going on to other parts of the country after the Easter weekend for the rest of their holiday, and others may be joining the tour from holidays they have already started – these tend to arrive by car, bus, motorbike, train, or scooter, ignoring the main party. But however you decide to travel, watch out for the Easter travel arrangements of public transport and remember that the roads may be very crowded, involving you in long delays. I well remember trying to get into Wales from England for a match on a Good Friday and being held up for a nail-biting length of time at the Severn Bridge by the holiday traffic.

Once you have settled into the hotel you will be amazed at the way in which even the most respectable members of the club hasten into second childhood when grouped on a rugby tour. They take over the bar, run round the hotel corridors with fire hoses, and get up to all sorts of childish pranks. Confusion and merriment take over. There was, for instance, the evening in Dawlish when our eighteen-stone lock forward, peering out into the night on his way to the gents, came across a clothes-line festooned with female underclothes. He took possession of some, went back to his room, stripped, and appeared on the landing wearing nothing but the hotel manageress's knickers. Someone now pretended the manageress was on her way up the stairs; whereupon our lock forward fled into his room and shut himself in the wardrobe. One of the party promptly turned the key of the door of the wardrobe, confining our lock to a dark prison which he did not appreciate. After a while the prisoner, imagining that he had by now eluded the manageress, tried to escape, but the wardrobe door would not open. Frustrated, he threw his shoulder at the door, the wardrobe toppled over, door downwards, and the hotel shook with the crash of wardrobe and eighteen-stone lock hitting the bedroom floor a violent blow. At this the manageress left her gin and tonic at the bar and rushed upstairs to find out what was happening. Thus it was that the owner of the knickers arrived at the open door of bedroom seven in time to see emerging from the wreckage a fat and sore lock forward looking very silly indeed.

The first tour breakfast can be 'interesting'. It is probably the first time you have ever seen all your team-mates reading newspapers, and it is certainly the first time you have ever seen middle-aged men dressed up in school blazers. The blazers are faded and so are their wearers, but the older members of the party do not seem to think it funny that they should wear blazers on tour. Nor did one of them think it funny at Dawlish when, while he was quietly reading his *Daily Telegraph*, a firework was surreptitiously – and irresponsibly – placed on his table under the shining silver lid which was meant to be keeping warm his sausages, eggs and bacon.

From *No Prisoners – A Background to Rugby Touring* by David Frost
(Pelham Books, London, 1978)

15
GREAT GROUNDS

A Smell All of its Own

John Robbie

If for obvious reasons, my own all-time favourite ground is Twickenham, I have a soft spot for the Arms Park, Murrayfield, Lansdowne Road, Parc des Princes, Loftus Stadium and Lancaster Park too. Nothing can replace the SCG in Sydney for me, however; when I see the Concord Oval I want to weep. Great games demand great venues and each rugby-playing country, apart from Australia, has its own great cathedral of the game. All rugby grounds have a distinct feeling and atmosphere to them, but John Robbie even manages to distinguish them by smell . . .

W.B.B.

One of the funny things about the major South African rugby grounds is that they each have a different smell. I first noticed it on the Lions tour.

I was used to Lansdowne Road, Twickers, Murrayfield and the Arms Park, and Parc des Princes, too. I know that each of those grounds is different – but they all smell the same. There is a dampness and a richness of the soil that, because I was so used to it, I never noticed or considered. Then I went to South Africa and, especially when you move away from the coast, you are aware of a change.

On the highveld the dryness hits you, not just in the atmosphere. It's in the turf, in the concrete; hell, it's even in the people. I love it, and my favourite ground in all the world is Loftus Versfeld in Pretoria. It's also my lucky ground, which helps. I first saw Loftus when the Lions played Northerns in 1980. I had replaced Colin Patterson who had flu; I was terrified, and will never forget the roar as we ran on to the field. I played well, though, and barring that bone-shaking mistake I made in taking on Pierre Edwards, it remains a treasured memory.

Ellis Park is also a highveld ground, but at a greater altitude than Pretoria. At Ellis Park I always detected a slight staleness in the air – and the pitch smells different. I once mentioned this to someone, and they explained that it was because of all the shit Transvaal play on it. But I think it's due to being situated in the old, run-down part of the city and also the totally enclosed design. Loftus has that huge open side and I think that lets the air in.

Bloemfontein's Free State stadium is depressing. I think all players hate playing on grounds that have an athletics track around them, because the crowd is so far away. In

Bloem you also have a cycling track to contend with, and you feel the lack of atmosphere immediately. Mind you, that could also be because there is rarely a full-house feeling there – even 20,000 or so get lost in its vastness. I always think of the pitch as yellow and hard, with a very sandy texture. I hated it.

Then we move to the coast. The city of Durban itself has a smell all of its own. I don't know if it's the humidity or the vegetation, but when you get out of the plane in Durban all this, mixed with the smell of the sea, produces a very spicy aroma. The ground is also very 'Durban' and of course as you leave it after a game the delicious smell of smoke and braaled meat creates a lasting memory.

Boet Erasmus in Port Elizabeth is a beautiful ground, but somehow the smell is of a small country rugby pitch. Somehow you don't smell buildings, you smell grass. It is sort of cut into a hill and there is a lot of earth around, and no doubt that's where the feeling comes from. It's huge, but doesn't smell huge.

Then, of course, there is Newlands. What a perfect ground for rugby. Even with the new stands and the perfect pitch they now have, it just smells of tradition. On reflection, there's also in my memory a paint smell. They are always painting something at Newlands on match day, always in blue and white and always by a rabid Province fan. That's the smell at Newlands: the paint of fanaticism.

Of all the provincial grounds I've been in, Newlands has the best people. You get the impression that all of them – the chap who directs you off the team bus, the lady who has just cleaned out the dressing-room, the programme sellers, union president Jan Pickard himself – all are happy and they are all Western Province fans. You don't get that at other grounds. Even at Loftus and at the Arms Park, it's hard to tell whether the people are working there out of love or for the pay. At Newlands you feel that the pay is not important, you really do. I loved playing at Newlands.

From *The Game of My Life* by John Robbie
(Pelham Books, London, 1989)

I Remember Lansdowne Road

John D. Sheridan

As I watched this new stand climb up, up, among the seagulls, up until it seemed to touch the rim of the mountains, I felt first that I deserved it and had earned it, and then that I had had some hand in the building of it. And so I had. All honour to those who had the courage to plan and sponsor this mighty enterprise, but a little honour too to me and the likes of me, for our custom is its best collateral and our loyalty a surer foundation than concrete.

The new stand will please everyone, but no one will welcome it more than those of us who have been coming to Lansdowne Road ever since we were in short trousers, and will keep coming as long as our legs will bear us up. Others may follow the crowd, but our urge is a fire in the blood that will know no cooling on this side of the grave.

I have been coming to internationals at Lansdowne Road now for more than thirty years. I saw Dicky Lloyd drop his last goal for Ireland, I watched the rise of the star that was Denis Cussen. Try me on the records and I will match you name for name.

If any ghosts come here on misty evenings, mine will surely be seen slinking out past the railings round the sacred sward to play some utterly negligible match on one of the unregarded back pitches. That was as far as I got, and it wasn't for want of trying. If the good fairy had offered me my choice of fame or wealth I would have settled for a green jersey: and if she were to ask me the same question now, and could do anything about my years and my varicose veins, I might make the same answer.

I remember my first trip to Twickenham. It cost me twenty-two shillings return, and for that I saw the Tower of London, Westminster Abbey, 10 Downing Street, and Larry McMahon's winning try.

But what I remember best is that touch of magic that marked international matches in Dublin, that strange electric feeling that brought a tingle to the spine and stretched Lansdowne Road to the Pillar. For us, the game began as soon as those cheerful mercenaries who sell the 'colours of the match' (and probably turn an honest penny during the off season by making a corner in shamrock and hot cross buns) took their stand in O'Connell Street and called public attention to the serious business of the day. Sometimes we bought our colours, and sometimes we made them, but we had to have them; we would as soon have gone to the match without trousers as without our insignia.

And we used to deplore the dark treachery of those who, towards one o'clock, lined up for trams that were going in the wrong direction – muddy-souled folk who, with a warped and treasonable sense of values, were prepared to spend the evening weeding their gardens or taking the dog for a walk. We wondered what they had in their veins instead of red blood.

The long wait before the match began (and because of our eagerness it was always a long wait) was no burden. It was, rather, a foretaste of ecstasy. And we had our own ways of passing the time. There was a band, provided by the management, but we preferred the impromptu comic opera provided by be-ribboned Englishmen, Scotsmen or Welshmen – old enough to know better, but still young at heart – who cavorted up and down the pitch and scored mighty tries against the half-hearted opposition of shamefaced policemen. Meanwhile, massed and swaying on the terraces, we greeted the holders of touch-line seats, to their obvious embarrassment, with tremendous and rhythmic shouts of 'Hard Hat', 'Hair Oil' and 'Mamma's Boy'; and once in a while there was a touch of pure genius, as when a small man arrived escorting two big women – and someone shouted 'Bigamist'! Those were the days.

And at one match I had a goal-line seat that was much nearer the pitch than the orthodox goal-line seats. It was in the days before crush barriers, and when the attendance was not quite as well regulated as it is now. The great press of humanity massed behind me started to crush down relentlessly, and wave after wave of us was pushed right up against the railings – and we had to choose between dying there or scrambling over. We felt very self-conscious out on the pitch, so we tucked ourselves down on the green sward behind the goal and tried to look as if we weren't there. And presently the English referee came over and asked me – asked me personally, picking me out from the whole mob of displaced persons – if I would mind moving back like a good chap and let the game go on. He was a very discerning referee – he knew a Rugby enthusiast when he saw one. So I let him have his game. I moved back a little, and the people behind me moved back a little, and we saw the match from ground level.

Today I shall watch it from a much higher perch, from a seat on the new stand that is flush with the rim of the mountains – this fine structure that has changed the geography of Lansdowne Road and opened a fresh chapter in its history. And I feel that I have helped to write that history, for it was written, not just by men in green jerseys, but by those who swayed on the terraces, who cheered and hoped and prayed, and who came away hoarse as drakes after both victory and defeat. We may not cheer as loudly as we used to, or take defeat as much to heart, but we can still manage an odd bellow and there is no doubt where our loyalties lie.

We are a part of Lansdowne Road – I and the likes of me. We are glad of its fine new stand, and as long as God lets us we will help to fill it. We earned it, and we deserve it. There is nothing about us to set us off from the rest of the crowd, but we still remember ancient glories. And we come, not from a love of spectacle and high drama that could be satisfied just as easily at a fireworks display or a race meeting, but from a fierce and unquenchable loyalty; not to follow the crowd, but because of a fire that will know no cooling on this side of the grave.

From the *Scotland/Ireland v. England/Wales programme*
(Irish RFU, 31 December 1955)

Not Now, You Silly Twit

Dave Allen

I'd have lit candles to Jack Kyle at one time, around about 1948–49 when Ireland had won two triple crowns. I remember an Englishman in the crowd at Lansdowne Road telling me that the reason why Ireland managed that remarkable double was that they'd not been involved in a war – 'While we've been rationed you lot have been eating steaks and eggs and butter. Your lot are therefore sturdier.' I've heard of many things being blamed for losing a game, but really, a war and starvation! They knock the crap out of the German Army and couldn't out of fifteen Irishmen.

I'm not really partisan. I don't care who wins as long as Ireland doesn't get beat. There's great atmosphere in Dublin on match days. I was there a couple of seasons ago when Ireland beat France. It was phenomenal. If you opened the door of a pub, the bodies just fell out and you had to push them all back and close the door. The whole city was jumping up and down.

There's great humour in the game. There were three Irishmen watching the 1951 Springboks at Lansdowne Road – two minutes to go and Ireland throwing everything at the South African line. Suddenly one says to his friend, 'Hey Shaun, Padders has dropped dead' . . . 'Ah he's missing the best part of the match.'

Cardiff Arms Park has a totally different atmosphere. It's sort of holy. I was there for the Scotland match, and a Welsh fella behind me was giving it some stick. 'Come on WALES!' If you remember Scotland got nine points and the shouts went down to a whisper, 'Come on Wales.' When Wales pulled back, so too did the volume of the shout. It was if he'd taken a tablet. He gradually came back as Wales came back.

Then, again, there's Twickenham. I was at that Springbok match against England and in that last fantastic couple of minutes when England were almost over the 'boks line, a demonstrator dashed on and stopped the game. An enormous fellow near me leapt to his feet: 'Not now, you silly twit.' You know, any other time, but not when England were poised for a score.

What I joke about at Twickenham – there's always a Rugby Type. He smacks of rugby and he generally wears a very long mackintosh and looks like he's had about five belts of whisky very quickly. He wears a check shirt and some form of club tie; and he's pompous, very pompous about the game, and he probably hasn't played since he was six or seven.

I've often thought if the GAA in Ireland and the Irish Rugby Union got together they could produce one hell of a side. There's great players in both. At the moment if a Gaelic football and hurling player is seen at a rugby match he can be banned for life. I don't go with that.

I played all three games at school. At a priests' college, the Holy Ghost Fathers and Carmelite Fathers taught Rugby Union and then I played Gaelic and hurling at the Christian Brothers School. Hurling's a great game to play. It doesn't matter how big you are or how small you are. You have a stick in your hand and so it levels you down. If a fellow gives you a cuff around the head, you eventually give him one back. You reach a line of respect. So it should be in all games.

I get great joy out of watching rugby and great disappointment too – that's when they won't play the ball. That's what I love about the French, even on their own line they take chances. The other team are so startled – sort of mesmerized. It's fabulous to watch. I'm not a rugby addict, but if I can, I arrange my work and some rugby to coincide – like I did last year in Australia when the Rugby League boys were there. I like Rugby League. I often wonder if the Union and the League should get together again, you know, take the best from both, eliminate the worst from both. You may get a super game just called Rugby.

From *Touchdown*
(RFU, London, 1970)

Excursion Train

John Morgan

The rain eased five minutes before the excursion train to Scotland for the Welsh Rugby match was due out of Swansea. The men who had been pretending they were waiting for the rain to ease ran from the ex-International's pub across the station yard swinging their flagons or carrying their crates like soldiers rushing ammunition to the guns. In the hallway an undergraduate stood holding a bunch of delicately wrapped leeks, looking very much like a man waiting for his mistress in a sensitive British film, but not talking like one. He had lost his ticket.

After a man had rushed through our crowded Pullman car shouting, 'Moses, Moses, where are you, Moses?' we settled down quietly for the twelve hours' journey through the night. Young men played cards for fun. In another car a frail middle-aged man, with his false teeth on the table in front of him, joined in singing 'I Believe', obviously not knowing the words. When 'Calon Lan' began he put his teeth back in his mouth. In the mixed car – the girls being of most ages – there was some shouting and a *bonhomie* so humid that, transmuted, it trickled down the window panes.

Two men, both over seventy years of age, at my table, after establishing that they had a mutual acquaintance of preachers and minor bards, began a recondite philological discussion in Welsh. The man in the grey suit and brilliant white collar, his face scrubbed until it shone, had postulated this argument; some Englishmen and some renegades say that Welsh is a dead language because it borrows from the English. Well, then, what about telephone? 'What about telephone indeed,' said his new friend, the man in the navy blue suit and striped flannel shirt.

'Telephone is from the Greek.'

'Those Greeks were a brilliant lot.'

'What is the English for telephone?'

'Ask you may.'

'Telephone!'

While they considered this point the man in the white collar offered me a Minto and his friend offered a Cymro Mint. I accepted both and offered a swig from my flagon. 'Strict TT,' they said.

'There is no "ph" in the Welsh alphabet,' said the white-collared man.

'You are quite right,' said the other.

'In Ireland they spell the word telephone with an "f". Now then.'

I left them to their discussion and their bags of sweets and moved down the train where men were arranged to sleep in remarkable postures. I settled myself down as some town passed by in the darkness and the rain.

A young man pounding the table and shouting, 'I'll never leave Wales again,' woke me. He had been ill all through the night. At another table a freshly shaved man was drinking beer out of a pint pot, eating last night's sandwiches, and reading about Formosa.

What does a man do when he arrives on a bitterly cold winter's morning in Edinburgh before dawn? He trails, hot sand in his eyes, in the train of tradition. He hands his bag through the luggage hatch and helps two solemn-faced jokers to lift their crate of Guinness into the same place. He then walks up Princes Street to Scott's Memorial, warms at a brazier, turns about and walks back in the dawn to a restaurant that opens at seven.

'Would you find this in Swansea? Would you find this in Cardiff?' demands a Welshman gone native. He has been here before and knows about this restaurant and is proud of that.

A man eats two breakfasts and reads what the native experts have to say about the match. He notes that the Scots have taken to trusting in miracles.

It is then time to gawk at the Firth of Forth Bridge, be restored by the first breezes and to ride back through the countryside into a city awake and alive with Welshmen. We join up with two compatriots who have been in Edinburgh two or three days, and walk the streets and the shops, staring at everything and listening to the people who actually speak with a Scotch accent as they do in the films.

Most of us have either scarlet berets or scarlet and white scarves, or leeks or daffodils. Some have all these things and also carry saucepans. Everybody is tremendously polite and cheerful. Even the rain stops and the sun shines. People in the know tell us that we must be at Murrayfield by two o'clock if we want a good view of Scotland being trodden into her own turf. And while, of course, we all feel sorry for poor Scotland, we don't feel all that sorry. 'Have a good journey up?' asks a man selling views of the Castle.

'Quiet,' says a customer.

'A very quiet journey, but God help us tonight if we win.' He pauses. 'Or especially if we lose.'

From *Report on Rugby* by John Morgan and Geoffrey Nicholson
(William Heinemann, London, 1959)

16
GREAT EXPECTATIONS

Pack Who March on Beer and Boasts

Alan Watkins

In many ways rugby is at a crossroads in its history. The great success of the World Cup has projected the game on to an ever bigger stage, but it has also contributed to the pressure that many feel will end in full-scale professionalism, at the top level at least.

Already rugby's higher profile has brought with it problems once thought to be the exclusive concern of other sports. Alan Watkins drew attention to the less savoury side of some modern rugby supporters, while Peter Bills highlighted a problem that many rugby men see as an inevitable consequence of the increasing competitiveness of club rugby.

W.B.B.

On the way to the ground, a member of the young group in front tossed a beer can over the fence into a Twickenham back garden. They all laughed at this feat. They then broke into song of a sort. The number they were attempting, 'Swing low, sweet Chariot', and the tunelessness of their rendition combined with the foulness of their prior language, clearly proclaimed them as supporters of new England. They went into the ground puffed up with the vainglorious boasting of Geoff Cooke and Will Carling – who is, it appears, to be accorded the privilege of that other former military man, the Duke of Marlborough, and appointed Captain for Life, though on Saturday's evidence with rather less justification.

Young England then sang 'God Save The Queen' with more spirit than I had ever heard before at Twickenham. They proceeded to whistle at Peter Dods when he was taking his kicks; to applaud the kicks of Jon Webb and Rob Andrew when they did not look remotely like going over; and – with more reason, it must be said – to boo Monsieur Maurette's more incomprehensible decisions, though only on that minority of occasions when they went against England.

You conclude from this that English rugby supporters are becoming more like the Welsh? Wrong: they are becoming more like English soccer supporters. Some day, mark my words, there will be a nasty incident. I am tempted to add: there certainly will be if Cooke (a manifestly decent man), Carling and their more undiscriminating admirers in the Press create unrealistic expectations among followers who – this being where they resemble not Welsh rugby supporters but English football fans – clearly have little notion of the game.

People who should know better, very different from the new, yobbish supporters of whom I write, also seem to lack any sense of history. Two years ago (though in April rather than February) Scotland came to London as a much-fancied team. England unexpectedly defeated them 21–12, Mike Harrison scoring a try, and Marcus Rose – who would almost certainly have won Saturday's match on his own – scoring a try also, two conversions and three penalties.

Two seasons later, Rose, Harrison, Jamie Salmon, Peter Williams, Richard Harding, Gary Pearce, Nigel Redman, Steve Bainbridge, John Hall and Gary Rees have been replaced by, respectively, Webb, Chris Oti, Carling, Andrew, Dewi Morris, Jeff Probyn, Peter Ackford, Wade Dooley, Mike Teague and Andy Robinson. Of these, only two – Probyn and Oti – are clear gains over their predecessors. Robinson in particular had a lamentable match, actually impeding the clean release of the ball on several occasions. When he learns to think as much as he runs, he will be an international flanker.

On the way back, Young England had changed their tune to 'Cockles and Mussels'. This was not, I think, a celebration of Ireland's win in Cardiff but, rather, an indication of some mental confusion. And who shall blame them?

Since my comments in these pages on the crowd's behaviour at the England–Scotland match, several friends and acquaintances have been kind enough to say that they agreed with me. They had noticed the same deterioration themselves. One of them took his teenage son, a Watford football supporter, on his first visit to Twickenham for an international. He said that no doubt he would observe a difference from what he was used to. The boy said afterwards that, yes, they were rather better behaved at Vicarage Road.

The outward and visible signs of the new rugby hooligan are: jeans, a ski-jacket, training shoes and a can of beer. Though he will probably be wearing a scarf, it is not normally a striped supporter's scarf. Nor does he go in much for rosettes, woolly hats or other indications of team or national loyalty. The true hooligan travels anonymously and travels light. He is not invariably male. Groups of half a dozen or so young men (they tend to be in their late teens or early twenties rather than youths) often carry a complement of one or two girls of the same age, similarly attired. They do not seem to exercise much moderating influence.

On Monday I listed the following: foul language, tossing a beer can over a fence, whistling at opposing place-kickers, booing the referee and generally displaying ignorance of the game. It does not do to be priggish about these matters: for instance, I have always thought it perfectly all right to boo the referee, provided the noise is both intended and understood as an expression of informed, even if partisan, dissent.

In Saturday's match, not only were many of the French referee's decisions incomprehensible, but much of the English frustration was understandable, for John Jeffrey, Finlay Calder and Derek White spent a good part of the game offside. This, rather than any ineptitude by Dewi Morris or Rob Andrew, was the reason why the English three-quarters so often took the ball standing still. Nevertheless, I doubt whether these technical considerations moved the ski-jacketed brigade, the boring criers of 'Eng-land, Eng-land': before long we shall no doubt be treated to 'Here we go'. They had come to Twickenham to see England win, to make a lot of noise and to get as drunk as they could.

I do not look back to any mythical golden age. I remember the days when, at the old, and unreconstructed Cardiff Arms Park, the prudent man wore stout shoes and hitched his trousers well above the heel, to lessen the perils of the urine which, shortly after kick-off, would trickle down the terraces like mountain streams. The England supporters of whom I write today may have drunk no more in quantity but they undoubtedly get drunker, they are younger and they know less, much less about the game than the *aficionados* of the old Arms Park, of St Helen's or, above all, of Stradey Park.

Drink is now becoming a serious problem at rugby matches. Spectators have their bags, though not their persons, perfunctorily searched as they enter the ground. Once inside, they can buy as much drink as they like – and they do. I am not puritanical about drink. *Au contraire*, as the late George Brown used to put it. But, oddly, I do not regard the consumption of alcohol as part of an afternoon's rugby. I do not enjoy sipping whisky from a hip-flask. At all events, the present policy of casual search and free availability afterwards is both dotty and unfair to soccer. Rugby should be treated exactly as soccer is.

From *The Independent*, February 1989

Time to Stop the Poaching

Peter Bills

Dudley Wood, the RFU's avuncular secretary, is a most proficient holder of his post, master of the after-dinner speech, especially the one-liner, and stout upholder of the laws of the game.

Wood's record as a sage voice on most matters of importance stands scrutiny by even his fiercest critic, which is all the more reason to express surprise that Wood displayed so disinterested, almost defeatist an attitude when he was asked at a recent Twickenham press briefing whether legislation might be brought in to restrict the movement of players between first class clubs.

Ever since I revealed in *The Times* that Jason Leonard was switching allegiances from Saracens to Harlequins, the rugby world has been agog and abuzz at the movement of players and what could be done about it.

Saracens, quite rightly, were outraged that Harlequins, a club they beat in last season's Courage First Division and also finished above in the final table, could so blatantly poach their leading player.

Of course, this was nothing new for Harlequins, a club which maintains its lofty perch within the game mainly by acquiring other clubs' best players. Winterbottom, Ackford, Skinner, Moore and Leonard are all fine forwards who have abandoned other clubs to go to the Stoop. A piece of research demonstrating just how many home-grown players Harlequins have in their full, first choice side might be both interesting and damning reading.

Saracens are justified in their fury, commendably suppressed in public for the most part, but fully and frankly revealed in private asides. What point is there, they wonder, in all the time, trouble, patience, effort and cost in producing an international player like Leonard or Dean Ryan if a competitor is to snatch him away. Better to save the money and forget the training and developing of young players.

I cannot think of a more burning issue in the game today in this country, for it goes to the heart of the amateur ethos and all those associated qualities such as decency, fair play, honour, ethics and such like. Yet it was extraordinary to hear Dudley Wood saying that there was little the authorities could do to stop this business.

How wrong too.

Would Leonard, whom we are told is desperate to play for England this season and in the World Cup, have changed clubs so readily had an eighteen-month ban been imposed for the move? Wood is right – you cannot stop players changing clubs and playing for whom they like in a democracy. But you can force them to serve a period of qualification, so as to deter all but the most determined.

Heaven preserve us from any more committees, but there is a crying need for one to oversee all these moves. For example, if a player can prove that he has been moved from Manchester to London by his employers then the game has no right to prevent him playing first class rugby for a new club. But we all know which players are in that category and which are moving simply for the 'inducements' on offer by the big boys.

Does Twickenham not wonder why France has a rule which restricts players appearing for new clubs, for twelve months? The wily French know too well that the most financially secure club would lure every top player and win every trophy in sight, unless that law operated. Without question, it has stopped many leading French players moving clubs in the last ten years.

By lamely intoning that nothing can be done, Wood hints at a reluctance to tackle so thorny an issue; is it that he and others are concerned at what they might find if they start digging in this particular area?

It is beholden upon the authorities to stamp out an increasing tendency which has no place in a game which prides itself on decency and a sense of fair play and justice. Inactivity on Twickenham's part will give a green light to the Harlequins of this world to continue their dubious activities.

From *Rugby News*, October 1990

Fawlty Towers

Gareth Edwards

The arguments about professionalism in rugby will rumble on for years to come. There are those who feel that anything short of 'pay for play' is now justified, while others still believe that the amateur principle is the only acceptable one. Players have always benefited indirectly from the 'freemasonry of rugby', but the question of the acceptability of compensation for income lost through playing rugby, for example, still seems as intractable as when it provoked the breakaway of what was to become the Rugby League, nearly a century ago.

What constitutes professionalism is also far from clear-cut. Gareth Edwards voices a frequent complaint from players about the attitude of rugby officialdom, while John Robbie argues that money does not necessarily a professional make, a point of view that brings him into conflict with one of the doyens of rugby reporting, Terry O'Connor.

W.B.B.

I would not dream of expressing an opinion of my own about events out in New Zealand '77, I was not there. However, I know that the Lions, all good friends of mine, came back disconsolate. They had one more assignment left, to play against the Barbarians at Twickenham in a game staged to raise money for the Queen's Jubilee. Although they had agreed to play the match before they had left for New Zealand, they suddenly shocked the rugby administrators by refusing to turn out. Basically the problem was that only fifteen Lions and replacements were invited to the celebrations. The Lions felt that the whole party should be there with their wives too or girl-friends. The cost out of a £200,000 gate would be negligible. They got their way in part, though they were booked into a modest hotel in Richmond. It was just another way of cutting costs at the players' expense. A couple of nights in Fawlty Towers! Some home-coming!

By the end of the game the dissatisfaction had grown. I am certain that the right attitude should have been, 'Right, let's give these boys, and their wives who have been without them for the whole summer, a great time: a reward for their efforts.'

No, we were all stuck in poky little rooms, set-menu food, and wine only if you paid for it yourself. I asked the committee representatives if we could have some wine on my table because the Frenchmen Rives and Skrela were with me. There was a discussion and then the judgement. 'Yes, the French can have some wine, and because you are with them you can have some too.' This simple incident emphasized the embarrassment we always felt with the French, who always gave us a magic time at no cost to us in France. I looked at the wine list and was in a mind to choose the very best and most expensive they had, but I compromised and selected a wine of medium price which we all liked. Would you believe it? – ten minutes later the wine waiter returned with a bottle of ordinary plonk. Someone along the line had slipped him the committee motto, 'We can't waste money on the players.' The French boys saw the funny side of it. I wanted them to get up and walk out of the hotel in protest. I was furious. Then I cooled down because no one wants to start thinking that way.

The Lions told us about some of the restrictions they had suffered on tour, but we did have fun and settled for a good night at the Hilton on Saturday after the game.

Now it was the glossy West End and the dinner was superb. At last I managed to do the Frenchmen a favour. The waiter at our table had a chat with me about the game. I asked him to give us a bit of extra attention and slipped him a pound note. I was thoroughly enjoying a full, tasty trout when there was a tug on my cuff. Jean-Claude Skrela had finished his in lightning time and he wanted another. A nod and a wink to my waiter friend, and trout number two was in front of Jean-Claude.

The day was a success, the dinner superb, and all went happily until later in the evening. We had all withdrawn to a bar to enjoy our drinks. Then an announcement came that at that bar we had to pay for everything we wanted from now on; it was suddenly a pay-bar. Gerald Davies, the Babas captain, went to complain to Micky Steele-Bodger, one of the committee. Quickly a barrel of beer was organized for the players. 'But neither my wife or I drink beer,' protested Gerald. When asked what he would drink, he said lager would suit him, but not for his wife.

The reply came after a brief investigation. 'I have fixed you a free pint of lager, but no more, but there is nothing else available unless you all pay.'

As always, we ended up passing a pound note for every drink we ordered across the bar – that was about the going rate at the Hilton, and of course, we all looked after the Frenchmen. I do not think they would have believed us this time if we confessed that we were spending all our own money at an official function, after helping to fill Twickenham to capacity that afternoon.

From *Gareth – An Autobiography* by Gareth Edwards
(Stanley Paul, London, 1978)

Am I a Professional at Heart?

John Robbie

The whole question of payment of rugby players has been discussed over and over again. In all the books I have read, the issue comes under the spotlight – and in all the books the writer very daringly proposes that some greater compensation for top players is needed. At the same time, the writer neatly side-steps any admission that he himself has received money.

Well, I'll say it up front. I have received money for playing rugby. Not a lot, I'll admit, but certainly enough to put me outside the fold as far as the rugby board are concerned. And before you think that all this took place in dastardly South Africa, where we all know that this evil practice goes on, let me state that I've received money in Ireland, England and New Zealand. However, before the rugby bailiffs arrive, let me also add that I've never received a cent that did not come either from rugby officialdom or with their certain knowledge. I've already told how I used to feel about this, but like all old players – or the vast majority, anyway – my views have changed.

Am I a professional at heart? Not at all. I've often said that although the game will go professional, and so it must, I'm equally glad that the vast majority of my career was as a true-blue amateur – with the exception of the odd five quid here and there. How can this be? Surely this statement is as Irish as Paddy's pig? Not at all.

Rugby is almost perfect. Schools, youth and club rugby must never change. It's great fun, people don't kill (although they can), and it embodies the amateur ideal. By the way, in this scenario I don't include the top Welsh or French clubs. What I mean is that the junior ranks of the game are fine. The big problems occur at the top: with World Cups, Welsh Cups and certainly Currie Cups, the pressure to win is enormous.

As each side gets better, so they put up the required standard to compete. In fact, I believe the strength of the current All Blacks will do more to push the game towards professionalism than anything else. Last year Wales, having shared the Five Nations, were absolutely destroyed in New Zealand, and now British rugby has a decision to make. Does it stay second division to the southern hemisphere, or does it get competitive? Well, just look at the national training squads in Wales and England for your answer. In the old days they used to meet a day before an international. Now they go on training camps to Spain and Portugal. The players are having to work harder and harder.

Meanwhile, up the road in the Rugby League, all is different – that game has been transformed, partly through TV. The players are making bucks and enjoying a great game and now national stardom. League names are just as big in England as Union ones are.

And after the tenth cap for Wales or the sixtieth, what's the difference? Jonathan Davies has gone to League, so has Adrian Hadley – my bet is that more will go too, because League is fulfilling a need. It offers another step further up the ladder for the top player. A cap is no longer enough reward for all the hours of training.

From *The Game of My Life* by John Robbie
(Pelham Books, London, 1989)

Terry O'Connor

David Lawrenson

The whole structure of the game has changed.

'In those early days people played rugby to get fit rather than the other way round. The introduction of leagues and cup competitions has changed the face of rugby football. Clubs now know that they can't live on their reputations as London Welsh have discovered.

'In my early days, Twickenham's attitude to the public wasn't what it is today. Up until four years ago their telephone number was ex-directory and the introduction of sponsors has revolutionized the game.

'There are dangers as things have moved towards a highly organized professional game, some of the spirit will go. But I don't think it will ever go completely because these changes only ever affect the top two per cent.

'A lot of people don't see the danger in moving to a professional role. There's no great virtue about being professional, it doesn't make you a better player. If they can avoid the curse of agents and ensure that you don't have people taking over clubs as in association football, then I think with good administration and well-paid top administrators, the game could survive.

'I'm not against players making money outside the game but there's a terrible danger if players are allowed to write columns in newspapers. Then you could get an agent saying to a player "Look, if you write an attacking piece, we could get five times the money." That's one of the curses of professional sport.'

One thing Terry does lament is the fact that there seem to be fewer real characters around in the sport. He feels that modern players may train harder but seem to have less fun.

'I prefer the Colin Meads approach, where he would drink a lot on Saturday night, because he loved his beer, and then pay for it by going off on a run on Sunday morning. Players don't drink as much these days, there's too much orange squash!'

Which seems as good a reason as any to retire.

From *Rugby News*, November 1990

Small Worlds

Geoffrey Moorhouse

Can the spirit of the game, evoked in the writings which opened this anthology, survive into the very different world of rugby to come? The answer, I am sure, is an emphatic 'yes'. People have always played rugby for fun and the vast majority will continue to do so, valuing the healthy exercise, the keen competition and the companionship of rugby above any material reward.

At the top levels, however, rugby players are already professional in their dedication and attitude, if not in the financial rewards they receive. Pressure will grow on the law-makers to make the game increasingly fast and attractive for non-specialist viewers, in the stands or by their television sets. It will be a shame if such law changes mean that rugby ceases to be a game that anyone of any shape or size can play, for that is one of its delights.

While the two codes of rugby may move closer together in the future, I do not share the belief of those who argue that they will one day be reunited. I believe in the amateur principle and I feel that there will always be a distinction between the two games. Just the same, as a Northerner, I have always enjoyed the banter between rugby union and rugby league supporters and, like Geoffrey Moorhouse and Alan Watkins, I enjoy rugby of both codes.

W.B.B.

Rugby Union is also at a crossroads, and one at which some painful decisions on which way to go will soon have to be made. (Perhaps, in the surrender to competitive league football, the crucial decision has already been made.) Its traditional autocracy is still going strong, manifested as unpleasantly as anywhere in the preposterous rule which withholds from Lewis Jones – one of the most honourable and excitingly talented players ever to put on football boots in any code – the privilege of a ticket at all international matches on Cardiff Arms Park, which is granted to all who have played for Wales; withheld from him, as from David Watkins and others in a similar position, only because he is tainted by having played Rugby League professionally. Now there's a mean spirit for you! But how much longer can it be sustained in the face of other happenings in the world of fifteen-a-side? For it is patently obvious that international rugger in these islands has become as shamelessly shamateur as it always has been in France, and that a day is not far distant when player power will demand that payment for services rendered must be out in the open and pretty substantial.

The New Zealand Rugby Union has already tied itself in knots in trying to pretend that the All Blacks have not been cleaning up dollars and other emoluments rather well in recent years. One of their captains, David Kirk, has even gone into cold print with the following opinion of what will be:

> It seems to me that the tide of social and political sentiment in many of the countries in which rugby is played is turning more and more to a belief in a meritocratic way of life. A way of life that provides opportunity and rewards success in due measure. Rugby players are not isolated from this social tide. Is it any wonder then that the world's top players may feel confused and in some senses alienated by a rugby meritocracy that ignores the principal medium of reward the whole world recognizes: money? A medium, incidentally, that by its nature acknowledges transitory excellence as deserving of long-term reward.

At this, a snort may be heard coming from the direction of Huddersfield, where a rather less brassy approach was adopted, and condemned, in 1895.

The roots of these grudges and resentments are often embedded in local history. The most notable of them is entangled in the origins of the game, as well as in the social and economic circumstances which gave it a distinctive character. It is a depressing fact of life that after almost one hundred years, and even after the removal of an official barrier separating amateur players of the two rugby codes, antipathy persists between some people in League and others in Union. I can detect lingering traces of it in myself. I get a satisfaction verging on the malicious whenever I contemplate the results of those two matches played by gracious (almost divine) permission during the war, between Combined Services sides representing the Rugby League versus the Rugby Union. We, it will be recalled, beat Them first of all at Headingley, in 1943, by eighteen points to eleven; and then, in the following year at Odsal, repeated the medicine to the tune of fifteen points to ten. We did so, what's more, by playing them at their own game; that is, at fifteen-a-side. It satisfies me enormously, childishly, to remember that; and I can scoff quite loudly when I pick up the *Playfair Rugby Football Annual* for the 1948–9 season – a Union publication – and see how they dealt with those fixtures in their retrospective look at what had been happening while the war was on.

The Headingley match they simply didn't notice. Of the Odsal game they remarked cryptically: 'Both sides composed of Service men and not truly representative.' Yes, it must have stung, when it happened not once, but twice: and I suppose it *might* have made a difference to the final score if the games had been truly representative. But we'll never know because, although the secretary of the Rugby League in those days, John Wilson, said at a luncheon before the game in Leeds that he saw no reason why the fixture should not become an annual event, Homo Twickiens would have none of it. His variant at Murrayfield had been even more forbidding, taking the view that Lance-Corporal Ernest Ward, Sergeant Stan Brogden, Sergeant Ike Owens, Sergeant-Instructor Trevor Foster & Co, while quite acceptable as subordinates in hostilities against Hitler, might dangerously pollute the likes of 2nd Lieutenant Bruce-Lockhart, Flight-Lieutenant Weighill and Officer-

Cadet Haydn Tanner on a football field. As Playfair noted in November 1939 the 'Scottish Union announced it saw no reason for departing from its ban on professionals in Services playing for or against amateur sides'.

Narrow little men of inadequate education, constipated with prejudice, continue to regard Rugby League like that even today, and I can spit with fury whenever I find myself downwind of one.

My position, when I am in that mood, would be more tenable were it not for the indisputable fact that our lot contains its quota of ignoramuses and bigots, too. Some would die rather than admit that in the splendid Rugby Union Varsity match of 1987 there was scrummaging that shamed the incompetent version commonly practised in the first division of the Rugby League championship; that every one of our professional packs could have learned much in this respect from those young Blues, as could some of our grade one referees from the man in charge at Twickenham that day, Roger Quittenton. We include a number who all but wet themselves with mirth whenever they see references to a certain Steele-Bodger, which puts them at the same level as juveniles who crease themselves every time they come across a name ending in ' . . . bottom'. There must be legions who are convinced that from the moment of the schism in 1895, nobody associated with Rugby Union has ever treated Rugby League with anything but the disdain of a Brahmin for an Untouchable.

The antipathies seem to exist everywhere but in Australia and in Papua New Guinea. The French grievance is that their Rugby Union is professional in all but name, much wealthier than Rugby League, and therefore holds the whip-hand in the recruitment of the best players: also that Union politicians were behind the notorious seizure of League assets and banning of the game itself by the Vichy Government in 1941. In New Zealand, where League is a totally amateur sport, it has been known for a Kiwi side to train on a Union ground before a Test against the Kangaroos, although Graham Lowe has told how, when his Kiwis and Brian Lochore's All Blacks had planned a get-together in an Auckland hotel, as both sides happened to be playing in the city that weekend, the idea was kiboshed by the New Zealand RFU. In Australia alone they appear to have long risen above such pettiness.

In the 1936 symposium of views on Rugby Union entitled *The Game Goes On* – edited by Captain H.B.T. Wakelam and including an article on 'Old Boy Football' by one E.W. Swanton – there is an illuminating piece by E.N. Greatorex, who toured the British Isles in 1927–8 with the Waratahs of New South Wales. He recounted the development of Rugby Union in his country, and made the point that it suffered severely when Rugby League began there, because nearly all the 1908 Wallabies went over to the thirteen-a-side game. In other words, the older body had as much reason for feeling sore as the English Rugby Union after 1895. He went on: 'The Australian Rugby Union, however, has no quarrel with the League. There is room for both games. Australians are impartial so far as football is concerned. The man who goes out to see a Rugby League international will turn up for a Rugby Union international.' That is as true today as it was half a century ago, producing a climate the rest of us should envy and try to imitate. In such a climate it has been quite natural for the Australian Rugby Union to ask the Queensland Rugby League if they might use Lang Park for a representative match in Brisbane, and for permission to be given. Would that the same civil behaviour were the rule rather than the exception in the northern hemisphere.

It is not beyond the bounds of possibility that we in the British Isles might get there one day; and it says much for the changing circumstances of our times that one can now speculate on a topic that has for too long been petrified in snobbery and recrimination.

From *At The George* by Geoffrey Moorhouse
(Hodder & Stoughton, Sevenoaks, 1989)

Professionalism Defined

Alan Watkins

In rugby, as in most other activities known to man, the same topics keep coming round like the washing-up. Thus South Africa, leagues and amateurism (real or false) have been endlessly talked about for the last decade and more. Occasionally some progress is made – or, to put it neutrally, some change occurs. But it is a slow business. On South Africa, attitudes have become firmer: it is difficult to imagine England visiting that country now, as they did as recently as 1984. On leagues, the question has been settled in England, though not yet in Wales. On amateurism, however, disparate and usually contrary opinions are flying about like, well, like fists at Sardis Road, Pontypridd.

The Bath club are proposing a kind of sunset home for old players – or, strictly, a trust fund to be distributed when players have ceased active football. From what I can make of this scheme, the people with most cause to celebrate will be the lawyers, who will surely be bringing out the vintage port in Lincoln's Inn.

Geoff Cooke, for his part, fails to see why players should not be allowed to receive cheques from publishers and bundles of banknotes from supermarkets, provided they are not paid for actually playing the game. This robust and, in my opinion, wholly defensible view has embarrassed Dudley Wood of the Rugby Football Union. There he was, on *Rugby Special*, trying in his customary charming manner to explain away Cooke, for all the world as if he were a member of the Cabinet maintaining that one of his junior ministers had not really meant what he said.

At the same time, Brian Thomas of Neath is, I read, offering his paid services to Welsh rugby clubs as a 'consultant'. This, it appears, does not impair his continuing amateur status within the game because his job is to be a consultant. It is all great nonsense, I am afraid, and I will tell you why. The mess rugby has got itself into derives from false notions of amateurism and professionalism.

A professional is not someone who receives payment for doing something: it is a person who earns his (or her) living substantially by the activity in question. Similarly, an amateur is not someone who receives no payment at all: it is a person who does something primarily for love. Though the derivations of words can be treacherous guides, 'amateur' comes from the Latin for 'lover'. I regard myself as a professional journalist but an amateur book writer.

Indeed, the entire discussion about the writing of books, by players and others, is based on two fallacies. The first fallacy is that the sole reason for writing a book is to make money. The second is that there is a lot of money to be made out of writing books. In fact the great Welsh players of the early 1970s did quite well for themselves from their literary activities. And, as Barry Norman likes to say, why not? Writing a book has nothing to do with amateurism and professionalism. At present, a player (past or contemporary) who is a journalist and writes a book retains his amateur status. A player who is a schoolmaster and does the same is cast into outer darkness, as Ian McLauchlan was. Yet even a supposedly professional writer, who churns out a book a year, often has to possess another source of income. On grounds of principle, the book-writing argument is easy to resolve in favour of complete freedom.

Nor do I shrink from the logic of my own definitions. Rugby League players may be paid but they are not truly professional sportsmen as players of, say, soccer, golf and tennis can be. The great majority do not earn their livings from the game. Even if Union players continue to be unpaid, I see no reason why there should not be interchangeability at every level. And so tomorrow we might be viewing Alan Tait, Martin Offiah and Peter Williams at Twickenham, and Jonathan Davies, Adrian Hadley and, possibly, David Bishop at Cardiff. Some hope! It will not happen in my lifetime, but some day it will.

From *The Independent*, February 1987